W9-DGS-561

FROM JAMESTOWN TO JEFFERSON

FROM JAMESTOWN
TO JEFFERSON

The Evolution of Religious
Freedom in Virginia

EDITED BY
Paul Rasor and Richard E. Bond

University of Virginia Press
CHARLOTTESVILLE AND LONDON

#6572708o6

University of Virginia Press
© 2011 by the Rector and Visitors of the University of Virginia
All rights reserved
Printed in the United States of America on acid-free paper

First published 2011

9 8 7 6 5 4 3 2 1

LIBRARY OF CONGRESS CATALOGING-IN-PUBLICATION DATA

From Jamestown to Jefferson : the evolution of religious freedom in Virginia / edited
by Paul Rasor and Richard E. Bond.

    p.   cm.

The origins of this volume lie in a semester-long symposium held during the fall
of 2007 at Virginia Wesleyan College in Norfolk, Virginia, entitled "From Jamestown to Jefferson: The Evolution of Religious Authority in Colonial Virginia." The
symposium was sponsored by the college's Center for the Study of Religious Freedom.

Includes bibliographical references and index.

ISBN 978-0-8139-3108-1 (pbk. : acid-free paper)—ISBN 978-0-8139-3118-0 (e-book)

1. Freedom of religion—Virginia—History—17th century. 2. Freedom of religion—
Virginia—History—18th century. 3. Church and state—Virginia—History—17th
century. 4. Church and state—Virginia—History—18th century. 5. Virginia—
Church history—17th century. 6. Virginia—Church history—18th century.
7. Jefferson, Thomas, 1743–1826—Social and political views. 8. Virginia. Act for
Establishing Religious Freedom. I. Rasor, Paul B. II. Bond, Richard E., 1977–
III. Virginia Wesleyan College. IV. Virginia Wesleyan College. Center for the Study
of Religious Freedom.

BR555.V8F76 2011
   232.44'209755—dc22

2010032805

CONTENTS

PREFACE

THE ORIGINS OF THIS VOLUME LIE IN A SEMESTER-LONG SYM-
posium held during the fall of 2007 at Virginia Wesleyan College
in Norfolk, Virginia, entitled "From Jamestown to Jefferson: The
Evolution of Religious Authority in Colonial Virginia." The symposium was sponsored by the college's Center for the Study of Religious Freedom and organized by Paul Rasor, director of the center,
and coordinated with a concurrent course in the history of Virginia taught by Richard E. Bond, assistant professor of history at
Virginia Wesleyan.

The symposium sought to present a coherent narrative of Virginia's historic religious journey. Each contributor was invited to
make a presentation on a specific theme as part of this project, and
each chapter in this volume was first presented in the form of a free
public lecture. The contributors took their assignments seriously,
preparing thorough, well-crafted papers and often adjusting their
own presentations in light of the others. This cooperative collegial-
ity continued as they revised and expanded their original papers
for publication here. The contributors are among the leading scholars of Virginia history, and their contributions reflect important
scholarship. We are indebted to all of them for their superb work,
their ongoing enthusiasm for this project, and their willingness to
engage us simultaneously as editors and colleagues.

Dick Holway, history and social sciences editor at the University of Virginia Press, masterfully shepherded the book through
its many stages of production, and we are grateful. We also want to
thank Raennah Mitchell, acquisitions assistant, for helping with
the necessary administrative aspects of the project, Mark Mones,

acting managing editor, and Morgan Myers, project editor, for responding promptly and clearly to our many technical questions, and Carol Sickman-Garner for her excellent copy editing. We are especially grateful to the anonymous reviewers whose comments improved the text in important ways.

Ann Shappell, the center's invaluable administrative assistant, performed superbly throughout the long process of planning and presenting the symposium, preparing follow-up reports, and proofreading manuscripts. We are grateful not only for her logistical support but also for her helpful insights and timely reminders. We also wish to acknowledge the support of Dr. Timothy G. O'Rourke, Vice President for Academic Affairs and Kenneth R. Perry Dean of the College, whose office provided funding for the indexing of this volume. The original symposium was supported in part by a grant from the Virginia Foundation for the Humanities, and we are grateful for its contribution to the center's work.

Paul Rasor and Rich Bond
Norfolk, Virginia, May 2010

FROM JAMESTOWN TO JEFFERSON

Introduction

PAUL RASOR AND RICHARD E. BOND

LESS THAN TWO WEEKS BEFORE HIS DEATH ON JULY 4, 1826, Thomas Jefferson wrote precise instructions for the inscription to be placed on his tombstone:

Here was buried
Thomas Jefferson
Author of the Declaration of American Independence
of the Statute of Virginia for Religious Freedom
& Father of the University of Virginia

It is remarkable that of all his accomplishments, including two terms as president of the United States, these are the few for which he "wish[ed] most to be remembered."[1] Commentators have often noted that Jefferson's epitaph is a fitting tribute to his lifelong goal of expanding political, educational, and religious liberty.[2] The Declaration of Independence has become a foundational document in international law, and its language emphasizing natural rights and democratic government has served as a clarion call for change throughout the world.[3] The University of Virginia, established in 1819, continues to combine a tradition of excellence with a commitment to accessibility to all.

The Statute for Religious Freedom, adopted by the Virginia General Assembly on January 16, 1786, is among the most important and enduring documents produced during the Revolutionary period. Though less well-known than the Declaration of Independence, it was equally revolutionary. It influenced the development of church-state relations in other states for the next several decades, and its core principles, freedom of conscience and church-state separation, created the model that would be followed by the new federal government. As Martin Marty has noted, the statute marked "an epochal shift in the Western world's approach to relations between civil and religious spheres of life."[4] Yet for all Jefferson's brilliance, this remarkable document did not arise in a vacuum. The statute, and more specifically the colonial Virginia context out of which it emerged, form the subject matter of this volume.

Jefferson's statute has received considerable scholarly attention over the years. Historians and legal scholars have stressed its intellectual origins, which lie mainly in a blend of Enlightenment concepts, such as religious toleration and the authority of individual human reason, and the theological commitments of the evangelical churches, including religious voluntarism and church autonomy, in its creation.[5] Historians of Virginia have also emphasized the importance of the Revolutionary context for its formation and eventual passage. Evangelical groups such as the Separate Baptists and colonial legislators combined philosophical, theological, and political ideologies to challenge the longstanding public support of the established Anglican Church.[6] These influences are important, but they do not tell the whole story. At a more fundamental level, Jefferson's statute was rooted in the Virginia colonial experience, which began with the landing at Cape Henry on April 26, 1607, and the founding of the Jamestown settlement a few short weeks later.

Each of the six chapters in this volume examines key events and players of Virginia's early religious landscape. The first four chapters highlight the complex interactions between and among the diverse religious groups within the Virginia colony, while the final chapters trace the seismic religious and legal changes unleashed by the statute's adoption. Taken as a whole, the volume suggests how the evolving political, social, and religious conditions in colonial Virginia gradually helped create a space within which this new understanding of religious freedom could emerge.

JEFFERSON originally composed the text of the statute in 1777, after returning to the Virginia legislature following his service in the Continental Congress. Employing the general drafting strategy he had used in the Declaration of Independence, which recites its philosophical and experiential justifications at length before arriving at the actual claim of independence in the final paragraph, Jefferson devotes more than three-fourths of the statute to the preamble, where he blends theological and political arguments in making his case. Here, as Merrill Peterson and Robert Vaughn have noted, "Jefferson poured all his rage against the cant and falsehood, the corruption and tyranny associated with the history of the alliance between church and state."[7] Beginning with the premise that "Almighty God hath created the mind free," he condemns the "impious presumption of legislators and rulers, civil as well as ecclesiastical, who being themselves but fallible and uninspired men, have assumed dominion over the faith of others, setting up their own opinions and modes of thinking as the only true and infallible, and as such endeavoring to impose them on others." Such forms of religious coercion are contrary to "the plan of the Holy author of our religion" and in the end "tend only to beget habits of hypocrisy and meanness" and "to corrupt the principles of that religion [they are] meant to encourage." For the same reason, forcing a citizen to support any church, even one "of his own religious persuasion," or barring a citizen from office based on religious belief, is both "sinful and tyrannical." "Our civil rights," Jefferson insists, "have no dependence on our religious opinions." The preamble concludes with the famous claim that "truth is great and will prevail if left to herself."

Only after setting the legislative stage in this manner does Jefferson arrive at the statute's operative provision:

> Be it enacted by the General Assembly, That no man shall be compelled to frequent or support any religious worship, place, or ministry whatsoever, nor shall be enforced, restrained, molested, or burthened in his body or goods, nor shall otherwise suffer on account of his religious opinions or belief; but that all men shall be free to profess, and by argument to maintain, their opinion in matters of religion, and that the same shall in no wise diminish, enlarge, or affect their civil capacities.[8]

This language is best known for affirming an individual right of conscience and disestablishing the Anglican Church. But it is also important to note that with this statutory language, Virginia became the first state to eliminate religious tests for public office. Discussing the legislative treatment of his statute in his autobiography, Jefferson noted that a proposal to amend the bill by adding a specific reference to "Jesus Christ" "was rejected by a great majority, in proof that they meant to comprehend, within the mantle of it's protection, the Jew and the Gentile, the Christian and Mahometan, the Hindoo, and infidel of every denomination."[9] This was a radical move. Religious test oaths were then commonplace in English and colonial practice, and non-Christians were barred from office in all the other original states.[10] Indeed, most limited public office to Protestants. Here, too, Virginia established a precedent that would be adopted in the U.S. Constitution one year later.[11]

Following its passage, the statute met with generally favorable reception on both domestic and international fronts. A typical response appeared in a Maine newspaper, which noted that the statute "afford[ed] an example of Legislative wisdom, and liberality never before known" and suggested that if governments had only possessed the wisdom to enact similar legislation earlier, "most of the evils which have disturbed the peace of the world, and obstructed human progress, would have been prevented."[12] As for its international reception, Jefferson noted with pride in a letter to his former mentor, George Wythe, that the statute was "extremely applauded" by representatives from several European nations, many of whom "have asked of me copies of it to send to their sovereigns." Encouraged by this reception, he had the statute translated into French and Italian and hoped the text would be reproduced in the new *Encyclopédie Méthodique,* to which Jefferson himself had contributed.[13]

Yet there were dissenting views. A "citizen of Philadelphia," for example, complained that the statute was "more a general declamation against all religion, than an attempt to fix the freedom of any on a liberal and just foundation." This writer noted "that a door is opened wide for the introduction of any tenets in religion, however degrading to Christianity," and warned that the Virginia Assembly might eventually "be held and administered by men professedly atheists, Mahometans, or of any other creed."[14] The Philadelphia critic was in principle correct; as noted above, the elimination of religious qualifications for office was precisely what Jefferson had in mind. One Canadian critic asked rhetorically whether the former colonies' passage "through the purgatory of rebellion . . . [made] them wiser and more worthy of imitation than before," reminding his readers that even in countries with an established church, "where different Sects were found, there a toleration of them was reasonable and necessary." Imagining that this was the case in Virginia, he saw no need for the statute.[15]

The Canadian critic raises some useful questions as we explore the statute's historical context. What sorts of "different Sects were found" in seventeenth- and eighteenth-century Virginia, and what forms of toleration were—and were not—practiced? What role did religion play in the daily lives of the adherents of these groups? In what ways did the established Anglican Church shape the religious life of colonial Virginia, and how was Anglican hegemony limited by the geographical and political realities of settlement? More generally, what kinds of religious diversity existed within and among the African, European, and Native American segments of the population during the colonial period? What were the political and social consequences of this diversity, and how were these consequences reflected—if at all—in the Statute for Religious Freedom? Finally, what were the consequences of the statute itself, both immediate and long-term, on the diverse religious groups in Virginia and for the nation?

While the volume as a whole tells a coherent story, we want to emphasize that the narrative consists of two overlapping threads: the increasing appearance of *religious diversity* in the Virginia colony and the increasing embrace of *religious toleration* that culminated in Jefferson's statute. We do not see these as causally linked; that is, increased diversity by itself did not lead directly to greater toleration or to the statute. Yet the two stories are interrelated, and we believe each can be understood more fully in light of the other.

One of the volume's recurring themes is the way various religious groups—both those within and those outside traditional power structures—influenced and responded to each other's presence. Thus, in addition to the colony's many Anglican adherents, who themselves demonstrated a remarkably varied range of beliefs and practices, Roman Catholics, Quakers, and Puritans were also present in the colony's earliest decades. Moreover, several dissenting Protestant groups began to appear in greater numbers during the eighteenth century. There was also a diversity broader than that represented by these traditionally recognized groups, including Native Americans who had their own religious traditions; slaves whose religious practices included Islamic, African, and newly created African American traditions; and European colonists who held magical and folk beliefs of various types. The religious practices of these groups reinforced both the colony's deep religiosity and its profound diversity. As a result, all groups, both those in power and those on the margins, had to adjust to the daily reality of each other's presence and to negotiate the inevitable tensions generated by such close contact as a normal feature of colonial life. In the end, this volume argues, colonial Virginia was more religious, more diverse, and by necessity (often) more tolerant than commonly supposed.

In light of this complex reality, we can see, for example, that while the Anglican Church played a central role in the political and social life of the colony, its influence was limited by the realities of colonial life and by the competing claims of other religious groups, to whom it responded in ways ranging from persecution to compromise and toleration. The volume thus emphasizes the interplay between the Anglican Church's power and the limits on that power within the colonial context, a process that continued even after enactment of the statute. By the same token, while the various "outsider" groups had no direct influence on the passage of Jefferson's statute, chapters 3, 4, and 5, when read together, make clear that this broad diversity and the established Anglican Church's varied responses to it were linked. In this context, the Separate Baptists' demands toward the end of the colonial period, for example, could be perceived by the established authorities as less threatening than they might have been and thus embraced.

None of these events by themselves can be said to have directly "caused" Jefferson's statute. Yet these ongoing challenges, as well as the sustained criticism of the Anglican establishment by the dissenting Protestants, became part of the context in which both the ecclesial and the civil authorities were eventually forced to accept the compromises the statute represented. Indeed, the statute had more profound implications for religious freedom than its supporters likely realized. While they may not have intended to protect all of the various outsider groups (though Jefferson himself clearly had some of these in mind), the statute helped set Virginia, and ultimately the nation, on the road to applying religious freedom to everyone.

This volume challenges many of the scholarly assumptions too often reflected in historians' treatment of religion in Virginia. Indeed, as Brent Tarter demonstrates, religion is barely visible in many of the standard accounts of Virginia's history. One reason for this is the widely used but overly simplistic model contrasting the mercantile origins of the English colonization of Virginia with the religious origins of the colonization of New England. This view is not without its basis in reality; both the Pilgrims who landed at Plymouth and the Puritans of the Massachusetts Bay Colony, for example, understood themselves as fulfilling a divine mission, while the original English settlers of Virginia seemed to lack such a clear religious purpose, and many did eventually make their fortunes from tobacco.[16] Yet reducing history to such simplistic narratives is at best misleading and at worst can lead to inaccuracies. As Tarter, Edward L. Bond, and Daniel L. Dreisbach remind us in this volume, these early Virginia settlers, like their New England counterparts, also understood themselves as divinely chosen.

Fortunately, the scholarly treatment of Virginia history has become more nuanced in recent years. A number of historians interested in the workings of class, race, and gender have broadened our understanding of the complex social, cultural, political, and economic dynamics at work in early Virginia. Scholars of race and class, for example, have shown that black slaves and the white poor were able to influence both large-scale political events and the smaller patterns of daily life to a greater degree than we once thought. Some have expanded upon Edmund Morgan's view that a dominant aristocratic English landholding class manipulated its way into power by pitting class- and race-based antagonisms against one another.[17] Moreover, some recent scholars studying the many poor and middling yeomen who dominated Virginia's white population in the eighteenth century argue that class struggle continued right up to the Revolution.[18] Other scholars have shown that both longstanding and relatively novel understandings of gender structured much of the legal and social landscape in early Virginia. Thus, while women's behavior, both real and imagined, was crucial to the implementation of a patriarchal culture and the ideological justification for racial chattel slavery, seventeenth-century gender imbalances provided many Chesapeake women with a temporary space in which to wield varied forms of economic and political power.[19]

Given these prevailing scholarly emphases, we feel that a comparable study of early Virginia religion is long overdue, and we offer this volume as a first step on what we hope will become a fruitful avenue of scholarly inquiry. In addition to providing greater insight into the role played by religion in early Virginia life, we argue that such study, by building upon the rich scholarly work in these other contexts, will deepen our understanding of the complex and dynamic relationships among the multiple and overlapping populations of this period. In retelling the story of Virginia's early religious history, this volume stresses the murkiness inherent in the complex amalgam of religious experiences that helped shape colonial life.

The Virginia colony thus offered a rich soil in which the Virginia Statute for Religious Freedom could take root and flower. By exploring the religious backgrounds of the generations of Virginians who lived before Jefferson penned his famous statute, this volume's contributors shed new light on the meaning of this important American document. The ideal of religious freedom, in the end, was not only a product of transatlantic ideals or a response to transformative revolutionary rhetoric. It also grew out of the daily religious practices and struggles that took place in the town halls, backwoods settlements, plantation houses, and slave quarters that dotted the seventeenth- and eighteenth-century Virginia landscape.

THIS VOLUME is not simply a collection of independent scholarly papers. As we note in the preface, each contributor was asked to address a specific theme as part of a coordinated series of public lectures. Several made adjustments to their own presentations in light of those that had come before, and all worked cooperatively as they revised and expanded their original papers for publication here. While we have not attempted to hide occasional differences in interpretation, the result of these cooperative efforts is that the chapters in this volume relate to and build on each other.

The volume moves roughly chronologically, beginning with the English settlers' first days after their landing at Cape Henry and continuing through the end of the colonial period and the passage of Jefferson's famous statute, though there is necessarily some overlap as the contributors take up recurring themes and revisit various groups from contrasting perspectives. In chapter 1, Brent Tarter argues that historians of early Virginia have typically paid little attention to religious beliefs and practices, often misinterpreting or missing altogether the evidence of religion that was right in front of them, focusing instead on political institutions and the economic and social structures of plantation culture. Tarter examines previously overlooked sources and argues that the English colonists saw themselves and their world as thoroughly religious in nature. Religion thus played a critical role in every aspect of early colonial life. The colonists' religious orientation influenced their political institutions, their governing laws and judicial procedures, their attitudes toward both the English and the Native peoples they encountered, the way they understood the events of their daily lives, including their response to hardship and suffering, and even their language. Religious and civil life, in other words, were inseparable. Tarter also examines the ways in which the Church of England adapted parish structures and clergy roles in light of colonial frontier conditions and notes especially the role of parish churches as local units of governance. Finally, he finds evidence of significant religious diversity in these early decades, even among Anglicans, and shows that religious differences were generally tolerated within a broad, though not unlimited, range.

In chapter 2, Edward L. Bond takes us beyond the colony's earliest decades and examines the role of religion in the daily lives of the colonists throughout the seventeenth century and into the eighteenth. He notes the ways in which widespread belief in the intervention of supernatural forces—both divine and demonic—shaped the colonists' understanding of the circumstances they encountered in their lives. These belief patterns were not only found among the poorer and uneducated classes but also reflected in the personal and official writings of legislators, governors, and ministers. Supernatural beliefs were blended with forms of religious belief and practice more familiar to our twenty-first-century perspective. Ministers performed their normal pastoral and preaching roles, the Anglican liturgy was repeated on a regular basis, offices and devotions were held, and the Book of Common Prayer guided both public worship and family devotional practice.

Yet, as Bond demonstrates, external factors also affected lived religious practice in several important ways. In addition to a shortage of clergy in the seventeenth century and the absence of ecclesial leadership throughout the colonial period, both the church and the general population had to adapt to the demands of the Virginia tobacco culture. The population was scattered along the rivers rather than concentrated in towns, and the large distances from parish churches meant that laypeople took on many roles normally assumed by the clergy. Religious books became prized possessions, especially for those not regularly served by the clergy. As a result of these and related circumstances, the Anglican Church was forced to relax its application of canon law and ecclesial authority. Nevertheless, Bond argues, the Church of England remained a strong and influential institution in Virginia through and even beyond the Revolution.

Philip D. Morgan steps outside the Protestant framework in chapter 3 and examines the place of heterodox religious groups in colonial Virginia. These include Indians, Africans and African Americans, and white colonists who practiced quasi-Christian or non-Christian forms of magic and other folk traditions, including witchcraft. Recognizing that "orthodoxy" is a problematic concept that largely depends on one's perspective, Morgan undertakes a comparative examination of the beliefs and practices of these groups and discusses their relationships to the Anglican establishment and the dissenting Protestants, including the racial implications of Protestant attitudes. Thus, the Protestants treated Native Americans primarily as objects of mission outreach, an effort that failed for both religious and cultural reasons. The gradual loss of native religious traditions is contrasted with the abrupt loss of

African traditions as a result of the Middle Passage. Yet surviving elements of African religions were often reinterpreted in ways that permitted appropriation of some Christian beliefs. This practice contributed to slave conversions to Christianity, though Christians remained a minority of the African American population throughout the colonial period. Persons whose religious practices were based in folk traditions such as magic or witchcraft were treated with suspicion and sometimes prosecuted in the seventeenth and early eighteenth centuries, but these forms of religious practice were eventually undermined by the culturally and politically dominant Protestants. Yet despite the growth and increasing dominance of Protestant groups in the period before the Revolution, these "unorthodox" forms of religious practice remained widespread. In fact, adherents of these groups constituted the majority of the Virginia population throughout the colonial period, a circumstance that both reflected and contributed to early Virginia's remarkable religious diversity.

In chapter 4, Monica Najar examines the practices and influence of the dissenting Protestant sects, focusing in particular on Quakers, Presbyterians, and Baptists. Though dissenters did not appear in large numbers until the mid-eighteenth century, they played a critical role in Virginia's colonial religious history. People were attracted to these groups despite—and often because of—the persecution and harassment they experienced. The enthusiastic and emotional worship style of the Baptists in particular appealed to many, and by taking their message directly to the people, these groups were able to reach large segments of the populace who were not well served by the established Anglicans. They also altered the common understanding of religious authority by empowering nonministers—including women—to testify and by redefining the church as a voluntary association of converted members rather than as based on residence in a parish.

Najar examines the contrasting strategies employed by the three major dissenting sects in response to licensing requirements and other restrictions imposed by established authorities. In the seventeenth century, Quaker perseverance in the face of persecution that included fines, whipping, and imprisonment revealed the limits of official tolerance and paved the way for Presbyterians and Baptists to continue the struggle a century later. For their part, Presbyterians generally complied with the restrictive toleration laws, signaling to the authorities that they were a respectable faith and thus not a threat to the establishment. Baptists, in contrast, were far more confrontational, challenging both the legal restrictions and the prevailing social conventions and thus prompting a harsher official response. Yet persecution reinforced their self-understanding as a people suffering for their faith, and this, in turn, attracted more members. More significantly, the Baptists celebrated women who joined them in defiance of their husbands' wishes, a stance that radically challenged the Southern model of godly womanhood and patriarchal power that linked the domestic and political struggles for liberty. Najar concludes that these sects collectively if unintentionally worked to undermine the rules and practices that supported the established authorities, especially those manifested in the official understanding and enforcement of religious toleration. While each of these dissenting groups pursued its own strategy with little connection to the others, all influenced the Virginia understanding of church-state relations and thus made significant contributions to Virginia's journey toward religious freedom.

In chapter 5, Thomas E. Buckley places Jefferson's statute in its Revolutionary context, showing how the final emergence of religious freedom in Virginia was linked to the larger struggle for political freedom. Key historical influences include the shifting power relationship between the established Anglican Church and the dissenting churches, the influence of Enlightenment thought on Jefferson and other Virginia political leaders, and the debates over the Virginia Declaration of Rights. Different models of the church-state relationship competed for dominance during this period, including the existing model of the established Anglican Church, a model of total church-state separation and complete disestablishment, and a middle position that recognized the freedom of all religious groups but provided state support for Christian ministry. Both Jefferson and the dissenting Protestants favored complete disestablishment, but for different reasons. Jefferson's position was based on Enlightenment philosophy and emphasized the political and legal equality of all religious groups; it sought to protect the state from church influence. The dissenters' view was grounded in the theological conviction that true religious belief cannot be coerced (a belief Jefferson shared); it sought to protect the church from state influence. Their shared goal created the political common ground that led to the adoption of the statute.

Formal disestablishment also had important consequences for the established Anglican Church, which in 1783 became the Protestant Episcopal Church. Removal of state support meant that the Anglican Church had to redefine its own forms of religious authority, yet it found itself largely unprepared to exercise the new freedom that had been thrust upon it. Buckley details the Anglican Church's internal struggle, linking it to the larger political and Revolutionary context. Finally, building on themes addressed in the previous chapters, Buckley notes that the formal separation of church and state did not mean the elimination of religion from social and cultural life. Jefferson agreed with the increasingly influential evangelicals that religion should continue to have an important place in public life and that a healthy democracy required the social inculcation of religious (Christian) values. As a result, despite the formal disestablishment of the Anglican Church, Virginia witnessed the social establishment of evangelical Christianity, an informal but powerful reality that dominated social and political life in the Commonwealth—and elsewhere in the new nation—throughout the next century and beyond.

The embracing of religious freedom in Virginia had widespread and lasting consequences, and in chapter 6 Daniel L. Dreisbach concludes the volume by examining several features of the Virginia experience that would become enduring themes in American self-understanding. These include the role of religion in the national narrative; the need to define the legal and political terms within which America's vast religious pluralism could best be accommodated; the idea that despite formal separation of church and state, religion remains necessary to support the social order and develop good citizens; and the establishment of religious liberty in place of mere religious toleration in the American polity. In each case, Virginia was the place where these themes were most thoroughly worked out. Thus, while Virginia was not the first American jurisdiction to formalize the separation of church and state, its transition from establishment to disestablishment had the most profound and lasting influence on the new nation. Dreisbach suggests that the final emergence of religious liberty in Virginia in the decade between 1776 and 1787 is one of the great stories in human history.

FOR ALL ITS critical importance, we must remember that Jefferson's Statute for Religious Freedom is but one point on a long and uneven historical journey. The struggle for religious freedom was not finished with the adoption of this statute in 1786, nor with the First Amendment to the U.S. Constitution in 1791, nor with Article 18 of the Universal Declaration of Human Rights in 1948. As one of us has written in another context, "Principles such as religious freedom are not self-defining. They carry only the meaning we give them."[20] Thus, while Jefferson's groundbreaking statute continues to influence the Supreme Court's interpretation of the First Amendment,[21] it is nevertheless the case that legal protection for religious freedom has weakened in the United States in recent years.[22] Indeed, many of the struggles of religious minorities in early Virginia discussed throughout this volume have a distinctly modern echo. The social and political space necessary for religious freedom to thrive must continually be renewed, and the historical lessons derived from the superb scholarship contained in these pages must continually be reexamined and relearned.

NOTES

1. Thomas Jefferson, "Epitaph, n.d.," American Memory Project, Library of Congress, http://memory.loc.gov/cgi-bin/ampage?collId=mtj1&fileName=mtj1 page055.db&recNum=1134&itemLink=%2Fammem%2Fcollections%2Fjeffer son_papers%2Fmtjser1.html&linkText=7&tempFile=./temp/~ammem_J7Su& filecode=mtj&next_filecode=mtj&itemnum=1&ndocs= 3 (accessed June 17, 2010). See Rhys Isaac, *The Transformation of Virginia 1740–1790* (Chapel Hill: University of North Carolina Press, 1982), 273–75.

2. Merrill D. Peterson, *Thomas Jefferson and the New Nation: A Biography* (New York: Oxford University Press, 1970), 988; Robert M. S. McDonald, "Thomas Jefferson and Historical Self-Construction: The Earth Belongs to the Living?" *Historian* 61 (1999): 300–302.

3. David Armitage, *The Declaration of Independence: A Global History* (Cambridge: Harvard University Press, 2008); Pauline Maier, *American Scripture: Making the Declaration of Independence* (New York: Vintage, 1997).

4. Martin E. Marty, "The Virginia Statute Two Hundred Years Later," in *The Virginia Statute for Religious Freedom: Its Evolution and Consequences in American History,* ed. Merrill D. Peterson and Robert C. Vaughn (New York: Cambridge University Press, 1988), 1.

5. See John Witte Jr., *Religion and the American Constitutional Experiment,* 2d ed. (Boulder, CO: Westview Press, 2004), 21–39.

6. See Isaac, *Transformation of Virginia,* 273–95; Thomas J. Curry, *The First Freedoms: Church and State in America to the Passage of the First Amendment* (New York: Oxford University Press, 1986), 134–58; Thomas E. Buckley, S.J., *Church and State in Revolutionary Virginia, 1776–1787* (Charlottesville: University Press of Virginia, 1977), 38–70; John A. Ragosta, *Wellspring of Liberty: How Virginia's Religious Dissenters Helped Win the American Revolution and Secured Religious Liberty* (New York: Oxford University Press, 2010).

7. Merrill D. Peterson and Robert C. Vaughn, "Introduction," in Peterson and Vaughn, *Virginia Statute for Religious Freedom,* ix.

8. William Waller Hening, ed., *The Statutes at Large: Being a Collection of All the Laws of Virginia, from the First Session of the Legislature, in the Year 1619, etc.* (Richmond, VA, 1809–23), 12:84–86.

9. Thomas Jefferson, *Autobiography,* in *Thomas Jefferson: Writings,* ed. Merrill D. Peterson (New York: Library of America, 1984), 40.

10. Gerald V. Bradley, "The No Religious Test Clause and the Constitution of Religious Liberty: A Machine That Has Gone of Itself," *Case Western Reserve Law Review* 37 (1987): 674–747. See also Daniel L. Dreisbach, "The Constitution's Forgotten Religion Clause: Reflections on the Article VI Religious Test Ban," *Journal of Church and State* 38 (1996): 261–95.

11. The U.S. Constitution, Art. 6, cl. 3 provides that "no religious Test shall ever be required as a Qualification to any Office of public Trust under the United States."

12. *Cumberland Gazette,* Dec. 1, 1786.

13. Jefferson was convinced that the international embrace of the statute "[would] produce considerable good even in these countries where ignorance, superstition, poverty and oppression of body and mind in every form, are so firmly settled on the mass of the people, that their redemption from them can never be hoped." Thomas Jefferson to George Wythe, Aug. 13, 1786, in *The Papers of Thomas Jefferson,* ed. Julian P. Boyd (Princeton, NJ: Princeton University Press, 1954), 10:244. For Jefferson's having the statute translated, see ibid., 10:603.

14. *Columbian Herald,* May 29, 1786. The author, who addressed his piece "to the Reverend Clergy of all Christian denominations in the City of Philadelphia, and to the Public Friends of the respectable Society called Quakers, in this Metropolis," spent considerable effort refuting the statute point by point; see the continued piece in ibid., June 1, 5, 8, 12, 1786.

15. *Massachusetts Centinel,* Apr. 26, 1786.

16. For useful discussions of the early histories of both regions, see Edmund S. Morgan, *American Slavery, American Freedom: The Ordeal of Colonial Virginia* (New York: W. W. Norton, 1975); Perry Miller, *The New England Mind: The Seventeenth*

Century (Cambridge: Harvard University Press, 1958). See also T. H. Breen, *Puritans and Adventurers: Change and Persistence in Early America* (New York: Oxford University Press, 1980); Jack P. Greene, *Pursuits of Happiness: The Social Development of Early Modern British Colonies and the Formation of American Culture* (Chapel Hill: University of North Carolina Press, 1988).

17. Morgan, *American Slavery, American Freedom.*

18. Useful introductory studies on race include Ira Berlin, *Many Thousands Gone: The First Two Centuries of Slavery in North America* (Cambridge: Harvard University Press, 2000); Philip D. Morgan, *Slave Counterpoint: Black Culture in the Eighteenth-Century Chesapeake and Lowcountry* (Chapel Hill: University of North Carolina Press, 1998); Anthony S. Parent, *Foul Means: The Formation of a Slave Society in Virginia, 1660–1740* (Chapel Hill: University of North Carolina Press, 2003); Mechal Sobel, *The World They Made Together: Black and White Values in Eighteenth-Century Virginia* (Princeton, NJ: Princeton University Press, 1989). See also Michael A. McDonnell, *The Politics of War: Race, Class, and Conflict in Revolutionary Virginia* (Chapel Hill: University of North Carolina Press, 2007); Woody Holton, *Forced Founders: Indians, Debtors, Slaves, and the Making of the American Revolution in Virginia* (Chapel Hill: University of North Carolina Press, 1999).

19. Useful places to begin to explore the role of gender include Kathleen Brown, *Good Wives, Nasty Wenches, and Anxious Patriarchs: Gender, Race, and Power in Colonial Virginia* (Chapel Hill: University of North Carolina Press, 1996); Mary Beth Norton, *Founding Mothers and Fathers: Gendered Power and the Forming of American Society* (New York: Alfred A. Knopf, 1996); Terri L. Snyder, *Brabbling Women: Disorderly Speech and the Law in Early Virginia* (Ithaca, NY: Cornell University Press, 2003).

20. Paul Rasor, "Center for the Study of Religious Freedom, Virginia Wesleyan College," http://www.vwc.edu/academics/csrf/index.php (accessed May 14, 2010).

21. The statute figures prominently in the Supreme Court's first modern establishment clause opinion, *Everson v. Board of Education,* 330 U.S. 1 (1947). A more recent example is *Rosenberger v. Rector and Visitors of the University of Virginia,* 515 U.S. 891 (1995) (Stevens, J., dissenting). See Cushing Strout, "Jeffersonian Religious Liberty and American Pluralism," in Peterson and Vaughn, *Virginia Statute for Religious Freedom,* 201–35.

22. See *Employment Division v. Smith,* 494 U.S. 872 (1990). Helpful recent treatments of the diminishing protection for religious freedom include Kent Greenawalt, *Free Exercise and Fairness,* vol. 1 of *Religion and the Constitution* (Princeton, NJ: Princeton University Press, 2006), 74–85, 439–43; and Erwin Chemerinsky, *Constitutional Law: Principles and Policies,* 3d ed. (New York: Aspen Publishers, 2006), 1258–62.

ONE   Evidence of Religion in
       Seventeenth-Century Virginia

BRENT TARTER

IN THE BEGINNING—THAT IS TO SAY, IN THE SPRING OF 1607
—Protestant Christianity got off to an inauspicious start in Virginia. Late in life, Captain John Smith penned a short recollection
of "how we beganne to preach the Gospell in Virginia." He wrote:

> Wee did hang an awning (which is an old saile) to three or foure
> trees to shadow us from the Sunne, our walls were rales of wood,
> our seats unhewed trees, till we cut plankes, our Pulpit a bar of
> wood nailed to two neighbouring trees, in foule weather we shifted
> into an old rotten tent . . . this was our Church, till we built a
> homely thing like a barne . . . yet wee had daily Common Prayer
> morning and evening, every Sunday two Sermons, and every three
> moneths the holy Communion, till our Minister died, but our
> Prayers daily, with an Homily on Sundaies; we continued two or
> three yeares after till more Preachers came.[1]

The study of religion in colonial Virginia also got off to an
inauspicious—or at least a very late—start. The first chronicler of
the colony's ecclesiastical history, William Meade, in his 1857 two-
volume *Old Churches, Ministers and Families of Virginia,* paid scant
attention to the colonists' religious beliefs in the seventeenth century.[2] Neither did his successor, George MacLaren Brydon, in the
1947 first volume of *Virginia's Mother Church and the Political Conditions under Which It Grew.*[3] Philip Alexander Bruce's 1910 two-
volume *Institutional History of Virginia in the Seventeenth Century*
describes the religious institutions of the colony and how civil authorities regulated the moral behavior of the colonists but does not

delve deeply into religious beliefs.[4] The modern histories of colonial Virginia, by Richard Lee Morton, and by Warren M. Billings, John E. Selby, and Thad W. Tate, include good accounts of the colonists' religious institutions, but little of substance on the religious beliefs and practices of seventeenth-century Virginians.[5] The same must regretfully be said about the most recent scholarly histories of Virginia, both published in the anniversary year 2007: Peter Wallenstein's *Cradle of America: Four Centuries of Virginia History*, and Ronald L. Heinemann, John G. Kolp, Anthony S. Parent Jr., and William G. Shade's *Old Dominion, New Commonwealth: A History of Virginia, 1607–2007*.[6]

What early historians of seventeenth-century Virginia too often saw when they looked at the surviving documents of Virginia's early history were evidences of individualism at work. They looked for and at the origins of plantation society or the development of representative political institutions, but most historians did not often look for, and therefore did not find or explain, the attitudes that English colonists and other early white Virginians had about religion. Most histories of seventeenth-century Virginia are consequently incomplete because they portray the first English colonists as not at all concerned about religion, but primarily or only about how settlers searched the watercourses for an easy route to the riches of the Orient, how they searched the ground for gold and precious metals, and how they eventually succeeded when they converted the colony into a tobacco strip mine.[7]

In looking for things to study other than the religious beliefs and practices of Virginia's colonists, most of those early historians made two big mistakes. The first was to assume, or to write as if they believed, that the residents of England who migrated to Virginia did not have any religious beliefs or that they forgetfully left them behind on the dock. It is a capital blunder to ignore the critical importance of the English Reformation for all seventeenth-century English men and women wherever they lived. By the time the first few English men and boys set foot in Virginia in 1607, three generations of English men and women had experienced tumultuous religious changes that rocked their native land to its political foundations and severed the relationship of a vast majority of the English people with the church headquartered in Rome.

The English Reformation and its consequences affected every English man and woman. It is inconceivable that the immigrants—both the literate ones and a goodly proportion of the nonliterate immigrants, too—were without religious beliefs that were important to them.

The other mistake of the early historians was to assume, or to write as if they believed, that a scarcity of evidence of the kind scholars employ to study religious beliefs in New England meant that there were few or no important religious beliefs in Virginia to study. There is a large body of written records about religious beliefs and practices in New England that preserve information about those religious beliefs and practices. Moreover, the physical and literary landscapes of New England invite attention to that region's religious history. If these important writings and artifacts had not survived, we would know much less than we do about religious life in colonial New England.

For a variety of reasons, the physical and literary landscapes of Virginia do not invite attention to the subject of religion. Yet for historians therefore to presume that religion was not important to seventeenth-century Virginians is a failure of imagination about research and resources. For example, there are not many surviving seventeenth-century Virginia church buildings, or any other kinds of buildings, for that matter, and there are but a few surviving early eighteenth-century church buildings. However, that does not mean that there *weren't* church buildings. Before the second third of the eighteenth century, most churches and other buildings in Virginia were of wooden, earth-fast construction. Those buildings left little evidence of their existence after they were enlarged or rebuilt or the timbers rotted or the structures burned.[8] The scarcity of native stone in the eastern portion of the colony also means that little aboveground evidence of graveyards remains to call attention to the sites of seventeenth-century churches.

The literary landscape of colonial Virginia also appears at first glance bare of enticing clues about religious beliefs and practices. There are almost no surviving seventeenth-century church archives, diaries, devotional records, private letters, or printed sermons and tracts, and the files of private and public correspondence that survive in British repositories did not become conveniently available for researchers until the Virginia Colonial Records Project micro-filmed them during the second half of the twentieth century. For its first century and a quarter, the colony did not even have a printing press through which ideas and disagreements could be aired and preserved for the convenience of later generations of scholars. Historians therefore did not find much evidence of the New England kind, and most of them did not think to look elsewhere for evidence of other kinds. Yet the very documents those historians read in search of information about the great landed families, tobacco production, trade, the slave system, westward movement, and the development of political institutions and practices all contain evidence about the colonists' religious beliefs and prac-tices. Historians' preoccupations with other subjects made them tone-deaf, as it were, to the echoes that the surviving documen-tary records contain about the religious beliefs of the people whom they studied.

If historians consciously or unconsciously began with an unex-amined assumption or reached an unexplained conclusion that re-ligious beliefs were not very important to those many thousands of seventeenth-century English-speaking Virginians, they committed a third mistake, because an absence of evidence is not necessarily evidence of an absence. In addition to the tone-deafness that af-flicted some historians of early Virginia, the dearth and difficulty of the evidence also muted the echoes and contributed to misper-ceptions about the colony's religious history. The evidence is con-spicuous for those who look for and recognize it when they see it.

A considerable body of surviving written evidence confirms the existence of church buildings throughout the settled Virginia landscape from fairly early dates. The surviving county records, including court order books, deed books, and will books, have references to churches scattered all through them. People some-times identified their places of residence or the locations of their property by the name of the parish or by a direction or distance from a church in the same way that they casually mentioned the courthouse or a watercourse or a neighbor's property line. Those references are easily overlooked because they are entirely routine. Frame churches were probably as familiar and unremark-able a part of the settled landscape as dwelling houses and sheds and barns and bad roads, none of which elicited comment unless something out of the ordinary happened to or near them. An even greater amount of evidence would be available if it were not for the propensity of frame and even brick courthouses to burn down, just like frame churches did, or if wars and floods had not also destroyed the contents of many of those courthouses. Seventeenth-century Virginia was as much a colony of churches as it was a colony of tobacco farms and courthouses, even though most of the histories of colonial Virginia portray courthouses as the centers of public life.

The existence of churches suggests the presence of clergymen. It is a standard feature of the literature on colonial Virginia, especially on the seventeenth century, to comment on the scarcity of clergymen. Ministers were, indeed, in short supply in some places and in some times, but court records and other government records are as likely to contain passing references to clergymen in their parishes as they are to include comments on a shortage of ministers of the gospel. The relative absence of early Virginia evidence is not clear evidence of an absence of early Virginia clergymen.

One influential study of American religious history has singled out the Eastern Shore counties as the one place in the colony where the institutions and beliefs of the Church of England functioned in an effective manner in the seventeenth century.[9] That there were churches and ministers on the Eastern Shore, and that white Virginians who lived there resided in an organized religious as well as an organized civil society, are beyond dispute. The local records clearly demonstrate that. But it may not be the case that life for those white Virginians on the Eastern Shore was significantly unlike life for white Virginians west of the bay. The one thing that clearly distinguishes the Eastern Shore from the remainder of seventeenth-century Virginia, other than physical separation of the two areas by an easily crossed body of water, is the survival for the Eastern Shore of a complete run of excellent local records that have in part been published and have long been studied. The records contain ample evidence of religious institutions performing their expected duties. It may be that the accessibility of the records is the unusual feature of the Eastern Shore, not that the Eastern Shore itself was unusual.[10]

The English men and women who colonized Virginia and their descendants believed themselves to be a chosen people in a biblical sense. Their nation, their church, and their faith were the one true Christian nation, church, and faith. God favored England, which was therefore the one true civilization. The English Reformation and its implications were as fundamentally a part of their lives as their language, dress, and political culture.[11] The linkage in their minds between true religion and civilization can be seen in documents from the very earliest days of the colony, when they recorded facts about those few English men who left the settlement and took up more-or-less permanent residence with the Indians. Scarcely any event caused the first English colonists more consternation or was more difficult for them to understand. The language they used to describe the abandonment of civilization for savagery, as well as the language they used to discuss differences between themselves and their Indian neighbors, was heavily freighted with religious meaning. They wrote about Christians and heathens and also about Englishmen and heathens. They wrote about Christians and Indians and also about Englishmen and Indians. They wrote about Christians and savages and about Englishmen and savages. The words *English* and *Christian* and variations on *civilization* identified one set of people and their culture. The words *savage* and *heathen* and *uncivilized* identified another. This religiously based language, which they also used in discussions involving persons of African origin or descent, clearly meant something significant to the English Protestants who used it.[12] English Virginians viewed themselves and their world through a thoroughly religious perspective. Religion and civilization were from their theological perspective inseparable.

EARLY RELIGIOUS CODES

Captain John Smith's account of the first worship service and subsequent descriptions of and regulations about the colonists' religious experiences deserve to be taken seriously as evidence of the colonists' religious beliefs and faith and of the thoroughly religious context in which they lived their lives, rather than merely as starting points for discussing other things. That is how historians have usually used those documents and how they missed some important clues. For instance, the famous—or infamous—*Lawes Divine, Morall and Martiall* are often cited and sometimes quoted to make a point about the brutal and dictatorial nature of the military regime instituted in 1610 to impose order on the chaotic colony. But the regulations and the language in which they were promulgated also indicate how inextricably intertwined governance was with religious beliefs and practices and how much the governors believed that English Protestantism was essential to the well-being of the colony and of the colonists.

The governor opened the code with this tangled sentence fragment, which emphasized the link between government and religion: "Where his Majestie like himselfe a most zealous Prince hath in his owne Realmes a principall care of true Religion, and reverence to God, and hath alwaies strictly commaunded his Generals and Governours, with all his forces wheresoever, to let their waies be like his ends, for the glorie of God."[13] The code required that the colonists "have a care that the Almightie God bee duly and daily served"; that "no man speake impiously or maliciously, against the holy and blessed Trinitie"; that "no man blaspheme Gods holy name upon paine of death, or use unlawfull oathes"; that no man "shall speake any word, or do any act, which may tend to the derision, or despight of Gods holy word upon paine of death"; that all colonists attend religious services twice daily; and that all clergymen "within this our Colonie, or Colonies, shall in the Forts, where they are resident, after divine Service, duly preach every Sabbath day in the forenoone, and Catechise in the afternoone, and weekly say the divine service, twice every day, and preach every Wednesday."[14] These religious regulations precede the strict rules governing personal behavior and prescribing severe punishment for violations. The following year the military commander added as an appendix a seven-page prayer that he ordered to be "duly said Morning and Evening upon the Court of Guard, either by the Captiane of the watch himselfe, or by some one of his principall officers."[15] Each twice-daily recitation of that prayer required between a quarter and half an hour.

In the summer of 1619, the first General Assembly also intermingled sacred and secular language with sacred and secular regulations. The Assembly met in the Jamestown church, probably because it was a convenient and capacious enough room, and there was no alternative. "Forasmuche as mens affaires doe little prosper where Gods service is neglected," the report of the opening proceedings stated, the members began their work with a prayer from the minister "that it would please God to guide & sanctifie all our proceedings, to his owne glory, and the good of this plantation."[16] In addition to the many regulations they adopted, including rules "against Idlenes, Gaming, drunkenes, & excesse in apparell," they made plans "for laying a surer foundation of the conversion of the Indians to Christian Religion" by placing Indian children in every town where they could be educated "in true religion and a civile course of life."[17] The Assembly also required all ministers in the colony (there may have then been four) to keep and annually report records of all christenings, burials, and marriages (a responsibility of ministers of the Church of England in the old country) and "duely read divine service, and exercise their Ministerial function, according to the Ecclesiasticall lawes and orders of the churche of Englande."[18] The Assembly ordered the ministers and the churchwardens to report all "ungodly disorders" and "skandalous offenses, as suspicions of whordomes, dishonest Company-keeping with weomen, & suche like."[19] In one of its final acts, the Assembly required that "All persons whatsoever upon the Sabaoth daye shall frequente divine service and sermons both forenoon and afternoon."[20]

One thing stands out in the laws of 1610 and 1619: Protestant Christianity was of fundamental importance to the rulers, and they expected it to be of fundamental importance to those whom they ruled. The language of those laws and the language of that time are replete with religious references, and the daily lives of the colonists were punctuated with the rhythms of religious rituals. A second thing lurks inconspicuously in the laws of 1619 and can easily be missed. The ministers and lay leaders, or churchwardens, were required to police the community for moral failings. This may be one of the first references to churchwardens in a Virginia document. What does the mention of churchwardens in the 1619 law mean? Where did they come from? Who appointed them? Had they been there all along? Did that act implicitly create them?

The Church of England treated the colony during the first decades of the seventeenth century as a place of missionary work
(ministers were missionaries to the Indians and also missionaries to the colonists),[21] and therefore the formal creation of parish
structures and modes of church governance may not have seemed
initially necessary. Yet the church needed local officials like churchwardens, and so somebody somehow designated some. As early as
1619, a rudimentary form of local church governance was in place
in Virginia, and it resembled, as would be expected, the forms of
local church governance in England. Few records and references
survive to document the development of local or colonial church
organization during the first half of the seventeenth century. It is
likely that each minister and congregation devised practices consistent with expectations they brought with them from England.
The word *parish* was also then a very new word in the colony, insofar as extant Virginia documents show.

In 1643 the General Assembly enacted what was probably the
first comprehensive law since 1619 (it is the earliest such statute
that survives) to regulate religious affairs "for the advancement of
God's glorie and the weale publique." The law required the colonists to attend church and specified the duties of ministers and
churchwardens. It also directed that "there be a vestrie held in each
parish, for the makeing of the leavies and assessments for such uses
as are requisite & necessary for the repairing of the churches, &c."[22]
The wording of the 1643 law suggests that in some or many or most
of the churches in the colony, but perhaps not yet all, a select number of lay members had begun taking responsibility for the parish.

That same statute also empowered vestries to select parish
ministers.[23] This action was undoubtedly a concession to local
circumstances because it was a departure from English custom,
and there was nobody else in the colony to exercise that essential
work on behalf of the church. The governor as well as the com-
manders of particular plantations had previously appointed some
ministers, but by the 1640s lay vestries in Virginia took responsibility for appointing clergymen. A 1652 act went further and
explicitly vested in parish vestries the power to act by "theire
owne orderinge and dispossall from time to time, as they shall
thinke ffitt," in all matters concerning the minister, the church,

the churchwardens, the poor, and the behavior of their parishioners.[24] There was no bishop or other ecclesiastical authority in the colony, there were no ecclesiastical courts, and it is unclear whether governors often attempted to exercise ecclesiastical jurisdiction in emergencies. As a consequence, there was virtually no church hierarchy in Virginia, and the congregations scattered around the bay and along the great rivers were largely self-governing until after the American Revolution.[25] The organization of the Church of England in Virginia during the seventeenth century resembled the organization of the Church of England in England only superficially, even at the local level.[26] In fact, it more nearly resembled the congregational churches in New England or the Church of Scotland.

Parishes as local units of governance were important in many ways. Lay vestries assumed responsibility for the poor and the orphaned and for the public roads. Ministers in the seventeenth century may also have conducted schools, as many of them did in the eighteenth century. It is difficult to imagine that a common school under the direction of a clergyman would not include instruction in the teachings of the Church of England. Literacy itself may be taken as prima facie evidence of a religious education. It is likely that until the middle of the seventeenth century the churches in Virginia, as in both old England and New England, allowed people suspected of crimes of morality, such as fornication or adultery, to purge themselves of sin and to cleanse the community of immorality by confessing in church in a ritual ceremony called compurgation.[27] For an undetermined number of years in the middle of the seventeenth century, some parishes even sent representatives to the General Assembly, just as counties did.[28] That frequently overlooked fact suggests just how important churches and parishes were to the people, who had to pay the expenses of their parochial burgesses, and how important parishes were to the General Assembly, which admitted their burgesses on equal terms with the county representatives.

In 1656 the Assembly required counties that had not already established boundaries for the parishes within their jurisdictions or created parishes for the local churches to do so forthwith.[29] This was a directive to complete the formal organization of the colonial church into a system of uniformly managed parishes. The wording of the law suggests that the development of local church government had proceeded at different paces and perhaps in different ways in the different localities. Some parishes already had settled boundaries and boards of superintending vestrymen, but perhaps some did not. The development of institutional and social structures in seventeenth-century Virginia was in many ways haphazard. English colonists brought with them knowledge of English social, economic, political, and religious practices and institutions, but when carving out of the New World enough space for them to live in and establish their own institutions and practices, they necessarily and slowly improvised.[30]

The 1656 statute has not gone unnoticed by historians, but they too often quote only the preamble, which notes that "there are many places destitute of ministers, and like still to continue soe, the people content not payinge their accustomed dues, which makes them negligent to procure those which should teach and instruct them."[31] This language is misread as evidence that seventeenth-century Virginia was a place where ministers were scarce and religion was not of enough importance that colonists were willing to pay ministers a salary. To draw that conclusion is to miss an essential fact: members of the Church of England could and did conduct their own religious services without an ordained minister. Recall that Captain John Smith wrote that during an extended period between the death of the colony's first minister and the arrival of another, the colonists held their daily prayer services, and somebody delivered a homily every Sunday.

The 1650s was no ordinary decade in Virginia or in England. During that decade Oliver Cromwell's Puritan Commonwealth attempted to suppress the performance of the church's liturgical worship service and the use of its Book of Common Prayer. Puritans held powerful political offices in Virginia, including the governorship, so what were vestrymen to do? What were Prayer Book ministers to do? It may have been that clergymen were in short supply or unwilling in sufficient numbers to take parishes in the colony at the rates parishioners could afford to pay. Alternatively, it might have been that vestrymen were of divided opinion or reluctant to choose a minister whose religious persuasion differed from their own. It is by no means clear whether or how Cromwell's government altered the religious landscape in Virginia, nor is it wise to presume from one legislative comment, even if repeated almost verbatim two years later, that there was a *chronic* shortage of clergymen in the colony throughout the century because parishioners did not care enough to hire them. In fact, the General Assembly in 1656 offered a bounty of twenty pounds sterling to every clergyman who would move to Virginia and take charge of a vacant parish, and it exempted clergymen and six of their servants from paying local taxes.[32] If clergymen were in short supply, it may have been the supply, not the demand, that was responsible.

PURITANS IN VIRGINIA

Puritans were in New England, but they were also in seventeenth-century Virginia. Historians' commonplace habit of dividing English Protestants into two distinct groups, Puritans and Anglicans, distorts the complex realities of the past. Between the mid-sixteenth and mid-seventeenth centuries, there was a wide continuum of beliefs among English Protestants about how much reform of the English church was the right amount to complete the English Reformation. Many English churchmen revered the solemn liturgical service of the ancient church, which they codified early in the years of the English Reformation in the Book of Common Prayer. The reforming impulse led other English Protestants to greater or lesser degrees of dissatisfaction with the formalities of the liturgical service. At the opposite end of the continuum were English Protestants who insisted on ridding the church, or purifying it, of most or all vestiges of its Catholic past. Some of them rejected the liturgical service and the Book of Common Prayer entirely. Most English Protestants, however, were somewhere between the extremes, and within that middle ground differences of opinion were oftentimes not so great as to disrupt congregations or communities.

It is probable that seventeenth-century Virginia numbered comparatively few of what in later centuries would have been regarded as high church Anglicans or the high Puritans who gave to New England a religious and political culture quite different from Virginia's. A wide middle ground predominated in which both

Prayer Book churchmen and many moderate Puritans felt quite comfortable. Some of the leading clergymen of the early years and some important planters and political leaders were sympathetic to, or in full agreement with, the reforming spirit characterized as Puritanism, and the founding Virginia Company had included among its many shareholders and most influential officers a large number of Puritans.[33] In 1641 and 1642, in Upper Norfolk County in the southeastern corner of Virginia, when the formalization of parish lines and structures was still in process, the people had become numerous enough to create three parishes, requiring them to recruit three ministers. In the spring of 1642, they wrote a letter to Puritans in New England asking the church worthies there to select three pastors to take over care of the souls in the three new parishes. The first signature on that letter is that of Richard Bennett, who was to be the Puritan governor of Virginia from 1652 to 1655, elected by the General Assembly.[34] As it turns out, the three ministers returned to New England fairly soon because their zealous beliefs made them incompatible with some Virginians.[35] But the important point about this episode and the lesson to be learned from the public career of Richard Bennett is that members of the Church of England in Virginia, with or without Puritan ideas, got along reasonably well most of the time, probably because their differences of opinion on religious matters did not often approach the intolerant extremes.

By the same token, some white Virginians, perhaps most, were comfortable with the Book of Common Prayer and the liturgical service, even though their worship services may have been simpler than the formalities the Book of Common Prayer prescribed. John Clayton, for instance, who was rector of James City Parish from 1684 to 1686, left evidence of the comparative informality of the worship services in Virginia when he stated that he believed that he was the first clergyman in the colony to use the full evening service of the Book of Common Prayer and "the first that wore a Surplice there."[36] That would have pleased early Puritans. It is entirely possible that in the first half of the seventeenth century, there may have been as many people in Virginia as in New England whom we could classify as Puritans, though Puritans of the reforming sort rather than Puritans of the separatist sort.

The liturgical services of the Church of England, the language of the Book of Common Prayer, and the emphasis on godly living and salvation may have given most Virginia Protestants few occasions to engage in theological disputes on fine points of doctrine or interpretation of Scripture or on parishioners' fitness for church membership. Hence, there may have been little in Virginia to begin with of the kind of disputation that reveals much about the religious beliefs of New Englanders. Through its services and the ministering of its clergy, the church sought to persuade parishioners to seek in their own ways the salvation that God offered to them. Even the Book of Common Prayer, which prescribed set biblical texts and prayers for each of the scores of devotional occasions throughout the year, left it to the discretion of individual clergymen (and perhaps of their more-or-less superintending congregations in Virginia) whether to deviate from the prescribed forms of worship by omitting or substituting texts.

The English Civil Wars of the 1640s can be thought of as a belated and bloody chapter of the English Reformation. The violence did not, by and large, spill over into Virginia, even though the colonial government remained loyal to the Crown long after Charles I lost his head. Virginians, however, who ultimately surrendered peacefully to the authority of Parliament in 1652, when they had no other choice, did not lose their heads.[37] While some government officials persecuted some Puritans, and a significant portion of Virginia's Puritans eventually moved to Maryland or dispersed into the Northern Neck during the 1640s, it is entirely possible or even probable that the avoidance of like violence in Virginia was as important as, or more important than, imposing religious uniformity.[38]

The same might be said of Virginia's newly elected Puritans. In 1652, the General Assembly elected Puritan Richard Bennett as governor. Edward Digges, who got along well with both Cromwell and Charles II, succeeded him in 1655, and Samuel Matthews, namesake son of a Puritan merchant and powerful political officeholder from before the Civil Wars, succeeded Digges in 1656.[39] It is not clear to what extent these officials enforced the discontinuance of the use of the Book of Common Prayer, either in private or in the churches, or imposed hardships on the royalists.

The striking thing is how comparatively nonviolent Virginia was during most of the decades that produced profound religious upheavals in old England. The church appears to have left most people alone with their beliefs. Protestants could reinforce their faith weekly, for those who attended church that regularly, or daily, for those who had a copy of the Book of Common Prayer and were inclined to observe its daily offices in their homes. A considerable variety of individual belief systems could dwell together peaceably enough in the colony's scattered and independent congregations. It is probably within that context that white seventeenth-century Virginians managed not to be at each others' throats very often about matters of religious belief and practice. It was not that they did not care about or believe in anything; it was that they did not always insist that everybody else care about and believe in precisely the same things and for exactly the same reasons.

THE ROLE OF THE PARISH

The parish, not the county, was the most local unit of government in the colony. Throughout the seventeenth century, almost every county included several parishes. In Virginia, parishes were much larger than in England, but in nearly every instance much smaller than any county. The vestrymen, churchwardens, parish clerks, and clergymen of those small vicinities—a word derived from *vicinage,* from church government—would have been personally known to most or all of the residents of the parish. The same probably could not have been said about all of the officers of the counties. It was at the parish or neighborhood level that many of the most important events of people's lives took place. The parish is where they married, where they baptized their babies, where they educated their children in the ways of God, where they buried their dead, where they closely scrutinized the quality of their neighbors' tobacco crops, and where they bartered chickens or grain or cloth or seed corn with their near neighbors, the same people with whom they attended church. The parish may have been the counterpart for colonial Virginians of the New England township, although scholars have not often thought to look on it as such.[40]

Colonial Virginians certainly did not underestimate the fundamental importance of the parish, either for its religious

responsibilities or for the community of interest that it represented in both sacred and secular affairs. In the spring of 1662, the
General Assembly passed a law intended to reduce the number of
locally divisive disputes about property lines. The Assembly ordered that the churchwardens of every parish assemble all of the
people who resided in the vicinity of each property line and that in
procession they perambulate the boundaries of all the landowners.
They jointly pointed out to one another the landmarks of their property boundaries, they renewed the slashes on the boundary trees,
and they did it all in a common endeavor that provided everybody
with the same information. If a difference of opinion arose during
the process, the churchwardens brought up documents and called
in two disinterested men to make a final determination. The law
required that the churchwardens do the same thing every fourth
year to refresh the marks and the memories and also to incorporate
new owners into the collective memory as they came of age or
moved into the parish or inherited property from owners who had
died.[41] The legislature elaborated, amended, and renewed the law
in 1691, 1705, 1744, and 1748.[42] The few surviving parish and county
records do not disclose whether the churchwardens observed the
letter of the law during the final third of the seventeenth century,
but they amply indicate that the processioning of the land, or "beating the bounds," as it was also called, was probably undertaken every fourth year, probably nearly everywhere, through the end of
the colonial period.[43]

After 1662 in Virginia, officials of the parishes of the Church
of England, not the surveyor or the sheriff or the justices of the
peace, had that important social responsibility in the guardian-
ship of real property. The collective community memory was of
such importance that the 1705 codification of the statutes directed
the churchwardens to record the results of their processioning in
a permanent book of record. After a boundary line had been publicly marked three consecutive times without objection, the landmarks could not be questioned in a court of law.[44] That the vox
populi of the parish might actually be of equal validity with written words on land grants, deeds, and surveys speaks powerfully to
the importance of the parish as a focus of community life.

"TRUE RELIGION AND A CIVILE COURSE OF LIFE"

If clergymen were scarce in some places and in some times, and if there were people who did not have or could not read from a family Book of Common Prayer, how pervasive or persuasive were the church's teachings among the white English-speaking residents of seventeenth-century Virginia? What did the occasional shortages of clergymen mean to devout Virginians who needed to marry their spouses, baptize their babies, educate their children, bury their dead, and safeguard their souls? Did the church, such as it was, with the aid of the state, of which it was a part, meet for the colony's white population the goal the Assembly had set in 1619 for the children of the colony's Indians, that they be trained "in true religion and a civile course of life"?

That is a rich phrase, one that concisely blends the essential objectives shared by the church and the state. For most seventeenth-century English Protestants, true religion was not possible without a civil course of life, nor was a civil course of life possible without true religion. As a chosen people, seventeenth-century English Protestants almost certainly could not have imagined religious and civic lives that were not entwined. The church and the state were not simply linked by a connective tissue that could be separated. Each was part of the other, and both were under the protection of the Crown and, in Virginia, of the Crown's personal deputy, the royal governor. Except during the Commonwealth years in the 1650s, the king was the head of the church and of the state. Through the combined and mutually reinforcing powers of the word and the sword, the king led and protected his people in true religion and a civil course of life.

That simple but essential fact of life for subjects of the English Crown was inescapable to any seventeenth-century Virginian with eyes to read or ears to hear. Laws required them to attend church services regularly, although it is impossible to know how many did so. Necessity or curiosity must have impelled many of them to frequent the regularly scheduled meetings of the county courts, which by the time the church's local governance was finally established were also firmly fixed as centrally important organs of the colony's government. At both places those Virginians would have heard sacred and secular texts read out loud; the mingling of sacred and secular language reinforced the fact that church and state—true religion and civilization—were one. They might very well have regarded "true religion and a civile course of life" as a singular rather than a plural phrase. Neither was possible without the other. The two were one, and the one was both, in parallel to their understanding of the Trinity.

Even at church, secular texts were read from the pulpits, just as they were read to the public at meetings of the county courts. After a session of the Assembly, scribes made copies of all the new laws so that the county clerks or sheriffs could read them to the residents. That is how they were published or made public. Proclamations concerning high matters of state, such as the deaths of sovereigns and the succession of new royal governors, and minor matters of police, such as the apprehension of thieves or runaway servants, were all read aloud at the courthouse, and parish clerks may also have read them at the church. People were accustomed to receiving information aurally.[45] They had to listen. And what they heard, regardless of the subject matter of the text, was clothed in language that mixed the sacred and the secular. Indictments charged that accused criminals acted at the instigation of the devil and without the fear of God before their eyes. Public documents were dated in the such-and-such year of our Lord and Savior and also in the such-and-such year of the reign of our Sovereign Lord the King. Public events were in some cases officially scheduled for a saint's day or for one of the days of the church calendar rather than on a specific day of a specific month. The 1662 law for processioning property lines, for example, ordered that it be done between Easter and Whitsunday, or Pentecost.[46] Such means of reckoning the rhythms of life not only testified to the importance of religious observances in the society at large but also presupposed a minimum degree of common knowledge about when those named days would come around, or at least that people would learn of the approach of such days through their regular attendance at church.

The combination of secular and sacred language and imagery abounds to such an extent in so many seventeenth-century documents that past historians may have neglected to inquire into its significance because of a presumption that religious references in secular documents were mere formalities or routine formularies. The language should be attended to, though; it is instructive and suggestive. For example, the taxes that county courts imposed for erecting courthouses and jails or arming the militia, and that vestries imposed for erecting churches or paying the minister or caring for the orphaned and the poor, were assessed at a rate of so much per able-bodied laborer. It was a poll tax, or a head tax, on people who by their own labor or by the labor of their able-bodied servants and slaves and children contributed to the colonial economy. English and Virginia laws and the record books that could be viewed at the courthouses and parish offices identified a taxable person as a "tithable," a term that originated in the church, not in the exchequer. Until 1781, in Virginia that adjective-made-noun identified every person who was required to pay all local taxes.

When men and women wrote their wills or dictated the terms of their wills to a clergyman or to some other person who could write, the opening words were almost always, "In the name of God." Wills nearly always provided for a decent Christian burial of the body and commended the soul to God before proceeding to provide for the payment of earthly debts and to dispose of earthly property. Those phrases and forms were the standard language of wills and can be dismissed on that account as lacking genuine religious meaning. Yet wills were read aloud to the family and perhaps also in court when it came time to settle a dead person's estate, and in a context of death those words may have worked as subtle reminders on the men and women who listened to them in these settings.

On other occasions in courthouses, men and women witnessed rituals that blended religious obligations with secular responsibilities, such as taking an oath before testifying in a case or before entering into the duties of an office. By the end of the century, following the so-called Glorious Revolution in 1689, all men before taking a public office had to swear three interlocking oaths: one of allegiance to the king, one disavowing allegiance to foreign princes (meaning the pope), and one disavowing belief in the Catholic doctrine of transubstantiation: in effect, one oath to the king, one oath to the church, and one oath to the Reformation. However repetitious or apparently routine the religious phrases and allusions in those documents and ceremonies, they were there because they originally had meaning and purpose, and they remained there as reminders of that meaning and purpose. They reinforced and comforted. They were ubiquitous and should not be dismissed as meaningless. If such language no longer carried any potent meaning, it might have been laid aside, but it was not.

RELIGION AMONG OTHER VIRGINIANS

Most white English-speaking residents of seventeenth-century Virginia were members of the Church of England, doubtless some more and some less committed and some inclined toward Puritanism. But these were not the only forms of religious practice among Virginians. African and Indian residents had a highly varied collection of religious and cultural heritages to which white English-speaking Virginians paid relatively little attention.[47] Further, not all white Virginians were native speakers of English or members of the Church of England. In the very first years of the colony, the Virginia Company sent artisans and craftsmen from other European countries to Jamestown, among whom were Poles, Germans, and Italian glassmakers, who today are the best known. Archaeological excavations of the original fort site have recovered religious artifacts that demonstrate the residence at the fort at a very early date of at least one Catholic.[48] It is not known whether the artifacts belonged to a Continental Catholic or to an English Catholic. Neither is it known whether any English Catholics who might have been present kept their affiliation a secret, or whether, if they disclosed their faith, it made any difference in how they fit into the largely English Protestant community.

Another thing we do not yet know is how Catholics from other countries were treated in the early years of the colony as a consequence of being Catholic. Perhaps, as in the case of the Italian glassmakers, usefulness outweighed the unsettling dangers of difference. English Protestant merchants and manufacturers certainly had no scruples about doing business with Continental Catholics, some of whom resided in England, even as some Protestant Englishmen resided for extended times in Catholic countries. The mercantile Bland family, for instance, who furnished the colony during the seventeenth century with one of its most important explorers, a customs collector, and a Speaker of the House of Burgesses, also had a branch of the family that resided for decades in Catholic Portugal and another that resided for a time in Spain and its colonies.[49] A few Catholics in the colony were probably not regarded as so dangerous as the presence of even one priest would have been.

For a few years early in the history of the neighboring colony of Maryland, Catholics predominated. By the middle of the seventeenth century, some Maryland Catholics moved to and resided unmolested on the south bank of the Potomac River at the northern edge of settled Virginia. They and their children and grandchildren became prosperous and respected planters, but they were never very numerous and posed no real threat to the colony's Protestant institutions and culture. There were no priests, as far as we know. This is not to say that English Virginians harbored no prejudices against Catholics, only that a prejudice against a church and a fear of its influence did not always extend with equal force to its quiet and peaceable members.[50] The English laws against Catholics taking part in public affairs in Virginia were sometimes ignored, and some Catholics served as high-ranking militia officers, practiced law, and sat on the county courts. Catholic George Brent was a major in the Stafford County militia, acting attorney general of the colony from the autumn of 1686 until the spring of 1688 (late in the reign of Catholic King James II), and a member of the House of Burgesses in the latter year.[51]

One group of white English-speaking Virginians did not initially fit in well and were not universally welcomed when they first arrived: the Friends, or Quakers. They arrived in the 1650s, when memories of the violence of the English Civil Wars were still fresh. The beliefs of the Friends directly connected each individual believer with God, and that equality of all believers and their immediate connection with God meant that Quakers perceived no need for ministers and engaged in no uniform formal worship service. It is possible that their religious beliefs alone would have made Quakers appear to be a threat to the stability and propriety and to the true religion and civil course of life the Church of England promoted. Their outward behavior certainly did. Quakers refused to abide by the legal requirement that they attend the services of the

Church of England. They eschewed virtually all of the outward manifestations of properly churched civilized Englishmen and engaged in a number of potentially disruptive practices. Not only did they have no minister and formal worship service, but they let anyone speak at meetings at any time, including women. They appeared, from the perspective of the Church of England, to be dangerous and subversive of good order.[52] At the spring 1660 Assembly session that restored Governor Sir William Berkeley to office after the collapse of the Puritan Commonwealth in England, the legislators passed "An Act for the Supressing the Quakers." It described them as "an unreasonable and turbulent sort of people" who taught "lies, miracles, false visions, prophecies and doctrines" that threatened "to destroy religion, laws, comunities and all bonds of civil societie."[53] Within a few years, however, the behavior of the Quakers in Virginia convinced most churchmen that they were no threat, and the larger society tolerated or absorbed them, as it did most of the Puritans and Catholics.[54]

Stability and order were prime objectives and key components of the version of English society that evolved in seventeenth-century Virginia, and the institutions and practices as well as the beliefs and habits of the Church of England were well matched to the social and political orders. Indeed, the nature of the church itself and its practices and teachings undoubtedly contributed significantly to the nature of the colonial culture. There was no ecclesiastical hierarchy in Virginia comparable to the political and social hierarchies evident in the structure of colonial government (in the conspicuous distinctions among militia officers, justices of the peace, sheriffs, burgesses, councilors, royal appointees, and governors) or in the society (among slaves, indentured servants, small farmers and artisans, and the great planter families). But within each neighborhood parish, there was a miniature hierarchy of parishioners, churchwardens, vestrymen, and clergy that almost perfectly replicated the county's political and social hierarchies and reinforced them. Even without a formal governing hierarchy, the church was an essential and reasonably strong institution during the seventeenth century. A strong decentralized church, every bit as much as a vigorous hierarchical Church, was compatible with the persistence and importance of religious faith. Without the

Church of England in colonial Virginia, the colony would not have been what it was.[55]

NOTES

1. Philip L. Barbour, ed., *The Complete Works of Captain John Smith, 1580–1631* (Chapel Hill: University of North Carolina Press, 1986), 3:295.

2. William Meade, *Old Churches, Ministers and Families of Virginia* (Philadelphia: J. B. Lippincott, 1857).

3. George MacLaren Brydon, *Virginia's Mother Church and the Political Conditions under Which It Grew* (Richmond: Virginia Historical Society, 1947–52).

4. Philip Alexander Bruce, *Institutional History of Virginia in the Seventeenth Century* (New York: G. P. Putnam's Sons, 1910).

5. Richard Lee Morton, *Colonial Virginia* (Chapel Hill: University of North Carolina Press, 1960); Warren M. Billings, John E. Selby, and Thad W. Tate, *Colonial Virginia: A History* (White Plains, NY: KTO Press, 1986).

6. Peter Wallenstein, *Cradle of America: Four Centuries of Virginia History* (Lawrence: University Press of Kansas, 2007); Ronald L. Heinemann, John G. Kolp, Anthony S. Parent Jr., and William G. Shade, *Old Dominion, New Commonwealth: A History of Virginia, 1607–2007* (Charlottesville: University of Virginia Press, 2007).

7. Credit where credit is due: Edmund S. Morgan and Marie Morgan, in "Our Shaky Beginnings," *New York Review of Books* (Apr. 26, 2007): 24, called Virginia after the 1610s "a kind of open-pit tobacco mine."

8. Dell Upton, *Holy Things and Profane: Anglican Parish Churches in Colonial Virginia* (Cambridge: MIT Press, 1986).

9. Jon Butler, *Awash in a Sea of Faith: Christianizing the American People* (Cambridge: Harvard University Press, 1990), 40–51.

10. Jon Kukla, "Perry on the Eastern Shore," a review of James Russell Perry, *The Formation of a Society on Virginia's Eastern Shore, 1615–1655* (Chapel Hill: University of North Carolina Press, 1990), in *Reviews in American History* 20 (1992): 297–302.

11. Edward L. Bond, *Damned Souls in a Tobacco Colony: Religion in Seventeenth-Century Virginia* (Macon, GA: Mercer University Press, 2000), 1–35.

12. Rebecca A. Goetz, "From Potential Christians to Hereditary Heathens: Religion and Race in the Early Chesapeake, 1590–1740" (Ph.D. diss., Harvard University, 2006).

13. *For the Colonie in Virginea Britannia. Lawes Divine, Morall and Martiall, &c.* (London: W. Burre, 1612), 1.

14. Ibid., 2–4.

15. Ibid., unnumbered pages following p. 89, which is misnumbered 41.

16. William J. Van Schreeven and George H. Reese, eds., *Proceedings of the General Assembly of Virginia, July 30–August 4, 1619* (Jamestown, VA: Jamestown Foundation, 1969), 14, 15 (transcription and facsimile of original in National Archives of Great Britain, Public Record Office, CO 1/1).

17. Ibid., 38, 39, 42, 43.

18. Ibid., 56, 57. The proceedings contain a reference to "the Ministers of the fower Incorporations" (ibid., 28, 29).

19. Ibid., 58, 59.

20. Ibid., 62, 63.

21. Edward L. Bond and Joan R. Gundersen, "The Episcopal Church in Virginia 1607–2007," *Virginia Magazine of History and Biography* 115 (2007): 174.

22. William Waller Hening, ed., *The Statutes at Large: Being a Collection of All the Laws of Virginia, from the First Session of the Legislature, in the Year 1619, etc.* (Richmond, VA, 1809–23), 1:240–43.

23. Ibid., 1:241–42.

24. Warren M. Billings, ed., "Some Acts Not in Hening's *Statutes*: The Acts of Assembly, April 1652, November 1652, and July 1653," *Virginia Magazine of History and Biography* 83 (1975): 31.

25. For the eighteenth century, see Joan Rezner Gundersen, "The Myth of the Independent Virginia Vestry," *Historical Magazine of the Protestant Episcopal Church* 44 (1975): 133–41.

26. Bond and Gundersen, "Episcopal Church in Virginia," 175–83.

27. John Ruston Pagan, *Anne Orthwood's Bastard: Sex and Law in Early Virginia* (Oxford: Oxford University Press, 2003), 120–22.

28. Hening, *Statutes at Large*, 1:421, 520–21.

29. Ibid., 1:400.

30. James P. P. Horn, *Adapting to a New World: English Society in the Seventeenth-Century Chesapeake* (Chapel Hill: University of North Carolina Press, 1994); Cary Carson, Joanne Bowen, Willie Graham, Martha McCartney, and Lorena Walsh, "New World, Real World: Improvising English Culture in Seventeenth-Century Virginia," *Journal of Southern History* 78 (2008): 31–88. See also Warren M. Billings, "The Growth of Political Institutions in Virginia, 1634 to 1676," *William and Mary Quarterly*, 3d ser., 31 (1974): 225–42; Jon Kukla, "The Founding of Virginia Counties—1634?" *Magazine of Virginia Genealogy* 22 (1984): 3–6.

31. Hening, *Statutes at Large*, 1:400.

32. Ibid., 1:418, 424.

33. Babette M. Levy, "Early Puritanism in the Southern and Island Colonies," *Proceedings of the American Antiquarian Society*, new ser., 70, part 1 (1960): esp. 92–122; Douglas Bradburn, "The Eschatological Origins of the English Empire," and Rebecca Anne Goetz, "A Puritan Virginia: The Role of English Religiosity in the Settlement of the Chesapeake," both papers presented at the Southern Historical Association annual convention, Richmond, VA, Nov. 1, 2007.

34. John T. Kneebone, et al., eds., *Dictionary of Virginia Biography* (Richmond: Library of Virginia, 1998–), 1:445–47.

35. Jon Butler, ed., "Two 1642 Letters from Virginia Puritans," *Proceedings of the Massachusetts Historical Society* 82 (1972): 99–109.

36. John Clayton, *The Defence of a Sermon, Preach'd upon the Receiving into the Communion of the Church of England, the Honourable Sir Terence Mac-Mahom, Bar-*

onet, and Christopher Dunn: Converts from the Church of Rome (Dublin: John Brocas, 1701), preface, unnumbered.

37. Steven D. Crow, "'Your Majesty's Good Subjects': A Reconsideration of Royalism in Virginia, 1642–1652," Virginia Magazine of History and Biography 87 (1979): 158–73.

38. See Kevin Butterfield, "Puritans and Religious Strife in the Early Chesapeake," Virginia Magazine of History and Biography 109 (2001): 5–36, which argues that Puritans and Prayer Brook churchmen in Virginia were less compatible.

39. Warren M. Billings, A Little Parliament: The Virginia General Assembly in the Seventeenth Century (Richmond: Library of Virginia, 2004), 76–78.

40. For the eighteenth century, see Clive Raymond Hallman, "The Vestry as a Unit of Local Government in Colonial Virginia" (Ph.D. diss., University of Georgia, 1987); John K. Nelson, Blessed Company: Parishes, Parsons, and Parishioners in Anglican Virginia, 1690–1776 (Chapel Hill: University of North Carolina Press, 2001), 13–16; Joan R. Gundersen, "The Non-Institutional Church: The Religious Role of Women in Eighteenth-Century Virginia," Historical Magazine of the Protestant Episcopal Church 51 (1982): 347–58.

41. Hening, Statutes at Large, 2:101–2.

42. Ibid., 3:82, 325–28, 530–34, 5:245–46, 426–30.

43. See William H. Seiler, "Land Processioning in Colonial Virginia," William and Mary Quarterly, 3d ser., 6 (1949): 416–36, which also contains evidence that after the disestablishment of the Church of England in 1786, local boards of overseers of the poor (who inherited one of the social responsibilities of the parishes) continued the practice. In King and Queen County, the court ordered that the property lines be processioned in 1867 and 1868 after the destruction of the local land records during the American Civil War; King and Queen County Processioners Report Book, 1867–1868, a 135-page manuscript volume in the King and Queen County Courthouse.

44. Hening, Statutes at Large, 3:326, 327.

45. David D. Hall, "The Chesapeake in the Seventeenth Century," in The Colonial Book in the Atlantic World, ed. Hugh Amory and David D. Hall, vol. 1 of A History of the Book in America (New York: Cambridge University Press, 2000), 57–65. See also Edward L. Bond's treatment of the auditory nature of Anglican worship in colonial Virginia in chapter 2 of the present volume.

46. Hening, Statues at Large, 2:102.

47. Philip D. Morgan discusses the practices of these groups in detail in chapter 3 of the present volume.

48. On public display in 2007 in the archaeological museum on Jamestown Island.

49. Neville Williams, "The Tribulations of John Bland, Merchant: London, Seville, Jamestown, Tangier, 1643–1680," Virginia Magazine of History and Biography 72 (1964): 19–41; Kneebone, et al., Dictionary of Virginia Biography, 2:5, 7–8, 14.

50. Owen Stanwood, "Papists, Indians, and Conspiratorial Politics in the Seventeenth-Century Chesapeake," paper presented at the Southern Historical Association annual convention, Richmond, VA, Nov. 1, 2007.

51. Bruce E. Steiner, "The Catholic Brents of Colonial Virginia: An Instance of Practical Toleration," *Virginia Magazine of History and Biography* 70 (1962): 387–409; Kneebone, et al., *Dictionary of Virginia Biography,* 2:215–16.

52. Bond, *Damned Souls,* 160–74.

53. Hening, *Statutes at Large,* 1:532–33.

54. For further discussion of Quaker practices, including Quakers' strategies for addressing their status as a dissenting sect, see Monica Najar's discussion in chapter 4 of the present volume.

55. Jon Kukla, "Order and Chaos in Early Virginia: Political and Social Stability in Pre-Restoration Virginia," *American Historical Review* 90 (1985): 275–98; Brent Tarter, "Reflections on the Church of England in Colonial Virginia," *Virginia Magazine of History and Biography* 112 (2004): 346–53; Alexander B. Haskell, "'The Affections of the People': Ideology and the Politics of State Building in Colonial Virginia, 1607–1754" (Ph.D. diss., Johns Hopkins University, 2004).

TWO   Lived Religion in Colonial Virginia

EDWARD L. BOND

LIVED RELIGION IN COLONIAL VIRGINIA TOOK MANY FORMS,
ranging from prayer and preaching and Bible reading to actions
people today might consider magical or superstitious. The "god-
centered" men and women of early modern England, the same
people who ventured to Virginia, focused intensely on religion
and the supernatural in ways that individuals in the twenty-first
century have a difficult time understanding.[1] Not only was their
religious commitment often very different, but the world they inhabited was also very different. Try to imagine a world in which it
simply was not possible to escape the supernatural, one in which
both divine and malevolent sources of supernatural power that
could protect, destroy, defend, or cure populated your cosmos, a
universe in which the natural world became a stage on which to
discern the will of God. Early modern English men and women
inhabited a universe in which these two approaches to the supernatural easily coexisted. They were devout believers, but they may
not yet have given up their belief in magic.

Lived religion in colonial Virginia, at least during the first several decades of the seventeenth century, began with the colonization venture itself, for English people then considered themselves
God's early modern Israel and North America their early modern
promised land. Using language that denied the difficulties of a
transatlantic crossing, supporters of the venture claimed that a benevolent deity had smoothed the way: "The passage into *Virginea* is
in true temper so faire, so safe, so secure, so easie, as though God
himself had built a bridge for men to passe from *England* to *Virginiea*."[2] Preaching before the Virginia Company of London, William

Crashaw articulated both a shared English faith and English hubris by proclaiming, "He that was *the God of Israel* is still *the God of England.*"[3] John Rolfe made the connection explicit, suggesting that an Anglophile deity had predestined England to possess and populate North America, perhaps even accomplishing the action before the English had ever set foot in Virginia: "What need wee then to fear, but to *goe up at once as a peculiar people* marked and chosen by the *finger* of God, to *possess* it?"[4] Faith in their friendship with a God they believed wanted them to settle the New World encouraged confidence among those who supported the colonization of Virginia. Like Abraham, whom the authors of a vast colonization literature urged the nation to emulate, they left home in faith, confident that if they cooperated with the deity they too would become a great nation with colonial possessions.[5] Bound for Virginia in 1623, one young man wrote that God had shown his favor on the voyage, revealing in the process how the natural world for men and women in the early modern period became a canvas on which to discern the will of God: "Wee hauinge the wynd faire (that messenger of God) hoised vp saile this daye and sailed some part of our Journeye."[6]

The supernatural world was not always so benevolent. Jamestown in the winter of 1609–10 was a desolate scene. The oppressive heat of the Virginia summer had given way to a brutal cold that chilled settlers to the bone, weakened them, and made them more susceptible to disease. As if the cold were not enough, the settlers' supplies of food had begun to dwindle. Many settlers had already perished. Those who yet clung to life could look around for themselves and see that too many people remained to survive on the meager supplies of grain on hand. They could feel the same lesson in their guts when the rations ran low and "that sharpe pricke of hunger" stayed with them throughout the day. Men saw death in their neighbors as well. A survivor of the "starving time" described the settlers as men who "Looked Lyke Anatomies Cryeinge owtt we are starved We are starved." Desperate for food, the survivors ate horses; when those ran out, they captured rats and mice or searched the forests for the occasional snake or lizard. Beyond desperation, some men found sustenance in the corpses of their former comrades. They sought warmth in the freezing winter by breaking apart the dwelling places of their dead friends and using the timbers for firewood. To make matters worse, the natives understood the difficulties the colonists endured and used circumstances to their advantage, attacking men who left the safety of James Fort.[7]

Virginia's early settlers did not reveal what they thought about in these difficult circumstances—buffeted by the cold, the hunger, and a gnawing fear of the unknown—but we can imagine. Would the bitter weather break? Would death come from a native's arrow? Would a supply ship soon arrive with food? Had God departed the universe? Worse still, had he brought the English here to die? The colony's early settlers knew the Old Testament well. Indeed, they often borrowed language from the stories of Abraham and Moses and the Israelites' conquest of the land of Canaan to describe their own colonizing venture in North America. At least some of these settlers, so well versed in the saga of Israel's salvation history, must have searched their Bibles for answers to their situation and compared themselves to the Hebrews during their flight from Egypt, wondering if they should adopt the Israelites' complaint: "you have brought us out into the wilderness to kill us with hunger."[8]

Confronted with this difficult situation, one man could endure the agony no longer. Pinched by hunger and overcome with despair, Hugh Pryse ran into the marketplace at Jamestown and blasphemed: "There is no God!" If a deity existed, Pryse said, he would not have allowed creatures made in his own image to suffer the miseries then afflicting England's colonists in Virginia. For men and women of the seventeenth century, Pryse's cry of agony and despair was the same as the unpardonable sin in Matthew's Gospel: "I say unto you. All manner of sin and blasphemy shall be forgiven unto men: but blasphemy against the Holy Ghost shall not be forgiven unto men." This sin took the form of two complementary opposites, pride and despair. Pride damned by making God irrelevant; despair damned by disavowing God's power to grant salvation. Hugh Pryse had murdered God by denying his existence.[9]

God, according to the account of the chronicler George Percy, took "his juste Judgment" later that afternoon when the blasphemer and a companion left the safety of the fort to search for food and were slain by Indians. There was nothing particularly strange about that. For months the natives had been attacking settlers who wandered away from the protection of James Fort. But Percy saw evidence of something more: wolves dismembered Pryse's corpse while leaving that of his companion untouched—clear evidence to Percy of God's disfavor.

Pryse's was but one death in a winter of deaths. But most men died anonymously, the nameless victims of starvation, disease, or attacks by the natives. Surely what made Pryse's death so noteworthy and suitable for detailed retelling was God's action in the case. Nonetheless, Percy related the tale in a cursory manner, adding a brief comment to suggest that he approved of the divine sanction visited upon Pryse. A man had blasphemed by denying God's existence, and God in turn took his revenge by sending death upon him and allowing wild beasts to desecrate his corpse. It was an unremarkable tale that the vast majority of men and women in the sixteenth and early seventeenth centuries would have found completely logical. It differed in no substantial way from thousands of other providences recounting the judgments that befell not only blasphemers but also adulterers, Sabbath-breakers, and cursers. Such lessons had formed the basis of countless sermons since the Middle Ages and were standard fare in contemporary devotional books.[10]

The Prince of Darkness was as real to the early modern mind as God, and just as immanent. He could act as an "agent of divine retribution" and was a thief of souls and a tempter. He could be summoned with an incautious word. Such fears were not paranoid fantasies, for English people could cite examples of people struck down after uttering oaths interpreted as the equivalent of dares.[11] And although Virginians rarely turned to Satan to explain the cause of events in their world, the York County Court deviated from that pattern in the late 1650s and early 1660s when it pointed to the devil as the reason for a series of indentured servant suicides, suggesting that Virginians, just like the Puritans in Massachusetts, could see in the devil an explanation for events. Mary Woddell, the court wrote, "not having God before hir eyes but being seduced by the Instigacon of the devill at Yorke aforesaid did voluntarily & felloniously drowne hir selfe in Yorke River."[12]

The supernatural world also influenced the uses and meanings of many traditional rituals. From time to time, Virginians in the colony's early years may have put the Church of England's communion service to use in a manner very different from modern understandings of that rite. Men and women in Tudor/Stuart England sometimes understood the Eucharist as a sort of poison ordeal. Accused criminals could testify to their innocence and then receive the sacrament to ratify their honesty on the assumption that a lie would invite God's judgment. Similar notions governed people who made agreements with one another, such as when newly married persons received communion in order to confirm the vows they had just made in the marriage service. More generally, communion as a poison ordeal carried an implied threat that anyone violating the peace of the community after sharing Christ's body and blood with their neighbors opened themselves to God's wrath. Persons who received the sacrament essentially swore by the Eucharistic elements that they would honor their agreements. To do otherwise turned the bread and wine from a foretaste of the heavenly banquet to a notice of divine sanction, what Italians called the "vendetta of God."[13]

Tremendously concerned with the problem of faction, settlers in early Virginia employed communion from time to time to mark the resolution of disputes, thus inviting God into their polity to terrify malcontents into maintaining harmonious relations with their neighbors. One such instance occurred in 1621 after a prolonged dispute between Governor George Yeardley and Captain William Powell, a burgess from James City. John Pory, secretary of the colony, described the religious element of their reconciliation when he reported that both men "receyved ye Sacrament" in pledge of their reconciliation and were "unwillinge, that ye matter should be in any way revyved; but desirous yt might be forevr buryed." This understanding of the Eucharist was apparently so common in early Virginia that even when facts dictated a different interpretation of events, some settlers nonetheless thought of communion as an "outward and visible pledge of reconciliation." John Smith, for example, related the usual series of events—conflict, resolution, and communion—after his admission to the resident council in 1607. Smith admitted that he had failed to get along with several of the leading planters. The Reverend Robert Hunt, however, had resolved the dispute, and Smith had then taken his place on the council. "The next day," Smith recounted, "all receaved the Communion." Smith erred on the date of the service. It happened eleven days after he joined the council, not one, but he nonetheless viewed the rite as part of the resolution of a conflict.[14]

There is also some evidence in seventeenth-century Virginia of curses, a powerful spiritual weapon. Based on the idea that merely articulating hostile words could cause physical harm, curses or maledictions had a long history. In the Middle Ages, curses took many forms. Priests cursed parishioners who neglected to pay their tithes; monks, since they could not carry weapons, relied on curses as a form of protection; monastic librarians sometimes attached curses to volumes under their care in order to protect their collections both from thieves and from scholars who kept the books too long; charters or deeds often included a curse upon individuals who violated the terms of the contract. John James of Virginia's Eastern Shore was apparently plagued by disagreements with his neighbors over the boundaries of his land and concluded a petition to the local court with a familiar Deuteronomic malediction: "Cursed is the man that removeth the mark of his Neighbors Land."[15] One early law code in the colony recognized the potent force of this weapon and outlawed curses; at the same time a lengthy prayer appended to the code directed a curse at Native Americans and English people who made sport of the colonization venture.[16] Following the Powhatan Uprising in 1622, a more violent curse appeared in the literature, one that asked God to help the English "roote out from being any longer a people" the colony's indigenous inhabitants. Such a curse asked for nothing less than the utter extirpation of the natives, their existence and memory.[17] So seriously did Virginians take curses that when an individual cursed "all those who wished well to the [Elizabeth City] parish" in 1635, he was banished to Maryland.[18]

Instructions sent to governors early in the seventeenth century sometimes tended toward magic rather than religion, using the language of influence and the ability to compel the supernatural rather than the language of entreaty and prayer. The Privy Council, for example, admonished Governor George Yeardley in 1623,

"In ye first place yu be carefull that Almighty God may be duly & daily served, both by yrselfe & all ye people undr yo charges, wch may draw down a Blessing upon all your endeavours."[19] To "draw down God's blessing" hints of the ability to compel the divine rather than to request or entreat the divine.

Both divine and demonic forces permeated the early modern cosmos, sometimes acting, but always watching and always present. They judged sinners, tempted souls, predicted the future, and, in the case of angels who pitched "their Tents round about our houses and dwellings," guarded Christians from the devil as they slept.[20] Judgments, magic, witchcraft, combat with the devil, and the use of various medieval spiritual weapons all comprised part of the mentality English settlers carried with them across the Atlantic to Virginia. Writing of popular religion in New England, David D. Hall has referred to this understanding of the cosmos as a "world of wonders."[21] While leaving far fewer examples than their countrymen to the north, Virginians nonetheless inhabited a similar supernatural world.[22]

INSTITUTIONAL FORMS OF LIVED RELIGION

Other forms of lived religion seem more typical of religious behavior to people in the twenty-first century, but they coexisted with an early modern belief that supernatural beings, both good and evil, could intervene in the world. Virginians prayed, they read the Bible and other devotional works, and they attended church. They wanted ministers to lead the services of the established Church of England. Colonists, however, endured a pastoral crisis that existed for over one hundred years. For much of the colonial period, in fact, Virginia was a missionary field, but that mission was not so much to Native Americans as to the English settlers who peopled the colony. Neither the English Crown nor the English church showed much interest until the mid-1680s in sending clergy to the colony. When Governor John Harvey suggested to the Privy Council in 1628 that the Crown cover ministers' transportation costs in order to encourage more ministers to settle in Virginia, he received a response that revealed the government's understanding of religion's place in the colonial venture: "such voluntary ministers may go over as will transport themselves at their own charge."[23]

The colony grew rapidly during the middle decades of the seventeenth century and by 1661 boasted a population of nearly twenty-five thousand; only ten or twelve of those people were ministers. Virginia's population had more than doubled to sixty-three thousand by 1697, but ministers served only twenty-two of the colony's nearly fifty parishes.[24] No wonder William Fitzhugh could write in 1687, "That which bears the greatest weight with me is the want of spirituall help & comforts, of which this fertile Country in everything else, is barren and unfruitful." Virginians tried hard to find clergy to fill their empty pulpits. Some individuals wrote to friends in England and asked them to help recruit suitable ministers for the colony. The General Assembly offered financial incentives both to clergy willing to come to Virginia and to citizens who successfully recruited a minister to serve a colonial cure (pastoral charge of a parish). To ministers, the Assembly offered a series of tax breaks for themselves and up to six servants; to individuals they offered a reward of twenty pounds sterling and reimbursement for the cost of transporting the clergyman from England to Virginia. County courts sometimes urged colonists traveling back to England to recruit ministers, as when the Lower Norfolk County Court asked Captain Thomas Willoughby to try and "pvide a Minister of God's word for us" while he was abroad.[25]

Governor William Berkeley came up with the most creative attempt to address the problem: he began ordaining deacons himself and may have followed Reformation precedent when he did so. Both Continental and English reformers, including Martin Luther and Archbishop of Canterbury Thomas Cranmer, had written that in an extreme situation the prince of a territory might step in and ordain bishops. Given both the shortage of clergy and Berkeley's low opinion of ministers sent from England to Virginia, it is entirely possible that the governor came to see himself in a desperate situation and acted as Virginia's prince to ordain deacons who could provide some form of clerical leadership for the colony's many vacant parishes.[26]

Virginia's Church of England also suffered from an absence of ecclesiastical leadership. No bishop resided in North America during the colonial period, nor did one ever make an episcopal visitation of the colonies. Absence of a resident bishop thus disrupted

Anglican religious life. Clergy went without the traditional measure of supervision, guidance, and advocacy. And since only a bishop could ordain men to the deaconate or to the priesthood, colonial men who wanted to pursue a career in the church had to travel to England for holy orders. Consecrating church buildings was also an episcopal function, and although some Virginia ministers agreed to perform this duty, the practice went beyond the bounds set by canon law. Not until the mid-1680s, when Henry Compton, the bishop of London, sent the Reverend John Clayton to the colony as his commissary or representative, did a member of the church hierarchy reside in North America. In fact, most previous bishops of London, to whom jurisdiction of the colonial church had fallen by tradition, since a previous bishop of London had been a member of the Virginia Company of London, had paid little attention to the colonial portion of their episcopal charge, hoping that the next incumbent of the see would take on the responsibility. Even commissaries found that their powers were limited, first by Virginia's tradition of lay authority over the church, and second by the lack of power invested in the office. Commissaries, for instance, could neither confirm nor ordain, and the shortage of clergy made it difficult for them to discipline the occasional wayward minister.[27]

These deficiencies meant that lived religion developed very differently in Virginia than back in the mother country. The absence of the traditional English ecclesiastical structure and the shortage of clergy were only two of the problems facing the colony's established church. Virginians had early on accommodated themselves to the demands of a tobacco culture, at one point in the 1620s even modifying the traditional church calendar so as not to interfere with the crop's growing season. "By reason of our necessities," the burgesses reasoned, when two holy days fell together on subsequent days "betwixt the feast of the annuntation of the blessed virgin [25 March] and St. Michael the archangell [29 September], then only the first to be observed."[28] Planting tobacco also dictated that planters settle themselves in a manner unlike people in England or New England. Instead of settling in towns, Virginians spread out along the colony's many rivers. Conscientious ministers worried about the impact that this accommodation to tobacco culture had both on the religious life of the laity and on their own abilities to serve their parishioners adequately. Roger Greene grew anxious about colonial laypeople, whom he described as "grow[ing] wilde in that Wildernesse" untended by a gardener, or in this case a minister. Their refusal to settle in towns meant that settlers endured the want "of Christian Neighborliness, of brotherly admonition, of holy Examples of religious Persons, of the Comfort of theirs, and the Ministers Administrations in Sicknesse, and Distresses, of the benefit of Christian Civil Conference and Commerce." Greene also pointed out the difficulties this caused ministers: "If they should spend time in visiting their remote and far distant habitations, they would have little or none left for their necessary Studies and to provide necessary spiritual food for the rest of their Flocks." Writing nearly a century after Greene, the Reverend James Maury gave some indication of the toll a large parish could take on a dedicated clergyman:

> Mine is the most extensive & inconvenient Parish in the Colony; that is regularly served. In it are three Churches & a Chappel, and Each of which equal Attendance is given. The Distances between these & the Glebe are 7, 12, 16 & 24 Miles; which, besides many long Rides to baptize & marry & bury, together with several others to Court & Warehouse on my own private Business, you'll find, upon a little Reflection, afford such an abundant Employment, that Intervals of Leisure & Repose are as short, as they are rare; which must unavoidably be still further diminished & curtailed by the necessary cares of a Family of no less than 8 children.[29]

The colonists' scattered manner of settling hindered the public practice of religion since it meant that most people lived a significant distance from the local parish church. Virginians lived like "*Hermites . . .* dispersedly and scatteringly seated upon the sides of Rivers," the Reverend Roger Greene complained, "as might make their due and constant attendance upon the publick worship and Service of God impossible to them."[30] The Reverend Alexander Forbes, minister of Isle of Wight Parish in the 1720s, echoed Greene's criticism: "the distance of the way may hinder many at sometimes who cannot be prepared to come X. XII. or XV miles [to church], tho' they might and would if they had but V. or VI."[31]

Parishes in Virginia were very large, and in most cases the parish's central or "mother" church was situated so far away from many of the inhabitants that they could not reasonably travel to and from church each Sabbath day. In order to take the church to the people, most parishes constructed smaller church buildings, or chapels of ease (this is what Maury meant when he referred to a chapel), at convenient spots in outlying areas, thus making it easier for many parishioners to attend church regularly. Still, this did not suit everyone. On one occasion in the 1730s, some residents of Spotsylvania County showed the high regard they held for traveling shorter rather than longer distances to church in a perverse way. Angry that an additional church building had been constructed in another area of the parish instead of in their neighborhood, they set fire to the new edifice, successfully damaging the structure enough to render it useless.[32]

Colonial parsons served their churches and chapels of ease on a rotating basis, often officiating and preaching first at one church and then at the others in their turn on successive Sundays, often delivering the same sermon to each church or chapel congregation in turn. James Maury, for example, preached the same sermon on prayer to one church in his parish on July 10, 1743, and then at another chapel the next Sunday.[33] In many areas of the colony, especially during the eighteenth century, this arrangement meant that many Virginians did not come into contact with the local minister more than once every three or four weeks. In the minister's absence, vestries hired clerks (pronounced *clark*) to read prayers and a sermon from either the Book of Homilies or the published works of an English divine.[34] The surviving evidence suggests that Virginians frequently did not attend church if the weather was bad or if the parish minister was not preaching that day. "Extremities of heat in Summer, frost and Snow in Winter, and tempestuous weather in both," as Roger Greene put it, often prevented settlers from traveling to church, as did "Rivers & Streams rendered impassable with much rain." The law, in fact, only required church attendance once every four weeks. Church attendance in eighteenth-century Virginia probably hovered at just over 50 percent.[35]

Nonetheless, when the minister of a parish led divine service and preached at his church or chapels of ease, his parishioners often filled the building. Of the twenty-nine Anglican clergy who responded to the bishop of London's queries in 1724, about 90 percent reported very strong attendance, suggesting a far greater desire for religion among members of Virginia's established church and a far greater attention to their vocation by clergy than historians have often suspected.[36] The Reverend Zachariah Brooke of St. Paul's Parish in Hanover County, for instance, shed light on both church attendance and service schedules when he noted, "each Sunday service is performed in the Churches and 9 months of the year on a working day at the Chappels[,] all of which are generally full, no less than 200 or 300 people at a time."[37] Another minister claimed that he could expect "pretty strong [attendance] in good weather," with more parishioners frequently showing up than the pews could accommodate.[38] Thomas Bayle of Newport Parish in Isle of Wight County followed a brutal schedule, holding services at all of his churches and chapels of ease each Sunday: three times in succession at his mother church to accommodate the five hundred parishioners there, two services at a church forty miles away, and once at the chapel that was located nineteen miles from his smaller church.[39] Other clergy described similar situations, noting, "I have known so great a number of them [parishioners] that there was not convenient room for them all within the Church," and "On Sunday mornings we have full congregations."[40]

Despite the shortage of clergy (a problem that declined in severity during the eighteenth century) and the absence of a resident bishop, the established church managed to provide for the spiritual welfare of Virginians. Until after the Revolutionary War, the Church of England was a strong institution in Virginia. In fact, despite the growth of the Baptists in the years before 1776, the Church of England may well have been at its strongest on the eve of the American Revolution. The church simply adapted to the new world.[41]

COMMUNAL RELIGIOUS PRACTICE

The Book of Common Prayer was the single greatest influence shaping the devotional lives of colonial Anglicans; only the Bible surpassed it as the book most commonly appearing in the colonists' libraries. Its liturgy repeated weekly at public worship and read each day privately by many individuals provided a constant source of structure for the spiritual life. Congregations and individual worshippers in private repeated the Apostles' Creed and the Lord's Prayer at each office, and in the lessons appointed for each day the Bible was read through each year. Anglican liturgy, in fact, echoed the Bible, with many of its prayers crafted from the words of Holy Scripture. Day after day, week after week, the Book of Common Prayer gave voice to the same themes in the same words that called the faithful to repentance at every office and offered them the means of grace. By repeating the same words at each office and by using the same words week after week, the set liturgies in the Book of Common Prayer were intended to work a gradual transformation in the lives of the faithful.[42] Unlike the evangelicals of the Great Awakening, Anglicans placed little emphasis on conversion, and their style of worship reflected this difference. Both as a devotional work and as a service book, the Book of Common Prayer aimed less at conversion than at assisting the presumably converted to maintain and deepen their faith. It served as the liturgy for a people thought to be Christian by virtue of their membership in the English commonwealth.[43] William Beveridge, a late seventeenth-century minister and sometime bishop of St. Asaph, explained in his discourse entitled *A Sermon concerning the Excellency and Usefulness of the Common Prayer* the design of prayer book worship to form and order the lives of English Christians. This process, however, occurred slowly, a gradual action rather than a sudden and dramatic change like that experienced by the apostle Paul on the road to Damascus or like the conversion experiences of the evangelicals of the Great Awakening. Because the set prayers worked this transformation through sound rather than through the more immediate agency of sight, necessity demanded the frequent repetition of the same words and phrases.[44] Beveridge, in fact, based his argument on the elusive epistemology of the spoken word:

> In order to our being *Edified,* so as to be made better and holier, whensoever we meet together upon a Religious account, it is necessary that the same good and holy Things be always inculcated and pressed upon us after one and the same manner. For we

cannot but all find by our own Experience, how difficult it is to fasten any thing that is truly good, either upon our selves or others, and that it is rarely, if ever, effected without frequent Repetitions of it. Whatsoever good things we hear only once, or now and then, though perhaps upon the hearing of them, they may swim for a while in our *Brains*, yet they seldom sink down into our *Hearts*, so as to move and sway the Affections, as it is necessary they should do, in order to our being *Edified* by them. Whereas by a *Set Form of Publick Devotions rightly composed,* as we are continually put in mind of all things necessary for us to know and do, so that it is always done by the same Words and Expressions, which by their constant use will imprint themselves so firmly in our Minds, that . . . they will still occur upon all occasions; which cannot but be very much for our *Christian Edification.*[45]

Hence, divine worship following the rites of the Book of Common Prayer was intended to grasp an individual's affections and thereby sway that person toward living a holy life. Not that this reorientation occurred simply by hearing or reading the offices each day or each week. Individuals had to participate willingly in the service. By opening their minds to the words they heard, they allowed the liturgy to bring their affections into a holy frame and temper.[46] Repeatedly using the same set, brief forms encouraged this process and allowed the faithful to "recollect" their prayers or, in Beveridge's words, to "look over our Prayers again, either in a Book, or in our Minds, where they are imprinted."[47] Some Anglican apologists argued that brief collects or "arrow-like prayers" required less time than the long extemporaneous effusions of the dissenters and therefore ran less risk of losing the auditors' attention.[48] Over time, spoken prayers taken from a set form thus gained the epistemological immediacy of sight.

Sermons supported the liturgy, urging parishioners to embrace the moral life, but not as an end in itself, as critics would have us believe. Unlike Puritans, who believed God had elected them, or Roman Catholics, who believed they had elected God, Anglicans followed a middle path: they believed that they cooperated with God to ensure their prior election by God. The moral life and the actions it engendered allowed Anglicans to cooperate with God in the drama of salvation. The Reverend Robert Paxton put the matter succinctly: "Everyone who perishes for want of mercy is his own murtherer & lost because he refused his own mercy."[49]

Church services in colonial Virginia were communal auditory events. Individual parishioners participated by hearing and offering the few responses available to them in the prayer book. In the late seventeenth and eighteenth centuries, the principal service in Virginia's Church of England would have been Morning Prayer. A typical Sunday worship service in colonial Virginia would have included Morning Prayer, Great Litany, Ante Communion or the communion service up to the point at which the Gospel was read, and a sermon. The sermon, usually read from a prepared text and delivered from the topmost tier of a "three-decker" pulpit, was often modeled on the discourses of Archbishop of Canterbury John Tillotson, the influential preacher whose pulpit oratory shaped the Anglican sermon for decades. Colonial parsons borrowed liberally from Tillotson's published works (as well as those of other English divines), sometimes transcribing lengthy passages from the archbishop's discourses to intersperse with their own original work. And like their model, Anglican sermons often explicated a single verse of scripture, most frequently one taken from the New Testament. James Blair, for example, published a lengthy series of sermons on the Sermon on the Mount and was readying a second collection, on the parables, for publication when he died in 1743.[50] Colonial laypeople enjoyed a good sermon and often stayed at home if the minister, who alone could preach an original discourse, was officiating at one of the parish's other churches or chapels of ease that Sunday.[51] Until the Great Awakening began to influence Anglican ministers, most of their sermons likely ran about twenty to thirty minutes, although among those Anglican ministers who sympathized with the Great Awakening, sermons probably were significantly longer.

In addition to Morning Prayer, ministers in Virginia also celebrated the Eucharist, generally three times each year, and presided over services that approximated confirmation. Ministers usually administered communion on Christmas, Easter, and Whitsunday (Pentecost), although some clergy reported in 1724 that they administered the sacrament six or eight times each year for each of their congregations.[52] Three celebrations of the sacrament each year seems to have been the norm. The Lord's Supper could be an awesome and frightening ritual, and ministers expected communicants to make serious preparations before receiving the sacrament. If colonial parsons followed the prayer book's instruction, they read an exhortation to their congregations from the Book of Common Prayer the Sunday before they planned to administer the sacrament in which they asked their parishioners "first, to examine your lives and conversations by the rule of God's commandments; and whereinsoever ye shall perceive yourselves to have offended, either by will, word, or deed, there to bewail your own sinfulness, and to confess yourselves to Almighty God, with full purpose of amendment of life." For those who "shall be religiously and devoutly disposed," the Exhortation referred to the Lord's Supper as "the most comfortable Sacrament." The Exhortation warned others to beware of receiving the body and blood of Christ: "if any of you be a blasphemer of God, an hinderer or slanderer of his Word, an adulterer, or be in malice, or envy, or in any other grievous crime, repent you of your sins, or else come not to that holy Table," for receiving the sacrament "doth nothing more else but increase your damnation."[53] Given the seriousness of these warnings, it is not surprising that comparatively few Virginians regularly approached the holy table to receive the sacrament. As Nicholas Beasley has recently pointed out, infrequent communion should not necessarily be interpreted as the absence of piety: "infrequency of communion is as likely to be indicative of excessive veneration as it is of disdain." Many colonists took the Exhortation's warnings seriously. William Byrd prepared for receiving communion by reading Jeremy Taylor's *The Worthy Communicant,* to which he had added a version of Psalm 51, a penitential psalm typically used on the first day of Lent in "A Commination, or Denouncing of God's Anger and Judgements against Sinners."[54]

In the eighteenth century, at least a few Virginia ministers also preached confirmation sermons, suggesting that they were instructing and then admitting young people to communion. If they followed English practice, persons admitted to communion would have been expected to recite and understand the Lord's Prayer, the Ten Commandments, and the Nicene Creed. While only a bishop could confirm a person, the Book of Common Prayer of 1662 made confirmation unnecessary as a condition for receiving the sacrament. Its rubrics noted: "And there shall none be admitted to the holy Communion, until such time as he be confirmed, or be ready and desirous to be confirmed."[55] Thus, the lack of a resident bishop did not prevent people from being confirmed and then receiving communion. Before the early 1800s, in fact, according to one authority on Christian initiation in the Anglican tradition, "confirmation was more often ignored than observed."[56] In short, our understanding of the rite today does not provide a good model for its use in the eighteenth century.

Prayer book services and sermons, of course, were the ideal. But practice was another matter. Since these were auditory events, older people who could not hear well were excused from church attendance. The county records contain several examples of deaf people brought to court for failing to attend church; the cases were dismissed when the court learned they were deaf. Nor were Virginia congregations necessarily the best behaved. Ministers throughout the colony preached discourses to their congregations that suggest a wide degree of inattention and irreligious behavior during divine service. James Blair, for example, accused members of his congregation of concentrating on the things of the world rather than the spirit when he chastised them for coming to church primarily to "feed their lustful Eyes" by exchanging "Undecent, Lascivious Glances, and Ogling Gestures."[57] In a sermon preached over a dozen times in the decade between 1770 and 1780, the evangelical Anglican Charles Clay of Albemarle County questioned the seriousness of his parishioners' Christianity when he asked, "Can you be [Christ's] Disciples when many of you, (might one Judge of your Devotion from the inattention Visible on your Countenances in time of Divine Service), w[oul]d give more head to a tale of Tom Thumb, Tom Hickerthreft [Hickathrift], or Jack the Giant-killer, than to any prayer, or to the best Sermon it was in the Power of Man to Preach?"[58] In another discourse preached no fewer than thirty-five times between 1769 and 1785, he described parishioners who failed to kneel or make the correct responses from the Book of Common Prayer during the service. Instead, he saw members of his congregation

hanging first on one hipp then on the other; leaning with their
Elbows on the pews or on the windows . . . or . . . Running in & out
to the great anoiance & disturbance of those whose minds are
piously inclined. . . . And while the Psalms for ye Day are Reading,
instead of having a book & answering in turn; are playing with
their Snuff box; dancing their foot with one leg across the other for
amusement; or twirling their Hat about; making their observations
on ye Congregation, whispering to the person that Sits next to
them; or Smiling & grinning at others yt [that] sits at a distance
from them.[59]

Clay further criticized parishioners who chit-chatted during the
service, the sauntering of women who enjoyed "talking & laughing
& pacing up & down" during baptisms, and the practice followed
by some of running in and out of the church during prayers.[60]
Other parishioners admitted sleeping at church. One of James
Blair's sermons so wearied William Byrd II in 1709 that Byrd went
home and confided to his diary: "Nothing could hinder me from
sleeping at church, though I took a great deal of pains against it."[61]
Not that laypeople were the only ones who fell short of the mark;
Byrd described another minister whose discourse or manner was
so tedious that he succeeded in preaching the "Congregation into
a Lethargy."[62] Given some of this behavior, we can understand
why John Page advised his son, "be not like some that when they
come first into the church, sink down on their seats, clap their
hats before their eyes, and scarce bow their knees: as if they come
to bless God, not to intreat God to bless them."[63]

Page also warned his son, however, that there was more to leading a holy life than hearing sermons: "This is not written against
frequent hearing of sermons, but to let you know that it is not the
only exercise of a Christian to hear a sermon, nor is that Lord's-day
well spent, that dispatcheth no other business for heaven. In heaven
there will be no sermons, yet in heaven there will be hallelujahs.
All God's service must not be narrowed up in hearing; it hath
greater latitude; there must be prayer, praise, adoration, and worship of God."[64] The Reverend William Douglas raised a similar
point when he asked his congregation, "How much less good will a
sermon do us if as soon as the hour of worship is ended, we run im-

mediately from God, & plunge our selves into worldly affairs, without giving our thoughts and leasure & leave to reflect on what we have heard?"[65]

PERSONAL AND FAMILY PRACTICES

Away from the sacred space of the public church, Virginians also engaged in family and private prayers. Devotional works and pulpit discourses both encouraged heads of families to lead public prayers in the household each day.[66] John Page (who was borrowing liberally from Richard Allestree's *The Whole Duty of Man*) recommended the practice to his son, pointing out that it was "as much his duty to provide for the souls of his wife, children and servants, as to provide food and raiment for their bodies." "Let no Christian man (especially you my son)," Page wrote, "keep so heathenish a family as not to have God daily worshipped in it."[67]

Family religion was particularly important for children. In rural areas like Virginia, church attendance was primarily an adult activity.[68] Therefore, family religion was likely a child's most significant introduction to the church and Christianity. Daily prayers introduced children to worship. And many parents taught their children the catechism, either from the Book of Common Prayer or from one of the many catechisms written by ministers in England, although ministers in rural Virginia often catechized young people during Lent.[69] When queried about how young Virginians learned religious truths in the colony, Sir William Berkeley, the colony's governor, indicated the importance of family religion, explaining that parents in Virginia followed "the same course that is taken in England out of towns; every man according to his ability instructing his children."[70] The Reverend Devereux Jarratt recounted a similar practice in his autobiography when he explained that his parents taught both him and his brothers "short prayers" and made "us perfect in repeating the *Church Catechism*." English minister John Lewis's catechism, *The Church Catechism Explain'd by Way of Question and Answer*, proved so popular in Virginia that by 1738 William Parks began publishing an inexpensive (no more than a shilling) reprint edition out of his Virginia press, advertising it in the *Virginia Gazette* as "being very proper for a New Year's Gift to Children."[71]

Many Virginians engaged in private devotions as well. William Byrd II read morning and evening prayer almost daily and often read John Tillotson's published sermons, noting on one occasion, "I read a sermon of Dr. Tillotson's which affected me very much and made me shed some tears of repentance."[72] For his closet devotions, Philip Ludwell kept a "poor little old prayer book," worn from use, to guide his private devotions.[73] James Blair, the bishop of London's commissary or representative in Virginia, recommended that his parishioners set aside words and approach God in "mental prayer" in their private devotions.[74] Blair himself was particularly fond of Psalms 136 and 140. Blair was an advocate of brief ejaculatory prayer, or repeating the same brief phrases in prayer, and one can almost imagine him praying the refrain of Psalm 136 throughout his day: "for his mercy endures for ever."[75] The commissary hoped his parishioners would make this type of prayer "as common as bodily Respiration; the one being as necessary for the Preservation of the spiritual, as the other is to the Preservation of the natural Life."[76] Some Virginians demonstrated their private piety by making public donations to their parish churches in the manner of William Hawkins, who left fifteen hundred pounds of tobacco to the vestry of York Parish to purchase a "Silver Flaggon . . . to be used and to remaine to and for the use of the Inhabitants of York Parish in the Church belonging thereto at Sacrament and other necessarie times and occasions."[77]

Thomas Ludwell confided his private religious thoughts in a letter in 1667, when he described the "most Dreadfull Hurry Cane" that struck the colony. Torrential rain fell. Hundreds of cattle drowned; clapboard buildings collapsed under the assault of nature's fury. Floodwaters covered lands over a mile from the nearest river. As destructive as this tempest was, it nonetheless fascinated Ludwell. The scene that came to his mind was that of the primordial chaos described in Genesis: "And the earth was without form and void; and darkness was upon the face of the deep." Shortly after the storm passed, Ludwell wrote down his impressions of the hurricane's fury. It was as though "all the Elements were at Strife," he wrote, contending with each other to see "which of them should do most towards the reduction of the creation into a Second Chaos, it was wonderfull to consider the contrary effects of that Storme."

Ludwell's letter reveals both his biblical literacy and his use of the word *wonderful,* a word that no longer conveys the power it did a few centuries ago. In the seventeenth century, *wonderful* conveyed a sense of wonder or awe, an acknowledgment of God's action that was at the same time both frightening and attractive.[78] As part of their private religion, Virginians, like Ludwell, from time to time noted how nature revealed the power of the creator, evoking in them feelings of wonder that both attracted them to the creator and frightened them. Governor John Page, for example, once said of the botanist John Clayton, "I have heard him say, whilst examining a flower, that he could not look into one, without seeing the display of infinite power and contrivance; and that he thought it impossible for a BOTANIST to be an ATHEIST."[79]

Instead of meeting with parishioners to offer spiritual advice, ministers wrote letters that might be considered counseling. James Maury, for example, sent a tattered and well-used translation of *The Imitation of Christ* to one of his ill parishioners, Mary Grymes, recommending to her "perusal the fifth Meditation in the short office for sick Persons, which Doctor Stanhope drew up for the ease of a Lady in your Circumstances, & hath published at the End of his Translation of Thomas à Kempis."[80] Ministers of both the established church and dissenting persuasions frequently distributed books to adherents throughout the colony, especially during the late seventeenth and eighteenth centuries. John Talbot, a missionary for the Society of the Propagation of the Gospel in Foreign Parts, wrote from Virginia in 1703 requesting prayer books "new or old, of all sorts & sizes," explaining that if he received these books he would "carry them 100 miles about and disperse them abroad to all that desired 'em . . .'tis a comfort to the People in the Wilderness to see that some body takes care of them."[81] For Alexander Forbes, books and tracts helped bring the church's teachings to people in areas where ministers could not regularly travel. In 1724 he wrote and asked the bishop of London, Edmund Gibson, to send him "such books and printed sermons according to the doctrine of the Church of England . . . to be dispersed and read among such remote Inhabitants of the parish as live at a great distance from all Churches and chapels, where God's word is commonly taught and read."[82] For the Reverend Edward Johnson of

Mulberry, a package of devotional books was a tremendous gift worthy of thanksgiving. After receiving a package of religious volumes from Virginia Ferrer in 1651, he wrote, "I went into the church and fell on my knees to pray for you and your religious family."[83]

Religious writings were possessions so highly sought after by some colonists that contention occasionally resulted. In 1658, for example, a dispute over two volumes of St. Augustine's works ended up in the York County court.[84] James Craig was shocked when he arrived at Lunenberg County's Cumberland Parish in 1759 and found numerous people "which by Reason of their Distance from any place of Divine Worship, had never or seldom, been at Church since they were baptized" and whom he found "ignorant of the very first Principles of Christianity." He pleaded with Commissary Thomas Dawson for books on baptism, the Lord's Supper, and the duties of godparents, as well as William Beveridge's often reprinted *Sermon Concerning the Usefulnes of the Common Prayer:* "I would freely give any Consideration to have these & such like Books to distribute among the people NOW!"[85]

Books in some ways became substitutes for ministers, who could not adequately serve their large colonial parishes and symbolized the efforts of the Church of England to reach a population assumed to be Christian but that was often unchurched, sometimes by circumstances, sometimes by choice. By reading English devotional works written by some of the great English preachers, Virginians may have felt that they were part of a vital trans-Atlantic religious culture associated with the London metropole rather than merely members of a rural colonial parish.

Thomas Dawson worried that no matter the quality of the books ministers distributed, those books could nonetheless be ignored or misused. Perhaps concerned about not only the use of the volumes but also the interpretations an infrequently instructed laity might find in religious books, he urged other ministers to take care when they gave tracts to parishioners, noting that they ought to "give some suitable Advice, and Instruction how to make use of this excellent Charity to the Purposes of a Christian Life. For . . . the best of Books when lightly given, will be lightly valued, and as lightly made use of."[86]

Quakers and Presbyterians, as well as Anglicans, attempted to expand the influence of religion by distributing religious texts. The Presbyterian Samuel Davies, for example, donated hundreds of devotional volumes to persons too poor to pay for the books themselves.[87] And Anglican clergy and Quaker missionaries engaged in pamphlet wars in the colony at the turn of the seventeenth century, distributing tracts particularly designed to combat specific titles handed out by their opponents. When Anglicans began circulating the anonymous anti-Quaker tract *The Snake in the Grass: or, Satan Transform'd into an Angel of Light. Discovering the Deep and Unsuspected Subtilty of the People Call'd Quakers,* Quakers retaliated by requesting and distributing copies of a response, *A Switch for the Snake.*[88] Sometimes the religious jousting between Anglicans and Quakers went beyond distributing pamphlets: Joseph Glaister, a Quaker missionary, and the Reverend Andrew Monro of Newport Parish held at least one formal religious disputation at Chuckatuck, drawing a large crowd that wished to hear the debate on a variety of topics, ranging from state support of clergy salaries to the legitimacy of baptism by water.[89] Religious leaders showed a willingness to debate the truths of religious doctrines and practices with one another in disputes that edified and entertained significant numbers of colonists. Longtime commissary James Blair, in fact, encouraged debates between people of different religious persuasions, so long as these were "done in a friendly and peaceable Manner, and with a Design to find out the Truth," and bemoaned the tendency of all Christians to "lay greater Stress upon some of those little Points, in which they differ, than upon the great Points of Christianity in which they are agreed."[90]

Other colonists purchased their own devotional books. Lewis Bayley's *The Practice of Piety,* works by Jeremy Taylor, and *A Week's Preparation Towards a Worthy Receiving of the Lord's Supper* were all popular in Virginia. In addition, some people owned books that today might be considered "occult." Ralph Wormley, Edmund Berkeley, Francis Nicholson, Mathew Hubbard, and the Reverend Thomas Teackle all owned volumes on astrology or alchemy, the latter then understood by some people as an "exacting spiritual discipline" that sought the practitioner's "spiritual transformation." Of course, book ownership does not indicate how these men used these alchemical volumes any more than ownership of devotional books indicated the spirituality of their owners.[91]

Women, as Joan Gundersen has pointed out, "made their religious influence felt through their role at home," since they could not serve on vestries, as wardens, or as ordained ministers. Women, for example, sometimes allowed clergy to hold services at their homes if there was no chapel of ease in the neighborhood. They also oversaw preparations for three important religious ceremonies often held at Virginians' homes rather than at the parish church or chapel: baptisms, marriages, and funerals. Although the church rubrics indicated that these services should be held at church, and Henry Compton, the bishop of London, had urged clergy in the 1670s to hold these services at the parish church, many Virginians continued to resist English practice, preferring to hold these at their homes instead. In addition, women sometimes served as leaders of family worship; read sermons aloud to their families; or, like the mothers of both Devereux Jarratt and Susanna Nelson Page, taught their children the catechism. Women also took on the task of catechizing slaves. Ann Wager, in fact, taught as the only teacher for fourteen years at a school for black children in Williamsburg supported by the Associates of Dr. Bray. Nor was engagement in theological arguments beyond the private role of women in Virginia. Extant sources frequently document religious discussions and arguments held among women, their spouses, friends, and others.[92]

Lived religion in colonial Virginia encompassed no single variety of religious experience. During the early seventeenth century, Virginians continued their practice of orthodox Christianity but combined with it elements of the supernatural world thought of as more medieval than modern. Both practices must have brought them comfort in the New World. Services led from the Book of Common Prayer linked Virginians to the London metropole, emphasizing their shared English identity even on the fringes of empire in the North American wilderness. That God heard their prayers in Virginia as well as in England, and that he could strike down people like Hugh Pryse in Virginia as well as in England, emphasized continuities with religious traditions rooted in the Old World. Lived religion in colonial Virginia also meant change. Through the mid-seventeenth century, Virginians who violated

God's moral laws routinely did penance in the public church just as they would have in England; by the late seventeenth century, however, public penance had given way to fines and corporal punishments. Virginians were forced to adapt their religious practices to the demands of a new continent and a new cash crop, to living on plantations rather than in towns, to seeing a minister lead services once every three weeks rather than weekly, and to increasing the role of the laity in church government. That they adapted (often in ways, as Brent Tarter has pointed out, that previous generations of historians overlooked) rather than abandoned their English religious practices should suggest to us the important and enduring place of religion in the lives of colonial Virginians.

NOTES

1. Stuart E. Prall, *Church and State in Tudor and Stuart England* (Arlington Heights, IL: Harlan Davidson, 1993), 1.

2. William Crashaw, *A Sermon Preached in London before the right honorable the Lord Laware, Lord Governour and Captaine Generall of Virginia* (London, 1610), E-1 (emphasis original).

3. Ibid., L-1 (emphasis original).

4. John Rolfe, *A True Relation of the State of Virginia lefte by Sir Thomas Dale Knight in May Last 1616; set forth with an introduction and notes by a group of Virginia librarians. . . .* (New Haven, CT: Yale University Press, 1951), 41 (emphasis original).

5. For a discussion of Abraham in the literature of the Virginia venture, see Edward L. Bond, *Damned Souls in a Tobacco Colony: Religion in Seventeenth-Century Virginia* (Macon, GA: Mercer University Press, 2000), 28–34, 41–42, 48.

6. Anthony Hinton to his mother, May 4, 1624, in *The Records of the Virginia Company of London,* ed. Susan Myra Kingsbury (Washington, DC, 1906–35), 4:164 (hereafter *RVCL*).

7. My account relies upon George Percy, "A Trewe Relaycon of the Procedeinges and Ocurrentes of Momente wch have hapned in Virginia from the Tyme Sr Thomas Gates was shippwrackte uppon the Bermudes anno 1609 untill my depture outt of the Country wch was in anno Dni 1612," *Tyler's Historical Quarterly and Genealogical Magazine* 3 (1922): 260–29.

8. Exodus 16:3. Biblical quotations are from the Geneva Bible. For the biblical culture of early modern England, see Christopher Hill, *The English Bible and the Seventeenth-Century Revolution* (New York: Penguin, 1994), 3–44. For Virginia as Canaan, see Karen Ordahl Kupperman, *Settling with the Indians: The Meeting of English and Indian Cultures in America, 1580–1640* (Totowa, NJ: Littlehampton Book Services, 1980), 166–67.

9. The biblical quotation is from Matthew 12:31. Christopher Marlowe, *Dr. Faustus*, vol. 2 of *The Complete Works of Christopher Marlowe*, ed. Roma Gill (New York: Oxford University Press, 1990), xxxv; Lewis Bayly, *The Practice of Piety: Directing a Christian how to walk, that he may please God*, 35th ed. (London, 1669), 122–23. This volume was known to be in Virginia before 1624. See William S. Powell, "Books in the Virginia Colony before 1624," *William and Mary Quarterly*, 3d ser., 5 (1948): 178–80 (hereafter *WMQ*).

10. Keith Thomas, *Religion and the Decline of Magic: Studies in Popular Belief in Sixteenth and Seventeenth Century England* (London: Weidenfield and Nicholson, 1971), 96–104. On blasphemy, see Leonard W. Levy, *Treason against God: A History of the Offense of Blasphemy* (New York: Schocken Books, 1981); Leonard W. Levy, *Blasphemy: Verbal Offense against the Sacred from Moses to Salmon Rushdie* (New York: Knopf, 1993).

11. Thomas, *Religion and the Decline of Magic*, 470–77, 520.

12. York County Deeds, Orders, and Wills, vol. 3, 1657–62, 25, 74, 88, Library of Virginia.

13. Thomas, *Religion and the Decline of Magic*, 44–45; Edward Muir, *Ritual in Early Modern Europe* (Cambridge: Cambridge University Press, 1997), 162–63.

14. George Thorpe and John Pory to Sir Edwin Sandys, May 9, 1621, in *RVCL*, 3:445; Alexander Brown, ed., *The Genesis of the United States* (New York: Russell and Russell, 1964), 2:969–71; Richard L. Morton, *Colonial Virginia* (Chapel Hill: University of North Carolina Press, 1960), 1:58–60; John Smith, *Proceedings of the English Colonie in Virginia [1606–1612]* (London, 1612), reprinted in *Complete Works of Captain John Smith (1580–1631)*, ed. Philip L. Barbour (Chapel Hill: University of North Carolina Press, 1986), 2:106, 115, 122–23, 149, 151.

15. Deuteronomy 27:17. See Thomas, *Religion and the Decline of Magic*, 502; James R. Perry, *Formation of a Society on Virginia's Eastern Shore, 1615–1665* (Chapel Hill: University of North Carolina Press, 1990), 113; Lester K. Little, *Benedictine Maledictions: Liturgical Cursing in Romanesque France* (Ithaca, NY: Cornell University Press, 1993), 61–62.

16. *For the Colonie in Virginiea Britannia. Lawes Divine, Morall and Martiall, &c.* (London, 1612), reprinted in *Tracts and Other Papers, Relating Principally to the Origin, Settlement, and Progress of the Colonies in North America, From The Discovery of the Country to 1776*, ed. Peter Force (Washington, DC, 1844), 3.2:10.

17. Treasurer and Council for Virginia to Governor and Council in Virginia, Aug. 1, 1622, in *RVCL*, 3:672; Little, *Benedictine Maledictions*, 68–69.

18. Charges by the Virginia Company against Governor Harvey, 1635, Bankes Manuscript 8, fol. 3, Bodleian Library, Oxford University.

19. Instructions of the Privy Council to Sir George Yeardley, Apr. 19, 1623, Public Records Office, National Archives of Great Britain, CO 5/1354, fol. 207. See also "Instructions to Sir Francis Wyatt," *Virginia Magazine of History and Biography* 11 (1903): 54 (hereafter *VMHB*); "Council for Virginia to Captain and Virginia Company going to Virginia, 10 December 1606," in Brown, *Genesis of the United States*, 1:85. Cf. "Instructions from Charles I to Sir William Berkeley," [Aug. 10,

1641], which uses language similar to that quoted above, to "Instructions from Charles II to Sir William Berkeley," Sept. 12, 1662, which does not reflect magical language. Both may be found in *The Papers of Sir William Berkeley, 1605–1677*, ed. Warren M. Billings (Richmond: Library of Virginia, 2007), 29, 177.

20. Colonel [Henry] Norwood, "A Voyage to Virginia," in Force, *Tracts and Others Papers*, 3.10:50.

21. David D. Hall, *Worlds of Wonder, Days of Judgment: Popular Religious Belief in Early New England* (Cambridge: Harvard University Press, 1989).

22. For more on the supernatural world of Virginia, see Edward L. Bond, "Source of Knowledge, Source of Power: The Supernatural World of English Virginia, 1607–1624," *VMHB* 108 (2000): 153–88, from which portions of the foregoing discussion were adapted in part; Darrett Rutman, "The Evolution of Religious Life in Virginia," *Lex et Scientia: Journal of the American Academy of Law* 14 (1978): 190–214; Richard Beale Davis, "The Devil in Virginia in the Seventeenth Century," *VMHB* 65 (1957): 131–49.

23. "Governor John Harvey's Propositions Touching Virginia, [1629]," and "Certaine Answeares to Capt. Harvey's Propositions Touching Virginia," both *VMHB* 7 (1900): 369–71.

24. R[oger] G[reene], *Virginia's Cure: or an Advisive Narrative Concerning Virginia . . .* (London, 1662), in Force, *Tracts and Other Papers*, 3.15:4–5; Samuel Clyde McCulloch, "James Blair's Plan of 1699 to Reform the Clergy of Virginia," *WMQ*, 3d ser., 4 (1947): 73, 76. For population estimates, see Edmund S. Morgan, *American Slavery, American Freedom: The Ordeal of Colonial Virginia* (New York: W. W. Norton, 1975), 404. See also John Frederick Woolverton, *Colonial Anglicanism in North America* (Detroit: Wayne State University Press, 1984), 246 n. 6.

25. William Fitzhugh to Captain Roger Jones, May 18, 1685, and William Fitzhugh to John Cooper, Aug. 20, 1690, both in *William Fitzhugh and His Chesapeake World, 1676–1701: The Fitzhugh Letters and Other Documents*, ed. Richard Beale Davis (Chapel Hill: University of North Carolina Press, 1963), 168, 268; William Waller Hening, ed., *The Statutes at Large: Being a Collection of All the Laws of Virginia, from the First Session of the Legislature, in the Year 1619, etc.* (Richmond, VA, 1809–1823), 1:418, 424. See also Joan R. Gundersen, "The Search for Good Men: Recruiting Ministers in Colonial Virginia," *Historical Magazine of the Protestant Episcopal Church* 48 (1979): 453–64.

26. Governor Francis Howard, Baron Howard of Effingham, to Nathaniel Crew?, n.d. [between 1685 and 1690], in *The Papers of Francis Howard, Baron Howard of Effingham, 1643–1695*, ed. Warren M. Billings (Richmond: Library of Virginia, 1989), 458.

27. Warren M. Billings, *Virginia's Viceroy: Their Majesties' Governor General: Francis Howard, Lord Howard of Effingham* (Fairfax, VA: University Publishing Association, 1991), 80; Arthur Lyon Cross, *The Anglican Episcopate and the American Colonies* (Harvard Historical Studies 9, 1902; repr., Hamden, CT: Archon Books, 1964), 10. On the consecration of churches and confirmation, see Hugh Jones, *The Present State of Virginia, From Whence is Inferred a Short View of Maryland and North*

Carolina, ed. Richard L. Morton (London, 1724; repr., Chapel Hill: University of North Carolina Press, 1956), 97.

28. Hening, *Statutes at Large*, 1:123.

29. G[reene], *Virginia's Cure*, 5–6, 17; Woolverton, *Colonial Anglicanism in North America*, 62; James Maury to William Douglas, May 31, 1758, Sol Fienstone Collection, David Library of the American Revolution, on deposit at the American Philosophical Society, Philadelphia, PA. Governor Alexander Spotswood thought the extent of Virginia's parishes might lead to civil faction, irreligion, and the rise of dissenters. See his prescient analysis in *Calendar of State Papers, Colonial Series, America and the West Indies, 1574–1739* (London, 1860–1994), 16:316. The glebe was the property devoted to the maintenance of the incumbent of a parish; in Virginia this usually meant land and a dwelling.

30. G[reene], *Virginia's Cure*, 4–5, 13–14 (emphasis original).

31. Alexander Forbes to Bishop Edmund Gibson, July 21, 1724, Fulham Palace Papers, 13:91, Lambeth Palace Library, London; William Stevens Perry, ed., *Historical Collections Relating to the American Colonial Church* (Hartford, 1870; repr., New York: AMS Press, 1969), 1:328.

32. Instructions of the Privy Council, PRO CO 5/1323, 48; John K. Nelson, *A Blessed Company: Parishes, Parsons, and Parishioners in Anglican Virginia, 1690–1776* (Chapel Hill: University of North Carolina Press, 2001), 17.

33. Edward L. Bond, ed., *Spreading the Gospel in Colonial Virginia: Preaching, Religion, and Community* (Lanham, MD: Lexington Books, 2005), 279, 309.

34. George MacLaren Brydon, *Virginia's Mother Church and the Political Conditions Under Which it Grew* (Richmond, VA: Church Historical Society, 1947–52), 1:372–73; David L. Holmes, "The Anglican Tradition in Colonial Virginia," in *Perspectives on American Religion and Culture*, ed. Peter W. Williams (Malden, MA: Blackwell, 1999), 69; Parke Rouse Jr., *James Blair of Virginia* (Chapel Hill: University of North Carolina Press, 1971), 28; Hening, *Statutes at Large*, 1:208, 241, 290, 2:44.

35. An act passed in 1699 reduced the legal requirement for church attendance to once every two months, but the once-a-month standard became law again in 1705. Hening, *Statutes at Large*, 3:170, 360; G[reene], *Virginia's Cure*, 4; Alexander Forbes to Bishop Gibson, July 21, 1724, Fulham Palace Papers, 12:27–30, 91; Patricia U. Bonomi and Peter R. Eisenstadt, "Church Adherence in the Eighteenth-Century British American Colonies," *WMQ*, 3d ser., 39 (1982): 254–57.

36. Responses to the queries may be found in the Fulham Palace Papers, 12:41–84, and Perry, *Historical Collections*, 1:261–318.

37. Fulham Palace Papers, 12:49–50.

38. Ibid., 12:79.

39. Ibid., 12:45.

40. Ibid., 12:54, 47.

41. Thomas E. Buckley treats the impact of the Revolution, and especially of Jefferson's statute, on the Church of England in chapter 5 of the present volume.

42. John Spurr, *The Restoration Church of England, 1646–1689* (New Haven, CT: Yale University Press, 1991), 334.

43. Ibid., 108. See also "Draft Representation of the Society for Propagating the Gospel in Foreign Parts to King George I," June 3, 1715, Fulham Palace Papers, 36:42–43.

44. William Beveridge, *A Sermon concerning the Excellency and Usefulness of the Common Prayer . . .* [1682] (London, 1779); Horton Davies, *Worship and Theology in England* (Princeton, NJ: Princeton University Press, 1961–1975), 2:196; James Blair, *Our Saviour's Divine Sermon on the Mount, Contain'd in the Vth, VIth, and VIIIth chapters of St. Matthew's Gospel, Explained; and the Practice of it Recommended in divers Sermons and Discourses* (London, 1722), 4:9.

45. Beveridge, *Excellency and Usefulness of the Common Prayer*, 7–8.

46. Ibid., 17, 21–23, 39.

47. Ibid., 11.

48. See Davies, *Worship and Theology in England*, 2:212; Blair, *Our Saviour's Divine Sermon on the Mount*, 4:9.

49. Bond, *Damned Souls in a Tobacco Colony*, 258; Robert Paxton, sermon no. 8, "Of Repentance," 8, Robert Paxton Manuscript Sermon book, Houghton Library, Harvard University. For a more detailed discussion of Anglican theology and religious practice in colonial Virginia, see Bond, *Damned Souls in a Tobacco Colony*, chapter 5.

50. Blair, *Our Saviour's Divine Sermon on the Mount*, 3:282.

51. Nelson, *Blessed Company*, 191–93, 201–7; David A. deSilva, "Archbishop John Tillotson and Reform of Ecclesiastical Oratory in the Seventeenth Century," *Anglican and Episcopal History* 75 (2006): 368–400.

52. See Answers to the bishop of London's queries, Fulham Palace Papers, 12:41–84.

53. Nicholas M. Beasley, *Christian Ritual and the Creation of British Slave Societies, 1650–1780* (Athens: University of Georgia Press, 2009), 90–92; The Book of Common Prayer (London, 1662), Exhortation in "The Order of the Administration of the Lord's Supper, or Holy Communion."

54. William Byrd's copy of Jeremy Taylor, *The Worthy Communicant*, 3, Virginia Historical Society.

55. "Thomas Dawson: A Confirmation Sermon," in Bond, *Spreading the Gospel*, 490–95 (original in Dawson Papers, 2:257–63, Library of Congress; Book of Common Prayer [London, 1662], "The Order of Confirmation").

56. David R. Holeton, "Initiation," in *The Study of Anglicanism*, rev. ed., ed. Stephen Sykes, John Booty, and Jonathan Knight (Minneapolis: Augsburg Fortress, 1988), 297–99.

57. Jacob M. Blosser, "Irreverent Empire: Anglican Inattention in an Atlantic World," *Church History* 77 (2008): 597.

58. Ibid., 607.

59. Ibid., 611.

60. Ibid.

61. Ibid., 616.

62. Ibid., 621.

63. John Page, *A Deed of Gift to My Dear Son, Captain Matt. Page* (1687; Philadelphia, 1856), in Bond, *Spreading the Gospel*, 94.

64. Ibid., 92–93.

65. Blosser, "Irreverent Empire," 609.

66. James Maury, "First Sermon on Public Prayer," 3, James Maury Manuscript Sermons, John D. Rockefeller Jr. Library, Colonial Williamsburg Foundation, Williamsburg, VA; Miles Selden, "The Great Duty of Publick Worship," 1, 11, Henry Heth Papers, Albert H. Small Special Collections Library, University of Virginia, Charlottesville.

67. Page, *Deed of Gift*, 96. See [Richard Allestree], *The Whole Duty of Man* (London, 1657; 1663), 116–17.

68. David Hein and Gardiner H. Shattuck Jr., *The Episcopalians* (New York: Church Publishing, 2004), 20.

69. See the various Answers to the bishop of London's Queries, Fulham Palace Papers, 12:46, 48, 51, 58, passim.

70. Hening, *Statutes at Large*, 2:517.

71. *Virginia Gazette*, Dec. 15–22, 1738, Feb. 9–16, 16–23, Feb. 23–Mar. 2, Mar. 2–9, 9–16, 1739.

72. Louis B. Wright and Marion Tinling, eds., *The Secret Dairy of William Byrd of Westover, 1709–1712* (Richmond, VA: Dietz Press, 1941), 175 and passim.

73. Phillip Ludwell to Phillip Ludwell II, Dec. 20, 1707, Lee Family Papers, section 5, Virginia Historical Society.

74. Blair, *Our Saviour's Divine Sermon on the Mount*, 4:9–10.

75. Ibid., 2:342–44, 3:239, 5:170–71.

76. Ibid., 2:344, 5:170–71 (quotation).

77. York County, Deeds, Orders, and Wills, vol. 1, 1633–57, 1691–94, 254.

78. Thomas Ludwell to Lord Berkeley of Stratton, Nov. 7, 1667, PRO CO 1/21, 282–83.

79. Edmund Berkeley and Dorothy Berkeley, *John Clayton: Pioneer of American Botany* (Chapel Hill: University of North Carolina Press, 1963), 28.

80. The Reverend James Maury to Mrs. Mary Grymes, 1768, in Bond, *Spreading the Gospel*, 263.

81. John Talbot to Richard Cunningham, May 3, 1703, ser. A, vol. 1, fol. 120, Society for the Propagation of the Gospel in Foreign Parts, American Papers, Lambeth Palace Library.

82. Alexander Forbes to Edmund Gibson, July 21, 1724, Fulham Palace Papers, 12:27–30.

83. Edward Johnson to Virginia Ferrer, Mar. 11, 1650/51, Ferrer Papers, 727, Virginia Colonial Records Project, Library of Virginia.

84. York County, Deeds, Orders, and Wills, 3:33.

85. James Craig to Thomas Dawson, Sept. 8, 1759, Dawson Papers, 2:217–18.

86. Ibid.

87. George William Pilcher, *Samuel Davies: Apostle of Dissent in Colonial Virginia* (Knoxville: University of Tennessee Press, 1971), 105.

88. Jay Worrall Jr., *The Friendly Virginians: America's First Quakers* (Athens, GA: Iberian Publishing, 1994), 98; [Charles Leslie], *The Snake in the Grass: or, Satan Transform'd into an Angel of Light. Discovering the Deep and Unsuspected Subtilty of the People Call'd Quakers* (London, 1696); Joseph Wyath, *Anguis Flagellatus: or, A Switch for the Snake. Being an Answer to the third and Last Edition of the Snake in the Grass. Wherein that Author's Injustice and Falshood, Both in Quotation and Story, are Discover'd and Obviated. And the Truth Doctrinally Deliver'd by Us, Stated and Maintained in Opposition to His Misrepresentation and Perversion* (London, 1699).

89. Thomas Story, *A Journal of the Life of Thomas Story: Containing an Account of His Remarkable Convincement of and Embracing the Principles of Truth, as Held by the People Called Quakers* (Newcastle upon Tyne, 1747), 392–98.

90. Blair, *Our Saviour's Divine Sermon on the Mount*, 1:212–14, 223, 5:44.

91. Jon Butler, "Magic, Astrology, and the Early American Religious Heritage, 1600–1760," *American Historical Review* 84 (1979): 327–29; Thomas, *Religion and the Decline of Magic*, 269–71. See also Jon Butler, "Thomas Teackle's 333 Books: A Great Library on Virginia's Eastern Shore, 1697," *WMQ*, 3d ser., 49 (1992): 449–91. John Catlett of Rappahanock County wrote an almanac that questioned "judicial astrology," or attempting to determine an individual's life by referring to the alignment of the stars at the time of the person's birth; see John Catlett to Thomas Catlett, Apr. 1, 1664, Letter, MS00/1664/April 1, John D. Rockefeller Jr. Library.

92. Joan R. Gundersen, "The Non-Institutional Church: The Religious Role of Women in Eighteenth-Century Virginia," *Historical Magazine of the Protestant Episcopal Church* 51 (1982): 347–57.

THREE Religious Diversity in Colonial Virginia: Red, Black, and White

PHILIP D. MORGAN

EARLY VIRGINIA WAS A PLACE OF STRIKING RELIGIOUS ECLEC-ticism. The colony contained little religious orthodoxy. Indeed, I was tempted to label this chapter "unorthodox religions" in colonial Virginia, but *unorthodox* is an awkward term, reflecting unease about how to describe a broad but inchoate phenomenon that is in opposition to the nominally orthodox. When orthodoxy is minor or not well established, is *unorthodoxy* the appropriate term? *Unorthodox* could be construed as meaning anything other than Protestantism. Anglicanism, which from the beginnings of the English colonial venture at Jamestown became the de facto established church—and therefore the very archetype of orthodoxy—generally considered Puritans and Presbyterians, even more so Baptists and Methodists, and still more definitely Quakers, as unorthodox. But at least these groups were Protestant, part of the same post-Reformation world that Anglicans inhabited. Those who were not Protestant—Catholics, many Africans and African Americans, most Native Americans, and a fair number of lay white people who shared quasi-Christian or non-Christian beliefs about magic and the occult—were the groups the leaders of Virginia considered most unorthodox. Obviously, there are vast differences between a Catholic priest and an Indian shaman, an African conjuror and a European cunning woman, but to differing degrees they were all regarded as beyond the pale of orthodox Protestantism. They were outsiders to its religious conventions. Heterodoxy and dissent, then, flourished in colonial Virginia, in an age of supposed Christian orthodoxy.

These various unorthodox groups almost certainly formed a majority of Virginia's population throughout the seventeenth and eighteenth centuries. Clearly, that was the case soon after the English arrived. At that point, the thirty thousand or so Indians who lived in what would become Virginia were the majority. Their religious beliefs and practices were normative. Orthodoxy and unorthodoxy, then, are primarily matters of perspective, dependent on whose vantage point is taken. As the Indian population declined over time and English numbers grew, Anglicans became more numerous, but still the colony's Anglican adherents, as Thomas E. Buckley has noted, probably "numbered at best a bare majority of the white population" on the eve of the American Revolution. Furthermore, as Africans and their descendants became a significant proportion of the population—rising to about 40 percent by the end of the colonial period—so the ranks of the unorthodox widened. Unorthodoxy, no matter what the perspective, was widespread.[1]

As much as religious heterogeneity was present in early Virginia, the colony was conceived in the midst of a great contest between Protestant England and Catholic Spain, and Anglicanism in England took a militant and aggressive stance not just against Catholics but also against so-called heathens. The established Anglican Church, with its state approval for one religion, tended to see the world in dualistic terms. It thus marked all other forms of belief as impure, at least to some degree, and considered many of them heretical. In a sermon published in London in 1610 promoting the Virginia experiment, William Crashaw urged the colonial leaders to "suffer no Papists; let them not nestle there; nay let the name of the Pope for Poperie be never heard of in Virginea."[2] Furthermore, influential people believed North America was the "place where Satan's throne is" and that Englishmen, by bringing Christianity to the land, participated in a spiritual conquest, liberating territory from the devil's stranglehold. Naturally, the English contrasted their humanity to the cruelty of the Spaniards; they expected that the Indians would experience only "faire and loving meanes suting to our English Natures." Nevertheless, John Smith announced that the Powhatans' "chiefe God" was none other than "the Divell," and Alexander Whitaker, the Anglican minister at

Henrico, described Algonquian priests as "a generation of vipers, even of Sathans owne brood."[3]

Among Anglo-Virginians, this dualism was often expressed in proto-racial terms. Thus, they generally subscribed to the notion that Africans were evil because of their heathenism and skin color. Furthermore, since some of the earliest Africans in the colony, acquired predatorily from the Iberians, were at least nominally Catholic, they labored under yet another stain. One English traveler to Africa claimed that the inhabitants "in colour so in condition are little other than Devils incarnate." When, in 1630, Hugh Davis "defiled his body" by having sexual intercourse with a black person, his crime was "dishonor of God" and "shame of Christians." A century later, when Virginia legislators denied blacks (and Indians) the ability to give court testimony, they cited their "base and corrupt natures" as justification. Anglo-Virginians easily lumped together Africans and Indians as associates of the devil.[4]

Anglo-Virginians even charged one another with being in league with the devil. In the seventeenth century, that allegation was usually applied to putative witches; in the eighteenth century, as witchcraft beliefs declined and religious passions heated, dissenters were generally at the center of such battles. Thus, in 1745, a Louisa County resident declared that the Church of England "is the works of the Devil and they that pin their faith in it are damned." New Light Presbyterians, according to Patrick Henry, minister in St. Paul's Parish, Hanover County, thundered out "in awful words" that "the old people [were] Grey-headed Devils, and all promiscuously, Damn'd double damn'd, whose [souls] are in hell though they are alive on earth, Lumps of hell-fire, incarnate Devils, 1000 times worse than Devils &c." The constant refrain in many a criminal court case was that the accused had been instigated to commit the deed by the devil. Satan stalked the Virginia landscape in many guises.[5]

Anglo-Virginians could—and did—deploy the language of barbarity and bestiality to demarcate themselves from Indians and Africans, but at the same time proto-racial thinking was seriously constrained by the orthodox Christian belief in the monogenesis, or unity, of human origins. All humans descended from a single ancestor. To suggest otherwise was to risk heresy. Biblical sources were a first resort for answering certain kinds of questions: Were Native Americans the descendants of the Lost Ten Tribes of Israel? Or were they wandering Tartars from northern Asia? Why were some people black, others tawny, and yet others white? Was the curse of Ham directed at Africans? As Colin Kidd notes, "During the early modern era, theological concerns helped to inhibit—and at the very least to circumscribe—the articulation of racial prejudices and the formulation of identities based upon race." Thus, when in 1743 John Mitchell, a Virginia physician, tried to explain racial differences with medical evidence, he still defended the notion that all people were "descended from the same stock." Enlightenment thinkers such as Thomas Jefferson would flirt with polygenist ideas of multiple human origins, but mainstream monogenesis was not easily overthrown.[6]

My aim in this chapter, then, is to survey the ranks of what can be termed the unorthodox or the heterodox and to reveal the varied attempts to bring such outsiders into the fold. I intend no value judgment when I divide the religious world into the orthodox and the unorthodox. Orthodoxy and its opposite are unquestionably in the eye of the beholder; there is no intention here of contributing to Protestant triumphalism. To the extent religion is defined as involving a belief in superhuman powers and a set of practices to invoke those otherworldly forces, then indubitably Native Americans, Africans, and Europeans all shared a religious worldview. Their religious practices varied—in many cases radically—but they all possessed a basic belief in supernatural powers, a conviction that such forces affected humans, and various techniques or strategies to approach and manipulate those otherworldly powers. Still, one form of Protestantism dominated the leadership of the Virginia colony, and its leaders attempted to impose their religious hegemony on others. My goal is to document the extent of religious diversity in the colony, touch on some of the ways orthodox Protestantism tried to suppress those groups it considered the most unorthodox, and reveal the extent of resistance to that attempt at suppression. These struggles and challenges set the stage for the movement for religious freedom in later Virginia—a story that will be told by others in this volume.[7]

INDIANS

In Tsenacommacah, which means "densely inhabited land" and represented most of what became eastern Virginia, Algonquian-speaking Indians believed in a spiritual power, to which they gave the term *manit* or *manitou*. All authority had its origins in the world of the spirits. The creator was Ahone, a beneficent, peaceable god, a provider, the ultimate source of manitou. But Ahone was a remote god, unconcerned with human affairs, too mysterious for humans to fathom. Another spirit, Okeus, dealt directly with humans. Okeus was widely present in natural events and could be approached by offering sacrifice. The English usually translated *Okeus* as "devil," but in the Algonquian worldview, Okeus, although he might be vengeful, was not evil. In everyday matters, however, Algonquians had less to do with Okeus than they did with *quiyoughcosughs*, lesser gods, who could take a variety of forms—as animals, objects, and humans. A Patawomeck Indian, for example, claimed that his chief god appeared as "a mightie great Hare," while his other four gods were the winds coming from the quarters of the earth.[8]

Indians reported that they had guardian spirits that took the form of various animals. They tattooed their bodies with images of animals; they fashioned their ceremonial clothes from feathers, animal skins, and shells; they smoked tobacco pipes with animal-shaped decorations; successful hunters made offerings at "alter stones" in gratitude for animals making themselves available as gifts to humans; they used animals or parts of animals as ornaments. The English named Nemattanew, a charismatic war leader whom Powhatans revered for his supernatural powers, "Jack of the feathers" because "he used to come into the felde all covered over with feathers and swans wings fastened unto his showlders, as thowghe he meante to flye." Another Powhatan man wore in his pierced ear a small green and yellow live snake that coiled round his neck and, according to the white observer, "familiarly" kissed his lips. The Indian conception of animals was part of a cosmology that merged the natural and the supernatural worlds.[9]

Not just animals and objects, but humans were also embodiments of spiritual power. In Tsenacommacah, the most important human representative of the spirit world was the paramount chief, a man whose title was Powhatan but who went by the name of Wahunsonacock when the English arrived. He was part-god. He was the overlord, the "keeper of many spirits," or *mamanatowick*, a word incorporating the term *manitou*. The material, the spiritual, and the political were inseparable in this one person; he embodied spiritual power and chiefly authority. Not just the paramount chief but all chiefs or *werowances* straddled the porous border between humans and spirits. They could enter the sacred precincts of the temples, where their corpses would be buried with pearls, copper, and bracelets—indications of their material standing and their share of divinity.[10]

The other key mediators between the human and spirit worlds were the shamans or priests or quiyoughcosughs (in human form). Through rituals, images, architecture, clothing, and bodily markings, they constantly reminded people of their hereditary and personal spiritual power. They tended the temples, which were not so much churches, for they were constructed like any other dwelling and the public did not attend them (they went to ceremonies held outdoors), but rather more akin to shrines, mortuary buildings, and treasure houses. The temples contained sacred images, the bones of deceased chiefs, and stored wealth. They represented ancestral, economic, and military power. Priests buttressed chiefly authority; they advised the werowances on all matters. They read omens, sought to influence the weather, healed the sick, and determined when to go to war. They conducted various rites and sacrifices, for example, tossing smoke and flame upward in an attempt to pacify the gods during storms, or deploying rattles and incantations to call for rain. When in 1616 Pocahontas and John Rolfe—by then a married couple—went to England, Uttamatomakkin, a high-ranking priest and Powhatan's son-in-law, accompanied them. He was an experienced counselor to Opechanchanough, Powhatan's brother, and he apparently held his own in theological debates in England, stating his preference for his "God" rather than the Christian version. His English debater noted ominously that he wore his "Devill-lock at the left eare." Notably, the prefix *uttama-* connotes spiritual" or "priestly," and the holiest temple site was at Uttamussak on the Pamunkey River.[11]

Not just priests, but ordinary people engaged in various rituals to approach the spirit world. They routinely sacrificed the first fruits of their corn. They smoked—or rather drank, as the contemporary term had it—tobacco, which also opened paths of communication to the gods. They customarily took a morning bath—something Europeans certainly did not do—in order to cleanse themselves spiritually and physically. Sweat lodges served the same function. They believed that their dreams connected them to the spirit world. Their coming-of-age ritual, known as the *huskanaw,* a vision quest where teenage boys left their village, searched out a sacred place, and there mortified themselves in a months-long endurance test until the spirit world took pity on and communicated with them, was a way to establish a personal relationship with a spirit. It was an important initiation rite, marking the transition between boyhood and manhood. People could also improve their access to divine power if they possessed copper, shell beads, or other potent objects. The reddest copper was especially prized, as were particularly white or dark beads.[12]

When the English arrived at Jamestown in 1607, they bore especially prized trade goods, and they also came at a moment of acute environmental crisis. The sixteenth and seventeenth centuries constituted a period of unprecedented ecological hardship. Much of the northern hemisphere had experienced cold so severe this period has been called the Little Ice Age. Severe droughts compounded the cold temperatures. The lack of rainfall in the sixteenth century was the most severe of the last five hundred years. No wonder, then, that Virginia Algonquians thought their "Gods were angrie." They must have been distressed and confused when their appeals for rain went unanswered. Furthermore, the guns and trade goods that the English possessed were especially attractive. The Christian God's apparent willingness to deploy his powers on behalf of the colonists made Christianity impressive. In many ways, then, the Algonquians should have been ripe for conversion.[13]

But the first mission to convert Virginia Indians, which had occurred in 1570, almost forty years before Jamestown was settled, did not augur well. In 1561, a Spanish ship had taken off a young Indian known as Paquiquineo, a high-ranking Paspahegh man from the very nation where Jamestown would be sited. He would go on to live in Havana, Mexico City, Madrid, and Seville; convert to Catholicism; and assume the name Don Luís de Velasco. In 1570 he returned to the Chesapeake Bay with a group of nine Spaniards, mostly Jesuits, who were the first to try to convert Native Americans in Ajacán, the Spanish name for Virginia. They established a settlement on what the English would later call the York River. Hardly had they settled when Don Luís abandoned the missionaries and moved to the village of a relative upriver. Even after nine years' absence, he quickly reverted to Indian ways in dress and habits and soon married many women. Early the next year, he led a war party that attacked the mission and killed all the priests, using their own iron hatchets to commit the deed. Don Luís showed ambivalence, continuing to honor the priests in some fashion—apparently burying them in a Christian manner—but refusing to accept significant cultural change. That the Algonquians killed all the missionaries but spared a young boy suggests that they murdered only those they felt were a cultural threat. The mission lasted no more than five months.[14]

If Jesuits, generally considered highly skilled in converting natives, were unsuccessful in Ajacán, Protestants were not likely to fare much better. Nevertheless, what is impressive early on in Jamestown is that the Protestant English mounted a credible religious mission to the Indians. A leading member of the Virginia Company, William Strachey, claimed that conversion of the Indians was the "principal" reason for going to Virginia. He highlighted the Indian man Kemps, a Paspahegh taken prisoner in 1609 but then released, who regularly came to Jamestown, where he attended daily prayers and kept the Sabbath. The English achieved their most notable success when in 1614 Powhatan's daughter Pocahontas, in Governor Thomas Dale's words, "renounced publickly her Countrey Idolatry, openly confessed her Christian faith," and then married John Rolfe. She became the most prominent figure in the English attempt to establish dominion and civility in Virginia. With her marriage and conversion to Christianity, followed by her change of name to Rebecca, she became an emblem of successful English outreach. Her wildly successful tour of England—she was the first Indian woman to go there—was highly promising, for the Rolfes secured enough money to initiate a serious Christian education program to the Indians. The promise was cut short when she died in 1617 at the age of twenty, never having returned to Virginia.[15]

Still, the mission went ahead. In 1621 George Thorpe, a former Member of Parliament and member of the Governor's Council, arrived in Virginia to head the mission. He proposed that Indian children should be placed in white households, converted and educated, and then returned to their villages to spread the word. The idea was that Indians could be brought to Christianity more readily if they adopted European manners and clothes. He built one chief an English-style house as a way of demonstrating the advantages of the newcomers' material culture. He laid plans for a preparatory college and eventually a university. In early 1622, Thorpe reported that Opechancanough, now the paramount chief after his brother's death four years earlier, promised that some Indians would come and live with the English. Apparently, a spokesperson for Opechancanough "willingly Acknowledged" that "their [religion] was not the right waye" and that "God loved [the English] better than them." Thorpe was optimistic, for he had learned that Indians understood the stars and constellations as Europeans did. In his more sober moments, however, Thorpe put his finger on the biggest problem, which was that the settlers gave the Indians "nothinge but maledictions and bitter execrations." And the optimism evaporated on March 22, 1622, when Opechancanough launched the great uprising that killed at least 350 settlers, about a third of the colony, although an Indian convert working for an English master revealed the plan just before it happened, so that at least some settlements were forewarned. The reported mutilation of Thorpe's body was notable; it was much like killing the Jesuits with their own axes. The most potent threat to the Indian way of life—the attempt to convert their children—was not just destroyed but desecrated.[16]

Thereafter, Europeans in Virginia largely kept the Algonquians at arm's length, although continuing to advocate and sometimes to implement conversion, while Indians for the most part continued to show only sporadic interest in becoming Christians. In 1654, when the king of the Roanoke Indians attended church one Sunday, prominent whites threatened to whip him, even though he had earlier offered his own son for baptism and an English education. In 1671 a white servant woman, who had given birth to an illegitimate child fathered by an Indian, wanted him to have nothing to do with the child, since, as she put it, he was "a Pagan." A few years later, Nathaniel Bacon inspired a frontier rebellion built on hatred of the "barbarous Heathen"; while it was directed mostly at Siouan-speaking Indians to the west, all Indians suffered the consequences. Thus, when the governor of Virginia reported in 1683 that the king of Pamunkey and most of his leading warriors wished to become Christians, he added that "they are so treacherous that there is no trust in them." With the founding of the College of William and Mary in the 1690s, Alexander Spotswood, who governed Virginia from 1710 to 1722, implemented a plan to have two sons from every tributary Indian town sent to Williamsburg to be educated. In 1711 he reported that about twenty Indian children were being educated there. A few years later, the Reverend Charles Griffin educated over one hundred Indian students, mostly Saponi, at the short-lived school Spotswood founded at Fort Christanna on the Meherrin River.

Yet the English success in converting Indians was limited. The basic problem was that Indians had to renounce their culture in order to convert. For some exceptional individuals, this is precisely what happened. Thus, in 1709, a Pamunkey shoemaker named Robin successfully petitioned Virginia's general court to remain in the colony and not be returned to the Pamunkeys, because he said his trade was useless to him there, and he would have to "forsake the company & conversation of the English . . . with wch he is much more Delighted than with the barbarous Customs & manners of Living of his own nation." Robin was the exception that proved the rule. Unable to assimilate Indians, Anglo-Virginians excluded the natives altogether, turning their backs on the conversion ideals that motivated Thorpe and Spotswood. Only as Indians dwindled in numbers did Anglo-Virginians recast the natives as romantic vestiges of the colony's past.[17]

In short, conversion never achieved much. Indians might ask the English to pray to their Christian God for rain, or they might incorporate some aspect of the newcomers' material culture, but they were not about to forsake their way of life. Like most polytheistic peoples, Native Americans had no objection to adding a foreign deity to their pantheon if it seemed to assure more efficient control of the natural universe. The wish was to improve their own culture by judicious borrowing—a gun, a piece of copper, a supernatural being—but not to change religious customs entirely. The whole structure of Indian life relied upon controlling the mysterious aspects of the world through a traditional body of beliefs that required the use of priests, temples, idols, and rituals. Minor innovations might be permitted, but wholesale change was never likely. Only if and when the structure of Indian life disintegrated, as began to happen over the course of the eighteenth century, did individual Indians such as the shoemaker Robin abandon their cultures and presumably their religions—although it is always possible that Robin's assimilation was in part strategic. In 1745, after spending some time on the Eastern Shore, Thomas Bacon, the Maryland Anglican, announced, "I have not so much heard of a single Indian in this whole province, who is converted to, and lives in the profession of the Christian faith." Another Anglican rector described Eastern Shore Indians as "extremely barbarous and obstinately ignorant of the Christian religion," adding that they had "an idolatrous catica [set of practices?] of their own." Native Americans tenaciously held to their traditional religious beliefs.[18]

AFRICANS AND AFRICAN AMERICANS

The religious worldview of Africans in the seventeenth and eighteenth centuries shared some features with that of Native Americans. Both groups drew no neat distinction between the sacred and the secular. The supernatural and the everyday formed an integrated whole in both Native American and African cultures. In addition, most West Africans, like Native Americans, believed in a creator divinity, a supreme being—although a number of African peoples believed in not one, but two supreme creators, and some had no concept of a supreme being at all. Furthermore, most African high gods, like their Native American counterparts, were thought to be remote and detached from everyday affairs, even if ultimately responsible for the design and preservation of the universe. For most Africans, again like most Native Americans, belief in a supreme being or beings was peripheral rather than central to religious life. The core of traditional African cosmology, much like that of the Native Americans, was a system of lesser spirits whose activities were supposed to make meaningful the events of the ordinary, everyday world. Perhaps even more than Native Americans, Africans emphasized the power of the ancestors, the living dead, to influence the fate of their descendants—but this difference was more a matter of degree than kind. Finally, since their religions were both polytheistic, Africans and Native Americans shared an adaptability, a responsiveness to new ideas, a pragmatism, and a willingness to experiment.

The major difference was that African religious systems did not survive the Middle Passage, whereas Native Americans, as much as their cultures disintegrated over time, were, by comparison, relatively advantaged by continuing to live in their ancestral lands. Africans could transport significant quantities of knowledge and information to the New World, but not their institutions, priesthoods, or temples, and certainly not whole religious systems. Such devastating loss has spurred one historian to speak of "an African spiritual holocaust that forever destroyed traditional African religious systems as *systems* in North America and that left slaves remarkably bereft of traditional collective religious practice." I do not go so far myself, but he has a point, certainly when comparing the situation of Africans and Indians in the new world. African religious systems were destroyed at the point enslaved Africans arrived in Virginia; the destruction of Native American religious systems took a much longer time.[19]

Two key religious developments occurred among Africans in Virginia. First, in response to the severe dislocations they faced, they expanded the role of the lesser spirits in their lives. In order to cope with their new situation, Africans in Virginia gave increased prominence to magic, whether it was by resort to folk healing, divination, or sorcery. Whites usually described these activities as conjuring, as fortune-telling, or even more pejoratively as poisoning. Whatever the label, the dispenser of roots, herbal medicines, or charms—the so-called conjuror—became a central figure within slave communities. Such individuals often had a close relationship with animals: snakes, spiders, and scorpions formed key ingredients of their fetishes; their use of charms—such as the raccoon *baculum* or penis bone, a possible fertility symbol, recovered from George Washington's Mount Vernon slave quarters—suggests a similar connection. They, like Indians, became notable for providing cures for snake bites, and they told animal tales.[20] When life appears unusually capricious and unpredictable, conditions are ripe for magical expression. The unpredictability of the slaves' world helps explain why Christianity had little initial appeal for most slaves. Until they could see that Christianity might symbolize an improvement in the conditions of their daily lives, or until it could serve as an expression of their situation and a message of hope for the future, it was unattractive. The religious worldview of most early American slaves was primarily magical, not Christian.

The second development that occurred among Africans in Virginia, when faced with the interpretative challenge of large-scale social change, was an expanded place for their notion of a supreme being, which ultimately facilitated conversion to Christianity. Such seems to have been the case for one Chesapeake African who prayed "to the God of his native country" every night, "though he said he ought to pray oftener; but that his God would excuse him for the non-performance," because he was now a slave in a foreign land. He was scathing toward Christianity, declaring it "altogether false, and indeed no religion at all." Rather, he lauded his people's faith, "which had been of old time delivered by the true God to a holy man, who was taken up into heaven for that purpose, and after he had received the divine communication, had returned to earth, and spent a hundred years in preaching and imparting the truth which had been revealed to him, to mankind." In spite of his aversion to Christianity, this old African seems to have appropriated some Christian terminology and themes.[21]

Whether this portrayal of the role of a supreme being in traditional African religion was accurate or a modification brought about by the experience of being captured and transferred to the New World is impossible to say. In fact, the situation was even more complex because some Africans had been exposed to Christianity before they left their homeland. Some syncretism of an African high god with the Christian God had therefore probably already occurred. A number of the first generation of Africans probably knew something of Catholicism. The first twenty or so Africans brought into Jamestown in 1619 came from a Portuguese slave ship, the *São João Bautista*, that had loaded its complement at Luanda, the coastal capital of the Portuguese colony of Angola in West-Central Africa. Some likely shared a rudimentary understanding of Catholicism, because Portuguese law required all slaves to be baptized before arriving in America. Furthermore, perhaps some Muslim slaves arrived in Virginia, for we know of at least one, Yarrow Mamout, who lived in Georgetown in the late eighteenth century, who also may have reinterpreted Christian dogma in the light of Islamic precepts, perhaps eliding an Islamic and a Christian God. Transplanted Africans, then, certainly conceived of a supreme being, in some cases a Christian or Islamic God or, more likely, an indigenous or syncretized high god. Perhaps they enlarged on this deity's role in response to the wrenching experiences of becoming New World slaves. This elaboration may well explain, at least in part, some slaves' emphasis on the awesome powers of the Creator—a true God, a great God, surfaces in their accounts. This belief in an all-powerful God, like the widespread resort to magic, was a way of making sense of a world over which the individual had little control.[22]

This probability of fusion between African high god and Christian God is not to deny that Christianity introduced new concepts to most African slaves' religious repertory. Most obviously, the emphasis on one God, so important to Christianity, was alien to the polytheism of African religions. In addition, most African cosmologies contained few speculations about the nature of life after death. The insistence of Christianity on the fear of hell and the delights of heaven introduced African Americans to radically new conceptions of the afterlife. This novelty certainly wrought its effect on an "old gray-headed" slave encountered by a traveler in the Northern Neck of Virginia in 1760. The slave reported that he "awaited the hour when it please God to call him to another life." Did he not wish for that time, the white man inquired, since it would release the slave from his sufferings? No, the slave replied, for "he was afraid to die." Did this fear stem from a bad conscience, a lack of honesty and fidelity? No, insisted the slave, he had done his duty; but he remained fearful, for "was not our Saviour himself afraid to die?" The profundity of this remark "sunk deep" into the white traveler's mind.[23]

Nor does the probability of fusion deny that a significant number of blacks became pious Christians, quite orthodox in their beliefs. Two of the earliest were "Antonio," who reached Virginia in 1621, and Mary, the woman who would become his wife, who arrived the following year. Their names suggest that their homeland was a region influenced by Portuguese Catholicism, and the names of their children—Richard and John, their two sons—indicate that they were Christians in Virginia. Indeed, their son John would later be allowed to testify in county court because he was baptized. Another example is John Phillip, "a Negro" baptized in England in 1612 and present in Virginia at least by 1624, when he testified in court, no doubt because he too was a Christian. Three years later, Phillip was found guilty of fornication with an English woman but was not whipped, presumably again because he was a Christian. The Eastern Shore free black Francis Paine (or Payne) wrote a will in 1673 that revealed exceptional piety: he bequeathed his soul to his "loveing Father, my creator and to Jesus Christ who by his blood and passion suffered for my sins." Through Christ's merit, he expected to "injoy that heavenly portion prepared for mee and all true beleevers," and he committed his body to a Christian burial.[24]

Although some black Virginians gained access to Christianity in the seventeenth century, they were the exceptions. Even after the law of 1667 stipulating that baptism of slaves did not "alter the condition of the person as to his bondage," most Virginia masters still failed to allow their slaves to be converted. Reaching out to slaves in Virginia in the late 1660s, the Reverend Morgan Godwyn encountered intransigence and racial hostility from their owners. You might as well baptize a "puppy," said one; converting a slave was like sprinkling water on a "black Bitch," said another. As Godwyn noted, ranking human creatures among "Brute Beasts" smacked of "Hellish Principles." At the very time Godwyn was trying to convert slaves, a direct transatlantic trade in Africans—who were less familiar with European ways than those who came via the West Indies—began to reach Virginia.[25]

By the eighteenth century, as the native-born became the majority among the enslaved population, Afro-Virginians showed greater awareness of Christian beliefs. In 1723, speaking for "a Sort of people that is Calld molatters which are baptized," brought up as Christians, and "followes the wayes and Rulles of the Chrch of England," an anonymous mulatto slave—who knew his or her Bible, particularly Exodus—wrote an extraordinary letter to the Bishop of London in which he or she complained that "wee are commandded to keep holey the Sabbath day and wee doo hardly know when it comes for our task mastrs are as hard with us as the Egypttions was with the Chilldann of Issarell." Asking for the bishop's help in releasing "us out of this Cruell Bondegg," the writer begged "for Jesus Christs his Sake." The writer knew the requirements for baptism, requesting that the bishop "settell one thing upon us which is that our childarn may be broatt up in the way of the Christtian faith and our desire is that they may be Larnd the Lords prayer the creed and the ten commandements and that they may appeare Every Lord's day att Church." The author even desired that "our Childarn be putt to Scool and . . . Larnd to Reed through the Bybell." Signing the letter would lead, the writer wryly noted, only to a swinging on the nearest "gallass tree."[26]

In 1730, a number of Virginia slaves apparently believed that the king of England had ordered their freedom. The rumor spread rapidly. That slaves put their faith in a distant monarch may have owed something to African hierarchical beliefs, but the rapidly growing number of creoles or native-born among them were probably also aware of the king's growing imperial power. Furthermore, they supposedly held "many Meetings and Consultations" and engaged in "loose discourses" concerning the king's order that Christianized slaves should be freed. Local ministers had emphasized that baptism failed to change temporal status, but many slaves thought that their owners had suppressed the king's declaration. In southeastern Tidewater, slaves chose officers to lead them in an insurrection. They were executed. The dangers of slaves believing in a radical Christian message seemed real to many white Virginians.[27]

Some masters thought that slaves were attracted to Christianity for instrumental purposes. They often derided slaves for "pretending" to be religious, but nonetheless they were also impressed by some slaves' sincerity. In the 1760s, James Gordon, a Presbyterian of Lancaster County, "had much conversation" with a neighbor's slave, "whose piety I have great opinion of." Even masters of runaway slaves could grudgingly acknowledge their fugitives' religiosity. Thus, in the 1770s, one master reported that his slave was a Baptist and could be expected to "show a little of it in Company"; another described his slave as "fond of talking about Religion," while Will missed "no opportunity of holding forth" on religious subjects. One Baptist minister was so impressed at a revival meeting by seeing an "old African," who was "truly religious," that he said he "would have given all to have been like one of them," even exchanging his freedom for their slave status.[28]

Despite the dangers of being misinterpreted, a number of Anglican clergymen and planters sought to encompass blacks within their religious communities—certainly more so than happened among Native Americans. Hundreds of slaves were baptized in scattered locales throughout Virginia: 200 in Accomack Parish on the Eastern Shore between 1709 and 1724; 354 in North Farnham Parish, Richmond County, in a short seven-year period from 1725 to 1732; 250 on the Burwell plantations in Gloucester, James City, and York counties between 1721 and 1768; 172 in St. James Parish, Goochland County, during 1738; 140 in six months at Hanover Parish in 1762; 315 in St. Mary's Parish, Caroline County, in one afternoon in 1766. One of the most notable efforts occurred between 1739 and 1775 in Albemarle Parish, which became part of Sussex County, where Reverend William Willie baptized 913 slaves. In the early years, he baptized only about one in twenty, but by the Revolution the number increased to about four out of five. Over time, it would seem, planters increasingly accepted infant slave baptism, partly no doubt in response to the wishes of enslaved parents. Virginia's capital seems to have undergone the most intensive proselytization. In the third quarter of the eighteenth century, almost 1,000 slaves received baptism in Bruton Parish, Williamsburg. In 1770, the Anglican minister of Gloucester County reported that infant and adult baptism was actually "in Fashion" among his black parishioners. Some slaves even learned to read and write. By the end of the colonial period, Williamsburg, Norfolk, and Fredericksburg hosted schools for enslaved children, though numbers of attendees were always small.[29]

The incorporative character of Anglicanism is evident in the practice of "churching"—a ceremony in which a new mother was formally welcomed back into the fold after giving birth and in which the community gave thanks—which at least one minister, Adam Dickie of Drysdale Parish, was willing to extend to enslaved women. He petitioned Anglican authorities in England for a ruling on whether baptized slave women were eligible for this religious ritual, a celebration of a safe delivery in a world where childbirth was dangerous and often life-threatening. New mothers, even enslaved ones, no doubt appreciated the attention and formal recognition.[30]

Dissenters probably made greater inroads among enslaved adults than Anglicans. In the second quarter of the eighteenth century, the Huguenots of Manekin Town baptized about 150 slaves. From 1748 to 1755, the Presbyterian reverend Samuel Davies baptized about 100 slaves in Hanover County. His efforts then gained momentum, for in 1757 he reportedly baptized 150 adult slaves in an eighteen-month period. Similar successes occurred in neighboring areas influenced by the charismatic Davies and his disciples. Slaves were attracted by the opportunity to sing their worship and to be taught reading, and, in Davies's words, a misplaced expectation of "equality with their Masters." The most extensive and successful conversion effort undoubtedly occurred in the 1760s, when New Light Baptists established their first beachhead in the Virginia Southside. Their message of redemption for all, their belief in personal salvation, and their emotionalism swept through the slave quarters, appealing to hundreds, perhaps even a few thousand, of enslaved Virginians. Separate Baptist churches in Virginia mushroomed almost eightfold, from seven in 1769 to fifty-four just five years later. Finally, on the eve of the American Revolution, Methodist circuit riders and their revival meetings also began to attract sizable followings among the enslaved.[31]

Granting the novelty of Christianity and the piety, even orthodoxy, of some of its enslaved adherents, a case can nevertheless be made not only that African slaves were predisposed toward Christianity because of developments within their traditional religious beliefs but also that they infused elements of their traditional religion into Christianity. Slaves, in other words, did not just accept Christianity wholesale, but did so on their own terms, retaining some of their old beliefs, transforming others, substituting the new for the old in yet others, and always engaging with their new milieu.

For example, African attitudes toward the dead merged with the new environment in complicated ways. In African societies, the dead played an active role in the lives of the living. In fact, African kin groups are often described as communities of both the living and the dead. No direct evidence exists that elaborate beliefs about dead ancestors or friends survived the Middle Passage, although a widespread conviction that death brought a return to Africa was one way to retain a link to ancestors and friends, but the importance of funerals and distinctive graveside practices suggests continuity with traditional beliefs. As early as 1687, Virginia officials registered unease at the "great numbers" of slaves who attended funerals. Mortuary practices—interring beads, jewelry, seeds or tobacco pipes, or marking graves with broken crockery, upturned bottles, seashells, and particular plants—demonstrate the close relation slaves saw between the living and the dead. These practices were ways of propitiating the dead, easing their journey to the spirit world, and of ensuring that they did not return to haunt the living. Graveside rites—what eighteenth-century whites described as crying, bawling, howling, rolling in the dirt, or excessive grief—again point to the distinctiveness of black funeral behavior.[32]

Highly expressive funeral practices are, however, not far removed from the typical behavior of eighteenth-century evangelicals. Trembling, quaking bodies, and tear-lined faces were characteristic features of revivalist meetings in general. Indeed, some white evangelical preachers thought that blacks imitated their white coreligionists in falling down, crying, shouting, bawling, beating their breasts, and fainting. Still, blacks so often exceeded whites in the expressiveness of their evangelicalism that difference also seems present, another way in which blacks merged the old with the new. Thus, some dramatic seizures—being poleaxed for hours, even days; foaming at the mouth; speaking in tongues—may well have owed more to African patterns of possession trance than to the range of physical responses found in white evangelicalism. Similarly, the choreographed response of African

American possession behavior—hollering, jumping, and other types of particularly expressive physicality—also suggests separate origins.[33]

Two broad developments, then, characterized the religious lives of black slaves in colonial Virginia. The first and most important was the enhanced role of magic. Before Christianity penetrated the world of slaves, magical beliefs and practices had assumed a prominent place that they would retain even after Christianization. Second, even when African slaves came into contact with Christianity, they did not accept it wholesale. Rather than adding a high god to their pantheon of lesser spirits, they elaborated on a traditional concept of a supreme being. If this development encouraged Africans and their descendants to adapt Christianity to their needs rather than having it thrust upon them, such discrimination was evident in their distinctive funeral practices and their expressive religious behavior. Slaves managed to preserve some deep-level principles from their African heritage. Much was lost: few priests and almost no collective rituals survived. But they engaged in a process of selective appropriation or structured improvisation in which values and practices were reinterpreted as they were incorporated.

EUROPEANS AND ANGLO-VIRGINIANS

Many Anglo-Virginians, like Africans and Native Americans, had a magical view of the world. Admittedly, the European God was a more interventionist one than the remote creator divinity in which most Africans or Native Americans believed. Still, like most people in the early modern world, Anglo-Virginians believed in signs, portents, omens, and wonders. They read divine interventions in natural calamities—comets, earthquakes, lightning, droughts, and so forth—and in singular but less cataclysmic prodigies such as monstrous births. Strange or unexplained phenomena might be premonitions sent by God to warn of difficult events in the near future. In 1644, for example, an anonymous colonist read an impending Indian attack into the blood found in a wash pail, blood that mysteriously failed to stain either hands or clothes. Furthermore, Anglo-Virginians generally believed that those with herbal knowledge could both heal and harm. They used charms and amulets to keep away disease. They read almanacs, the most popular books of the day, which told them when to plant, bleed, marry, or have sex. By following the almanac's guide to the stars, they could predict the future. Systems of belief in natural and supernatural forces overlapped; Christianity coexisted with a world that included magic, astrology, divination, and occult forces in general.[34]

The English view of animals was also closer to that of Indians and Africans than is usually supposed. The orthodox Christian view was a doctrine of dominion over the realm of creatures, but the English were also heirs to rich folkloric traditions that identified animals as having significant predictive powers. Thus, owls were portents of death; black cats and ravens signified bad luck; low-flying birds or restless livestock suggested rain in the air. But while the English assumed that animals could serve as signs, symbols, and portents, they generally avoided granting specific supernatural powers to animals, with perhaps a couple of exceptions. The stories about rattlesnake "gazing" that emerged in late seventeenth-century America are one example. By fixing their eyes steadfastly on their prey—whether animal or human—the snake, it was thought, could "gaze" its victim into a stupor that allowed it to attack its victim more readily. The other exception was the persistent belief that animal familiars served as diabolic accomplices to witches. The witch's special "teat" was the means by which her animal familiar sucked her blood.[35]

As this example indicates, many Anglo-Virginians believed in witchcraft, even if the colony witnessed none of the spectacular prosecutions that occurred in New England. Thus, in 1626, the Virginia General Court examined the many alleged acts of maleficium committed by Goodwife Wright of Kickotan. Many witnesses testified to her ability to predict events and her ability to commit harm by magical means, but in the end the magistrates refused to prosecute her for occult practices. Other cases appeared over the course of the seventeenth century: one witness described how only a horseshoe over his door had protected his sick wife from a neighboring female witch; another attributed the death of some of his livestock to a witch; and a third spoke of witches riding him along the seashore. Witchcraft accusations were particularly prevalent in

Norfolk County, such that in 1655 the county's justices ordered any-one making a false accusation to pay a fine of one thousand pounds of tobacco. In 1705 two Virginia juries examined Grace Sherwood for witches' marks and supposedly found them. When the court subjected her to the infamous dunking test, she floated and was therefore bound over for trial on witchcraft charges. Even as late as 1740, in Augusta County, Virginia, witchcraft and occult accusations surfaced, but by then they were the province of gossip and rumor, not legal action.[36]

Over the course of the colonial period, clerical authorities, Protestant reformers, and elite gentlemen undermined the authority of the cunning folk, fortune-tellers, special healers, and witches. Prophecy, alchemy, and astrology joined witchcraft as subjects for attack because they all threatened to supplant theology with magic. Significant shifts in Enlightenment philosophy, theology, jurisprudence, and experimental science at the end of the seventeenth century led gentlemen to interpret prodigies and providences not as direct interventions from God, but rather as morally neutral anomalies or as examples of God's sound handiwork. In elite circles, magic became superstition that needed to be stamped out. Yet, by the same token, magic also went underground; it became folklore and did not so much disappear as become marginalized. Some superstitious practices displayed Catholic as well as pagan influences, only adding to the reasons why Protestant reformers would detest such gestures as the sign of the cross.[37]

Catholicism was suspect, then, in early Virginia, even if closet Catholics were almost certainly present and usually tolerated. Based on the number of crucifixes, rosary beads, and religious medallions recovered at early Jamestown, several Catholics lived in the early colony. As one indication of the ambivalence accorded them, one resident complained in 1620 of a neighbor who "smells to[o] much of Rome, as he attempts to work miracles with his Cru-cyfixe," but the resident governor took no action. On the other hand, perhaps the unpopularity of Edward Maria Wingfield—note the middle name—as first president of the council owed something to his suspected Catholic leanings. Also in the earliest years of Jamestown, another council member, Captain George Kendall, was tried and convicted of mutiny: he appears to have had Catholic sympathies, even if his primary offense was acting as a spy for the Spanish. The Church of England, of course, always retained some Catholic elements, not least the yearly rhythm of the cyclical calendar, which, even if much purged of its many saints' days, still celebrated events such as Advent, Christmas, Epiphany, Lent, Easter, and Ascension Day. A number of notable Anglican ministers in Virginia—James Marye, a Frenchman; John Garzia and Anthony Gavin, both seemingly Spaniards—were former Catholic priests. Furthermore, in another hint of the degree of tolerance extended to local Catholics, a merchant saw no need to hide from his county court that he had bought a silver crucifix from a local doctor. Virginia's statute of 1641 regarding Catholic recusants (those who refused to attend Anglican services) was fairly latitudinarian. While it banished priests and disabled lay Catholics from holding political office, it nevertheless allowed Catholic laypeople to remain in the colony. Fears of popery and popish plots—encouraged by the arrival of Scots, who were often suspected of Jacobite sympathies, by repeated wars with Catholic France, as well as by proximity to Maryland and its Catholic associations—kept the few Catholic families in Virginia on the defensive. When in 1691 a "Professed Papist," defined as a "contemner and slighter" of public worship, won custody of an orphan in a Virginia court, the child's godfather condemned the decision so that he could raise the child in the "true principals" of Christianity.[38]

From an Anglican perspective, Quakers constituted another threat, not as profound as Catholicism but dangerous nevertheless. Rejecting hierarchy, espousing pacifism, believing in spiritual equality, Quakers seemed to subvert the traditional order. In 1660 a law banned Quaker meetings on the grounds that Quakers were a "turbulent" people, promoting "lies, miracles, false visions, prophecies and doctrines" that would destroy all the bonds of civil society. Rumors circulated that Quakers included blacks in their religious meetings. A notable case of interracial fraternization and sex that occurred in 1681 in Henrico County had a Quaker woman at its center. In 1662, one Quaker missionary, imprisoned in Jamestown, complained of being "chained to an Indian" who was charged with murder. Linking Quakers to Native Americans and African Americans was not far-fetched in the minds of Anglican leaders.

All three groups posed a challenge to the established order, and alliances among them were to be expected, although over time Quakers managed to gain grudging acceptance from Virginia's leaders—not the case for the other two groups.[39]

Compared to Indian and African worlds, where there really was no conception of sacred and secular, for they merged inextricably, Anglo-Virginians inherited a post-Reformation Protestant culture that radically assaulted, if not totally dismantled, the established balance between the two. The gap between sacred and profane, supernatural and natural, inexorably widened in Anglo-Virginian culture. Accordingly, unbelief, atheism, and irreligion were possible among Anglo-Virginians in ways difficult to conceive for Indians and Africans. Thus, during the starving time of 1609–10, one anguished and despairing Jamestown settler ran around the settlement, exclaiming, "There is no God!" It is hard to imagine Indians or Africans making such a claim. And on occasion throughout the colonial period, some Virginians such as Thomas Newhouse of Lower Norfolk could be heard declaiming that "a great part of the Bible was false," or a Lancaster County blacksmith could describe Jesus Christ as a "Son of A Whore, & that his mother is A bitch." While atheism and free-thinking were possible for Anglo-Virginians, they do not seem to have been widespread. Only one person, for example, seems to have been suspected of blasphemy in early York County: he received punishment for slandering a minister, declining religious instruction, and refusing communion. Still, white Virginians exhibited a fair measure of religious skepticism, relativism, and indifference; had Anglicans instituted ecclesiastical courts in Virginia, we might have the same rich individual stories of just such beliefs and behaviors that Stuart Schwartz has been able to mine from Inquisition records in the Iberian Atlantic world.[40]

Early Virginians were certainly not noted for their piety. In the beginning, the harsh times, which led to isolated cases of cannibalism—even a case of a man butchering, salting, and then eating part of his wife—help explain the extent of irreligion. Some Englishmen even preferred the company of heathen Indians to their own countrymen: they "went native," as it were. Reversion to paganism seemed possible. On one occasion in 1609, Jamestown residents fought among themselves, laboring under a "fantasy," supposedly fostered by Indian "charms," that some of their company had actually become Indians. The prevalence of young men, hardly a group of the population known for their spiritual ardor, added to the reputation for impiety. The harsh penalties for blasphemy and gaming were indicative of the degree of spiritual indifference. Even into the eighteenth century, the prevalence of hunting, gambling, and irregular attendance at church spoke of spiritual laxity in Virginia. For most of the eighteenth century, custom and the law required attendance at church only once every month. Still, grand juries in many counties were fairly diligent in prosecuting for nonattendance at church. The average county—more so in the Tidewater than in the Piedmont—identified about seven to nine individuals a year for failure to attend church. Most were found guilty and fined. If the numbers of persons charged with disturbing the Sabbath, swearing, drunkenness, and sexual offense are counted, they outnumbered the nonattenders. Church meetings were, however, hardly devout—much business was transacted at them; family prayers were unusual in most households, it would seem; Sundays were as much days of rest and conviviality, of pleasure and amusement, as they were days of devotion. According to Philip Fithian, "All the lower class of People, & the servants, & the Slaves," considered the Sabbath "a Day of Pleasure & amusement." As Rhys Isaac puts it, "Virginians, whatever their rank, generally did not affect postures of grave piety and . . . on Sunday at church they took for granted the close proximity of the profane to the sacred."[41]

IN AN AGE when religious systems everywhere were tinged with magical beliefs and practices, Christian orthodoxy was rare. Colonial Virginia, especially, was home to three sets of folk—Native Americans, Africans and their descendants, and a large part of the Anglo-Virginian population—who inhabited a world as much magical as it was Christian. These three groups were truly unorthodox, at least from the perspective of those in power in the Anglican Church. Over time, their magical worlds came under severe attack, as gentlemen increasingly and publicly disavowed their practice. White gentlemen gradually brought the lower orders of their own communities within the fold. No longer can it be maintained that by, say, the middle of the eighteenth century, most Anglo-Virginians were unchurched. Rather, a major sacralization of the Virginia landscape—an Anglican renaissance, evident in new buildings, the arrival of church bells, more ministers, as well as a vigorous growth of dissenter congregations—had occurred.[42]

At the same time, white authorities increasingly fostered contempt for Indians and blacks. In 1667 the Virginia legislature passed a law that baptism would not affect the bondage of slaves, either blacks or Indians. Three years later, the legislature prohibited free blacks and Indians, "though baptized," from owning Christian servants. And then, in 1730, the legislature responded to instances in which "negroes, mulattos, and Indians have lately been frequently allowed to give testimony as lawful witnesses in the General Court, and other courts of the colony, when they have professed themselves to be christians." They banned their testimony (except in the trial of slaves for capital offenses) on the grounds that "they are people of such base and corrupt natures that the credit of their testimony cannot be certainly depended upon." Virginia authorities, then, established a rough congruity between Christianity and whiteness on the one hand as against heathenism and nonwhiteness on the other. They had to deal with the exceptions: those few Indians and rather more numerous blacks who became Christians and had to be restricted in their rights because of their alleged "base and corrupt natures."[43]

Nevertheless, the congruity was never watertight. In the early seventeenth century, some whites ran off to the Indians, attracted in part by their customs. In the eighteenth century, other whites, most notably evangelicals, were influenced by black religiosity. One white preacher noted that Harry Hoosier, or "Black Harry," as he was known, a black Methodist preacher, was "a wonder of grace" who "excited and won the attention" of many an audience. Furthermore, since Indians and Africans were thought to be close to nature—Indians in fact were often said to be "naturals," and Africans were often characterized as "cunning"—they were considered most able to know nature's hidden processes. Indians were generally viewed more positively than blacks in this regard, at least by the eighteenth century, but since both straddled the divide between human and nonhuman, both were thought to be in close touch with the animal world, sensually alert, good hunters, and knowledgeable about venoms, poisons, and their cures. As magic became off-limits to the white population, it increasingly became the province of Indians and blacks. On the other hand, while few Indians were converted in colonial Virginia, many blacks did join Christian congregations. Over time, increasing numbers of black Christians, albeit always a minority among the African American population, meant that orthodoxy gradually encompassed more African Americans than Indians.[44]

Orthodoxy was on the rise, then, but heterodoxy was still predominant on the eve of the Revolution. The growth of the Anglican establishment in colonial Virginia supposedly embraced all. Everyone was a parishioner. Even Native Americans, when they had lived among the English for years, could be considered parishioners. Thus, in 1769, Hungars Parish in Northampton County on the Eastern Shore took care of aged, sick, and disabled Gingaskin Indians in their midst, to the point that the Virginia legislature authorized the vestry to take two hundred acres of the Indians' six hundred acres to lease out for their support. While this was more land grab than altruism, nevertheless these Indians were considered part of the community, at least to some degree. By the eighteenth century, most Anglo-Virginians, it seems, had their children baptized, although almost no Indians and still a minority of African Americans followed suit. Most whites probably attended church fairly infrequently and took communion even less, but many outwardly conformed and thought of themselves as Anglicans. Thomas Jefferson characteristically exaggerated when he reckoned that two-thirds of white Virginians were dissenters from the established church on the eve of the Revolution; dissenters had made notable inroads, but Anglicans were more numerous than he acknowledged. But more telling is that by 1780 about 220,000 African Americans resided in Virginia, slightly over 40 percent of the total population of 580,000, and most of them were still strangers to Christianity, despite some impressive efforts at baptism. If, as Christine Heyrman notes, "by the most generous estimate, . . . fewer than one-tenth of all African Americans had joined Baptist, Methodist, or Presbyterian churches by the 1810s," then the proportion must have been much less in the 1770s. In short, religious heterogeneity was still the norm in Virginia on the eve of the Revolution, much as it had been from the beginnings of the colonial experiment.[45]

NOTES

1. Thomas E. Buckley, S.J., *Church and State in Revolutionary Virginia, 1776– 1787* (Charlottesville: University of Virginia Press, 1977), 8–9 (quote); Jon Butler, *Awash in a Sea of Faith: Christianizing the American People* (Cambridge: Harvard University Press, 1990), 98–128, 164–93; James D. Rice, *Nature and History in the Potomac Country: From Hunter-Gatherers to the Age of Jefferson* (Baltimore: Johns Hopkins University Press, 2009), 48.

2. William Crashaw, *A Sermon Preached in London before the right honorable the Lord Laware, Lord Governour and Captaine Generall of Virginea* (London, 1610), sig. L recto. See also Edward L. Bond, *Damned Souls in a Tobacco Colony: Religion in Seventeenth-Century Virginia* (Macon, GA: Mercer University Press, 2000), 61; John Parker, "Religion and the Virginia Colony," in *The Westward Enterprise: English Activities in Ireland, the Atlantic, and America, 1480–1650*, ed. Kenneth R. Andrews, et al. (Detroit: Wayne State University Press, 1979), 245–70; Darrett B. Rutman, "The Evolution of Religious Life in Early Virginia," *Lex and Scientia: Journal of the American Academy of Law* 14 (1978): 190–214, reprinted as "Magic, Christianity, and Church in Early Virginia," in *Small Worlds, Large Questions: Explorations in Early American Social History, 1600–1850*, ed. Darrett B. Rutman with Anita H. Rutman (Charlottesville: University of Virginia Press, 1994), 134–57.

3. Crashaw, *Sermon Preached in London*, sig. K-4 verso (quote); [Robert Johnson], *Nova Britannia: Offering Most Excellent Fruits by Planting in Virginia* (London, 1609), sig. C, fols. 1–2 (quote), as cited in Edmund S. Morgan, *American Slavery, American Freedom: The Ordeal of Colonial Virginia* (New York: W. W. Norton, 1975), 47; Philip L. Barbour, ed., *The Complete Works of Captain John Smith (1580–1631)* (Chapel Hill: University of North Carolina Press, 1986), 1:169 (quote); Alexander Whitaker, *Good Newes from Virginia . . .* (London, 1613), 26 (quote). Thomas Harriot described Indian priests as "coniuerrs or iuglers . . . verye familiar with devils" and noted their fastening "a small black birde above one of their ears as a badge of their office," thereby suggesting an animal familiar, often associated with witchcraft: Thomas Harriot, *A Briefe and True Report of the New Found Land of Virginia* (1590), ed. Paul Hulton, [54] (plate XI). See also Richard Beale Davis, "The Devil in Virginia in the Seventeenth Century," *Virginia Magazine of History and Biography* 65 (1957): 131–49 (hereafter *VMHB*).

4. Thomas Herbert, *Some Years Travels into Divers Parts of Africa, and Asia the Great . . .* (London, 1677), 10 (quote); Warren M. Billings, ed., *The Old Dominion in the Seventeenth Century: A Documentary History of Virginia, 1606–1700* (Chapel Hill: University of North Carolina Press, 2007), 190 (quote); William Waller Hening, ed., *The Statutes at Large: Being a Collection of all the Laws of Virginia* (Richmond: Samuel Pleasants, 1809–23), 4:326–27 (quote).

5. John K. Nelson, *A Blessed Company: Parishes, Parsons, and Parishioners in Anglican Virginia, 1690–1776* (Chapel Hill: University of North Carolina Press, 2001), 276, 288; Davis, "Devil in Virginia," 148. See Edward L. Bond's treatment of this theme in chapter 2 of the present volume.

6. Colin Kidd, *The Forging of Races: Race and Scripture in the Protestant Atlantic World, 1600–2000* (New York: Cambridge University Press, 2006), esp. 54–120, quotes on 57 and 91. For racial attitudes more broadly, the literature is extensive; see the magisterial Winthrop D. Jordan, *White over Black: American Attitudes toward the Negro 1550–1812* (Chapel Hill: University of North Carolina Press, 1968), and the special issue "Constructing Race: Differentiating Peoples in the Early Modern World," *William and Mary Quarterly*, 3d ser., 54 (1997): 3–252 (hereafter *WMQ*).

7. Edward L. Bond describes the supernatural world of the English colonists in chapter 2 of the present volume; Monica Najar details the dissenting Protestant groups' resistance to the Anglican establishment in chapter 4. The final appearance and both short- and long-term consequences of Jefferson's Statute for Religious Freedom are treated by Thomas E. Buckley and Daniel L. Dreisbach in chapters 5 and 6.

8. Helen C. Rountree, *The Powhatan Indians of Virginia: Their Traditional Culture* (Norman: University of Oklahoma Press, 1989), 130–39; Frederic W. Gleach, *Powhatan's World and Colonial Virginia: Conflict of Cultures* (Lincoln: University of Nebraska Press, 1997), 35–43; Margaret Holmes Williamson, *Powhatan Lords of Life and Death: Command and Consent in Seventeenth-Century Virginia* (Lincoln: University of Nebraska Press, 2003), 42, 164, 173–201, 218–22, 234–47; James D. Rice, "Escape from Tsenacommacah: Chesapeake Algonquians and the Powhatan Menace," in *The Atlantic World and Virginia, 1550–1624*, ed. Peter C. Mancall (Chapel Hill: University of North Carolina Press, 2007), 112–13; Rice, *Nature and History in the Potomac Country*, 1–2, 57–58.

9. Virginia DeJohn Anderson, *Creatures of Empire: How Domestic Animals Transformed Early America* (New York: Oxford University Press, 2004), 17–31; Karen Ordahl Kupperman, *The Jamestown Project* (Cambridge: Harvard University Press, 2007), 305 (quote). See also Shepard Krech III, *Spirits of the Air: Birds and American Indians in the South* (Athens: University of Georgia Press, 2009).

10. In addition to works cited in n. 8, see Bernard Sheehan, *Savagism and Civility: Indians and Englishmen in Colonial Virginia* (Cambridge: Cambridge University Press, 1980), esp. 37–64, 116–43; Helen C. Rountree, "Powhatan Priests and English Rectors: World Views and Congregations in Conflict," *American Indian Quarterly* 16 (1992): 485–500; James P. P. Horn, *A Land as God Made It: Jamestown and the Birth of America* (New York: Basic Books, 2005), 20–22; Camilla Townsend, *Pocahontas and the Powhatan Dilemma* (New York: Hill and Wang, 2004), 21.

11. Rountree, *Powhatan Indians of Virginia*, 130–39; Helen C. Rountree, *Pocahontas, Powhatan, Opechancanough: Three Indian Lives Changed by Jamestown* (Charlottesville: University of Virginia Press, 2005), 17, 19, 22, 69–70, 154; Alden T. Vaughan, *Transatlantic Encounters: American Indians in Britain, 1500–1776* (New York: Cambridge University Press, 2006), 92.

12. Karen Ordahl Kupperman, *Indians and English: Facing Off in Early America* (Ithaca, NY: Cornell University Press, 2000), 113–14.

13. Kupperman, *Jamestown Project*, 165–82; Rountree, *Pocahontas, Powhatan, Opechancanough*, 135.

14. Clifford M. Lewis and Albert J. Loomie, *The Spanish Jesuit Mission in Virginia, 1570–1572* (Chapel Hill: University of North Carolina Press, 1953); Charlotte M. Grady, "Spanish Jesuits in Virginia: The Mission that Failed," *VMHB* 96 (1988): 131–54; Paul E. Hoffman, *A New Andalucia and a Way to the Orient: The American Southeast during the Sixteenth Century* (Baton Rouge, LA: Pergamon Press, 1990), 262–66; Seth W. Mallios, "Exchange and Violence at Ajacan, Roanoke, and Jamestown," in *Indian and European Contact in Context*, ed. Dennis B. Blanton and Julia A. King (Gainesville: University Press of Florida, 2004), 126–48; Horn, *Land as God Made It*, 3–8; Kupperman, *Jamestown Project*, 103–5.

15. William Strachey, *The Histoirie of Travell into Virginia Britania* [1612], ed. Louis B. Wright and Virginia Freund (London: Hakluyt Society, 1953), 2, 61–62; "A letter of Sir Thomas Dale," in *Hakluytus Posthumus or Purchas His Pilgrimes . . .* , ed. Samuel Purchas (Glasgow: J. MacLehose and Sons, 1906), 19:106; Vaughan, *Transatlantic Encounters*, 42–56, 77–96. Few marriages between English men and Indian women followed; one exception was Reverend John Bass's marriage to the daughter of a Nansemond chief in 1638. Helen C. Rountree and E. Randolph Turner III, *Before and after Jamestown: Virginia's Powhatans and Their Predecessors* (Gainesville: University Press of Florida, 2002), 151–52. On the extent of intermarriage with Indians, see David D. Smits, "'Abominable Mixture': Toward the Repudiation of Anglo-Indian Intermarriage in Seventeenth-Century Virginia," *VMHB* 95 (1987): 157–92; Richard Godbeer, *Sexual Revolution in Early America* (Baltimore: Johns Hopkins University Press, 2002), 154–89.

16. Kupperman, *Jamestown Project*, 295–99, 306–7; George Thorpe and John Pory to Edwin Sandys, May 15–16, 1621, in *Records of the Virginia Company of London*, ed. Susan Myra Kingsbury (Washington, DC, 1906–35), 3:346.

17. Francis Yeardley to John Ferrar, May 8, 1654, Rawlinson Mss A-14, ff 84–87, Oxford University, as cited in Bond, *Damned Souls in a Tobacco Colony*, 170; John Ruston Pagan, *Anne Orthwood's Bastard: Sex and Law in Early Virginia* (New York: Oxford University Press, 2003), 108–9; W. Stitt Robinson Jr., "Indian Education and Missions in Colonial Virginia," *Journal of Southern History* 18 (1952): 152–68; Margaret Connell Szasz, *Indian Education in the American Colonies, 1607–1783* (Albuquerque: University of New Mexico Press, 1988), 69–77; Karen A. Stuart, "'So Good a Work': The Brafferton School, 1691–1777" (M.A. thesis, College of William and Mary, 1984); Owen Stanwood, "Captives and Slaves: Indian Labor, Cultural Conversion, and the Plantation Revolution in Virginia," *VMHB* 114 (2006): 435–63.

18. Nancy Oestreich Lurie, "Indian Cultural Adjustment to European Civilization," in *Seventeenth-Century America: Essays in Colonial America*, ed. James Morton Smith (Chapel Hill: University of North Carolina Press, 1959), 33–60, esp. 45; Reverend Thomas Bacon, *Sermons Addressed to Masters and Servants . . .* (Winchester, VA, 1813), 12; William Stevens Perry, *Papers Relating to the History of the*

Church in Colonial Delaware (n.p., 1878), 36, as cited in Helen C. Rountree and Thomas E. Davidson, *Eastern Shore Indians of Virginia and Maryland* (Charlottesville: University of Virginia Press, 1997), 133. For ossuaries and their incorporation of European materials, see Stephen R. Potter, "Early English Effects on Virginia Algonquian Exchange and Tribute in the Tidewater Potomac," in *Powhatan's Mantle: Indians in the Colonial Southeast*, rev. ed., ed. Gregory A. Waselkov, Peter H. Wood., and M. Thomas Hatley (Lincoln: University of Nebraska Press, 2006), 215–41; Stephen R. Potter, *Commoners, Tribute, and Chiefs: The Development of Algonquian Culture in the Potomac Valley* (Charlottesville: University of Virginia Press, 1993), 198–223.

19. Butler, *Awash in a Sea of Faith*, 129–63. Cf. Sylvia R. Frey and Betty Wood, *Come Shouting to Zion: African American Protestantism in the American South and British Caribbean to 1830* (Chapel Hill: University of North Carolina Press, 1998), esp. 35–62, and Albert J. Raboteau, *Slave Religion: The "Invisible Institution" in the Antebellum South* (New York: Oxford University Press, 1978), 3–92.

20. Philip D. Morgan, *Slave Counterpoint: Black Culture in the Eighteenth-Century Chesapeake and Lowcountry* (Chapel Hill: University of North Carolina Press, 1998), 610–31.

21. Charles Ball, *Fifty Years in Chains* (New York: Mnemosyne Publishing, 1970), 21–22. For the general argument, see Morgan, *Slave Counterpoint*, 631–57.

22. Linda M. Heywood and John K. Thornton, *Central Africans, Atlantic Creoles, and the Foundation of the Americas, 1585–1660* (New York: Cambridge University Press, 2007), 5–9, 242–48, 270–89; James H. Johnston, "Every Picture Tells a Story: A Narrative Portrait of Yarrow Mamout," *Maryland Historical Magazine* 103 (2008), 416–31 (hereafter *MHM*).

23. Andrew Burnaby, *Travels through the Middle Settlements in North-America, in the Years 1759 and 1760 . . .* , 3d ed. [1775] (London, 1798), 66–67.

24. Joseph Douglas Deal, *Race and Class in Colonial Virginia: Indians, Englishmen, and Africans on the Eastern Shore during the Seventeenth Century* (New York: Garland, 1993), 217–50; T. H. Breen and Stephen Innes, *"Myne Owne Ground": Race and Freedom on Virginia's Eastern Shore, 1640–1676* (New York: Oxford University Press, 1980), 7–18, 87; H. R. McIlwaine, ed., *Minutes of the Council and General Court of Colonial Virginia, 1622–1637, 1670–1676* (Richmond: Library of Virginia, 1924), 33, 155. For Paine's will, see Billings, *Old Dominion in the Seventeenth Century*, 181–82.

25. Billings, *Old Dominion in the Seventeenth Century*, 204; Morgan Godwyn, *The Negro's & Indians' Advocate, Sueing for Their Admission into the Church* (London, 1680), 38; Alden T. Vaughan, "Slaveholders' 'Hellish Principles': A Seventeenth-Century Critique," in *Roots of American Racism: Essays on the Colonial Experience* (New York: Oxford University Press, 1995): 55–81, esp. 66.

26. Thomas N. Ingersoll, " 'Releese us out of this Cruell Bondegg': An Appeal from Virginia in 1723," *WMQ*, 3d ser., 51 (1994): 777–82.

27. Frey and Wood, *Come Shouting to Zion*, 70; Morgan, *Slave Counterpoint*, 649; Nelson, *Blessed Company*, 263–64; Anthony S. Parent, *Foul Means: The Formation of*

a *Slave Society in Virginia, 1660–1740* (Chapel Hill: University of North Carolina Press, 2003), 159–62; Brendan McConville, *The King's Three Faces: The Rise and Fall of Royal America, 1688–1776* (Chapel Hill: University of North Carolina Press, 2006), 177. For the breadth of this traditional appeal to an emancipating king, see David Barry Gaspar and David Patrick Geggus, eds., *A Turbulent Time: The French Revolution and the Greater Caribbean* (Bloomington: Indiana University Press, 1997), 8–9.

28. "Journal of Col. James Gordon," *WMQ*, 1st ser., 11 (1902–3): 227; John Evans Sr., *Virginia Gazette* (Purdie and Dixon), postscript, July 21, 1774; John Scott, ibid., Dec. 1, 1774; John Murchie, ibid., June 13, 1777; Jewel L. Spangler, *Virginians Reborn: Anglican Monopoly, Evangelical Dissent, and the Rise of the Baptists in the Late Eighteenth Century* (Charlottesville: University of Virginia Press, 2008), 271 n. 31.

29. Nelson, *Blessed Company*, 264–67, 269; Lorena S. Walsh, *From Calabar to Carter's Grove: The History of a Virginia Slave Community* (Charlottesville: University of Virginia Press, 1997), 153–58; William Stevens Perry, ed., *Papers relating to the history of the Church in Virginia, A.D. 1650–1776* (Geneva, NY, 1870), 360; Thad W. Tate, *The Negro in Eighteenth-Century Williamsburg* (Williamsburg: University Press of Virginia, 1965), 65–85; Rebecca Anne Goetz, "From Potential Christians to Hereditary Heathens: Religion and Race in the Early Chesapeake, 1590–1740" (Ph.D. diss., Harvard University, 2006), 253–60; Rev. Thomas Baker to John Waring, Apr. 23, 1770, in John C. Van Horne, ed., *Religious Philanthropy and Colonial Slavery: The American Correspondence of the Associates of Dr. Bray, 1717–1777* (Urbana: University of Illinois Press, 1985), 289 (quote), 144–326 (schools). For opposition to the baptism of slaves and its gradual retreat by the 1720s, see Parent, *Foul Means*, 236–64.

30. Adam Dickie to Bishop of London, June 27, 1732, Fulham Papers, vol. XII, nos. 182–83, Lambeth Palace Library, London, as cited in Lauren F. Winner, *A Cheerful and Comfortable Faith: Anglican Religious Practice in the Elite Households of Eighteenth-Century Virginia* (New Haven, CT: Yale University Press, 2010), 47–49, 198 n. 24. My thanks to Ms. Winner for allowing me to see her important book in manuscript.

31. R. A. Brock, comp., *Documents Chiefly Unpublished, Relating to the Huguenot Emigration to Virginia* (Richmond: Virginia Historical Society, 1886), 79–110; Morgan, *Slave Counterpoint*, 426–28; Frey and Wood, *Come Shouting to Zion*, 95–103, 106–12; Jeffrey H. Richards, "Samuel Davies and the Transatlantic Campaign for Slave Literacy in Virginia," *VMHB* 111 (2003): 338–78; Spangler, *Virginians Reborn*, 54, 72–73, 158–65, 250 n. 16 (for another measure of Baptist growth), 259 n. 18; Monica Najar, *Evangelizing the South: A Social History of Church and State in Early America* (New York: Oxford University Press, 2008), 54–56; Charles F. Irons, *The Origins of Proslavery Christianity: White and Black Evangelicals in Colonial and Antebellum Virginia* (Chapel Hill: University of North Carolina Press, 2008), 33–44; Nelson, *Blessed Company*, 285. For Methodism, see Dee E. Andrews, *The Methodists and Revolutionary America, 1760–1800: The Shaping of an Evangelical Culture*

(Princeton, NJ: Princeton University Press, 2000); Cynthia Anne Lyerly, *Methodism and the Southern Mind, 1770–1810* (New York: Oxford University Press, 1998). Janet Lindman Moore notes, "African Americans generally did not become members of Baptist churches in large numbers until after the American Revolution." See *Bodies of Belief: Baptist Community in Early America* (Philadelphia: University of Pennsylvania Press, 2008), 113; also see 131–32, 134, 136.

32. Billings, *Old Dominion in the Seventeenth Century*, 186; Morgan, *Slave Counterpoint*, 642–44; Frey and Wood, *Come Shouting to Zion*, 51–54.

33. Morgan, *Slave Counterpoint*, 645–46.

34. Edward L. Bond, "Source of Knowledge, Source of Power: The Supernatural World of English Virginia, 1607–1624," *VMHB* 108 (2000): 105–38; Kathleen S. Murphy, "Prodigies and Portents: Providentialism in the Eighteenth-Century Chesapeake," *MHM* 97, (2002): 397–421; Joseph Frank, ed., "News from Virginny, 1644," *VMHB* 65 (1957): 86–87; Butler, *Awash in a Sea of Faith*, 80. See Edward L. Bond's treatment of the role of the supernatural among early Virginia Christians in chapter 2 of the present volume.

35. Anderson, *Creatures of Empire*, 45–57; Butler, *Awash in a Sea of Faith*, 86–87.

36. Butler, *Awash in a Sea of Faith*, 68–69, 73–74, 83, 85–86; Bond, *Damned Souls*, 156–57; Horn, *Adapting to a New World*, 411–18.

37. Butler, *Awash in a Sea of Faith*, 89–97; Keith Thomas, *Religion and the Decline of Magic* (New York: Charles Scribner's Sons, 1971), 570–83.

38. Edward L. Bond, ed., *Spreading the Gospel in Colonial Virginia: Preaching, Religion, and Community* (Lanham, MD: Lexington Books, 2005), 10, 113, 133, 139; Kupperman, *Jamestown Project*, 219–20, 265; Nelson, *Blessed Company*, 92, 97–98, 159–60, 373 n. 23, 376 n. 67; Joan R. Gunderson, "Anthony Gavin's *A Master-Key to Popery*: A Virginia Parson's Best Seller," *VMHB* 82 (1974): 39–46; Bruce E. Steiner, "The Catholic Brents of Colonial Virginia: An Instance of Practical Toleration," *VMHB* 70 (1962): 404–7; Gerald P. Fogarty, *Commonwealth Catholicism: A History of the Catholic Church in Virginia* (Notre Dame, IN: University of Notre Dame Press, 2001); William P. Palmer, ed., *Calendar of Virginia State Papers and Other Manuscripts* (New York, 1875–93), 1:31.

39. Hening, *Statutes at Large*, 1:532–3; Kenneth L. Carroll, "Quakerism on the Eastern Shore of Virginia," *VMHB* 74 (1966): 170–89; Billings, *Old Dominion in the Seventeenth Century*, 190–93; Kenneth L. Carroll, ed., "A Quaker in Seventeenth-Century Virginia: Four Remonstrances by George Wilson," *WMQ*, 3d ser., 33 (1976): 130; Bond, *Damned Souls*, 160–74; Horn, *Adapting to the New World*, 394–99. See Monica Najar's extended treatment of Quakers in chapter 4 of the present volume.

40. Horn, *Adapting to a New World*, 400–406; Bond, *Damned Souls*, 32, 134; Nelson, *Blessed Company*, 275; Stuart Schwartz, *All Can Be Saved: Religious Toleration and Salvation in the Iberian Atlantic World* (New Haven, CT: Yale University Press, 2008); "Critical Forum," *WMQ*, 3d ser., 66 (2009): 409–33.

41. George Percy, "A Trewe Relaycon (1625)," *Tyler's Quarterly Historical and Genealogical Magazine* 3, no. 3 (1922), 269; Reverend Alexander Whitaker to Reverend William Crashaw, Aug. 9, 1611, in *The Genesis of the United States*, ed. Alexander

Brown (New York, 1898), 1:498–99; Nelson, *Blessed Company*, 244–52; Hunter D. Farish, ed., *Journal and Letters of Philip Vickers Fithian: A Plantation Tutor of the Old Dominion, 1773–1774* (Charlottesville: Colonial Williamsburg, 1957), 137; Rhys Isaac, *The Transformation of Virginia, 1740–1790* (Chapel Hill: University of North Carolina Press, 1982), 60–61.

42. Butler, *Awash in a Sea of Faith*, esp. 98–128; Nelson, *Blessed Company*, 7–9, passim.

43. Hening, *Statutes at Large*, 2:260, 283, 4:326–27.

44. Journal of Thomas Haskins, Nov. 21, 1784, Library of Congress (for more on "Black Harry" and other influences of black evangelicals on their white brethren, see Morgan, *Slave Counterpoint*, 428–30, 654–55); Susan Scott Parrish, *American Curiosity: Cultures of Natural History in the Colonial British Atlantic World* (Chapel Hill: University of North Carolina Press, 2006), 215–306.

45. Nelson, *Blessed Company*, 433–34 n. 7; Thomas Jefferson, *Notes on the State of Virginia*, ed. William Peden (Chapel Hill: University of North Carolina Press, 1954), 158; Christine Leigh Heyrman, *Southern Cross: The Beginnings of the Bible Belt* (New York: Knopf, 1997), 5.

FOUR Sectarians and Strategies of Dissent
in Colonial Virginia

MONICA NAJAR

IN THE 1760S AND 1770S, AS VIRGINIANS JOINED OTHER COL-
onists in laying claim to a host of natural and civil rights, many
dissenters in the colony argued that persecution for religious beliefs was actually becoming more frequent and intense. Baptists
reported their meetings were disrupted by armed men and malicious activity. Ministers were threatened with bullwhips, clubs,
and guns. One minister was nearly drowned, a number were
whipped, and at least one was shot. Many preachers were hauled
into court, facing charges such as heresy, sedition, disturbing the
peace, and being a public nuisance or vagabond; some were fined
and others imprisoned. Danger came from another direction for
dissenting Baptist women. Several women reported that their
husbands fiercely and at times violently opposed their desire to be
baptized. The husband of one woman from North Garden, Virginia,
whipped his wife for being baptized in defiance of his wishes. Another woman hid her membership from her husband for four years,
insisting he would kill her if he found out. As Baptists carefully
recorded these incidents, they described a world in which the battle
for religious freedom was fought in their neighborhoods, in the
courts, and in their homes.

The persecution of dissenters was not a new phenomenon in
eighteenth-century Virginia. A century earlier, Quakers had experienced similar persecution, hostility, violence, and government
regulation of their meetings. In the 1660s and 1670s, missionaries
languished in prisons, some female Friends were threatened by
neighbors and banished from the colony, and believers faced a
government that sought to curtail their ability to give testimony

by prosecuting not only Quakers, but those who aided them as well. This reoccurring pattern of local and civil opposition to sectarian groups might suggest that little had changed in the colony, despite the passing of more than one hundred years, the adoption of the English Toleration Act in 1689, and the growth of an increasingly heterodox religious population. With the desire for religious orthodoxy seemingly so entrenched in Virginia society, how was it that the young state came to embrace religious freedom?

This chapter argues that while Virginia's dissenting sects did not work together in meaningful ways until the close of the colonial era, they collectively, if not collaboratively, constructed a multipronged assault on Virginia's understanding of toleration by challenging definitions and exposing contradictions. By doing so, dissenters ultimately ensured that colonial and Anglican authorities had to diligently maintain and defend the religious establishment. As early as the mid-seventeenth century, Quakers highlighted the discordance between the right to freely worship and the right to freely practice their faith outside their meeting houses, a distinction that Baptists would find significant a century later. In the eighteenth century, Presbyterians developed a strategy that forced Virginia authorities to abide more consistently by the terms of the Toleration Act, and this encouraged other dissenting groups to appeal for the same protections. Capitalizing on the existing privileges, evangelical Baptists shifted their demand away from mere toleration toward a broadly defined religious freedom.

Evangelicals embraced a multifaceted campaign for religious freedom, one that occurred not just in statehouses and courthouses, but also in the homes and families of believers. Baptists, in particular, were concerned as much with the domestic right to free exercise of conscience as they were with formal legal rights. While historians exploring the struggle for religious freedom have typically focused on the political and legal issues and on the ministers who played prominent roles, the Baptists themselves did not always do so. They assiduously recorded the stories of women who fought for religious freedom, positioning them alongside the stories of persecuted preachers. Baptists' goals were primarily religious and spiritual rather than social or legal in nature. Yet their struggle had important social implications. As Baptists heralded women's efforts to join churches and to participate in early evangelical activities, women's religious roles became an integral part of the conflicts between dissenting sects and the established church. Thus, Baptists came to espouse new gender norms in their efforts to resist persecution and to evangelize the population. This chapter will first explore why the numbers of dissenters increased through the late colonial period before turning to the experiences and strategies of three major dissenting groups—Quakers, Presbyterians, and Baptists—and finally to the role of women and gender ideologies in the last decades of the conflict.

THE APPEALS OF NONCONFORMITY

Sectarian diversity was a fact of life in colonial Virginia. To be sure, the Church of England was established by law, supported by taxes, and embraced by many as the path to heavenly salvation as well as earthly stability. And yet persons of a variety of faiths and leanings made their way to Virginia. The Anglican Church struggled to meet the needs of the population, hampered by a geographically dispersed populace, a shortage of ordained ministers, and the financial demands of the parish system. This was particularly true in the backcountry, where some parishes encompassed hundreds of miles. Thus, not only could Sundays pass without the presence of an Anglican minister; so too could births, marriages, and deaths. In a region too sparsely settled to support a local minister, nonconformists sometimes found the geography encouraging, even if the sociopolitical terrain was not. These areas were breeding grounds for nonconformity, drawing in dissenters and lacking the institutions to enforce orthodoxy among the population. Thus, throughout the colonial era, Anglican civil and religious authorities lamented, but could not eliminate, the increasing numbers of nonconformists.

While groups as diverse as Moravians, Covenanters, Mennonites, Anabaptists, Papists, Methodists, and German Lutherans were present in eighteenth-century colonial Virginia, the major dissenting sects were the Society of Friends, the Presbyterians, and the Baptists. The Society of Friends (or Quakers) began to proselytize in Virginia in the mid-seventeenth century, finding ready converts in the southeastern corner of the colony and building small but devout communities of believers. The Quakers were able to sustain their religious communities with relatively meager human and financial resources. They met in houses, so they did not need to build or maintain a dedicated place of worship. Accepting no sacraments, they required no communion vessels. Believing that a divine spirit resides in all people, they did not need an ordained and paid ministry. The Quakers initially faced great hostility, and not only because of their perceived heresies. They seemed intent on being a subversive population: they were pacifists and did not attend musters, and they refused to use titles, recognize social hierarchies, or give oaths.[1]

At the turn of the eighteenth century, Presbyterians were scattered along the eastern shore in sufficient numbers to maintain a few congregations and ministers. However, two important but independent factors contributed to significant growth by midcentury. In the 1730s, Scotch-Irish migrants from the Shenandoah Valley traveled south into the Virginia backcountry, bringing Presbyterianism with them. When a revival of separate origins began in 1740, they drew in new converts who established additional church communities with a committed, devout laity. They believed that faith should be felt as well as learned. Thus, they valued a heartfelt experience of piety and a conversion experience; at the same time, Presbyterians expected an orthodox, educated clergy to lead congregations and valued careful exegesis of the Bible and religious texts. With ministers to shepherd congregants and regional presbyteries to ordain and guide individual ministers, they constructed a church structure that helped them build orderly local churches and ordain trained clergy in the colonies.

A generation later, the Baptists' growth followed a similar pattern. In the early eighteenth century, they had only a few small and loosely organized churches. Influenced by a number of traveling ministers from northern churches, as well as an infusion of migrating Baptists, these struggling churches were brought into greater alignment with the theology and practices of the northern Particular Baptists. The newly reorganized and energized churches were Calvinist, and as they strengthened their own doctrinal orthodoxy and increased the demands of membership, they inspired more fervor and interest from their congregants and neighbors.

Religious fervor also increased with the arrival of a group of evangelical Separate Baptists, a group institutionally unaffiliated with the Particulars. Fervent missionaries, they had traveled from New England to Virginia, where they found curious audiences and ready converts. In just a few years, they had three churches with nine hundred converts, some of whom became preachers themselves and spread the faith to other parts of Virginia and beyond.[2] Despite the differences between the two groups, these Baptists shared a number of beliefs. They believed that salvation came through a profound experience of God's grace in a conversion experience and that salvation was protected by membership in a godly covenanted church that contained only converted members. Thus, church membership could not be earned by family attendance or even good behavior. So too salvation and membership could not be earned by infant baptism, and Baptists instead insisted upon adult baptism by immersion. These shared beliefs allowed for the two groups of Baptists to work together to spread their faith and evangelize Virginians. The astonishingly rapid growth of the Presbyterians and Baptists created a profound shift in Virginia's religious landscape and had significant consequences for church-state relations and American religious history.

It is worth noting that there was also a very small number of Methodists in the late colonial era. Beginning as an evangelical strain within the Church of England, they had much in common with other evangelicals, particularly the Baptists. While they numbered only about one thousand by the time of the Revolution, they would soon become the fastest-growing sect in the new state. However, the Methodists insisted throughout the colonial era that they were not dissenters, but still officially part of the Church of England. Accordingly, they are not treated in this chapter.[3]

Why were Virginians drawn to these sects, particularly in the late colonial era when the Church of England was building more churches and strengthening its parish system? While no one answer applies to all of the varied sects or explains the motivations of the diverse individuals who joined them, recent scholarship has provided valuable insights. To begin, we should be wary of portrayals of the Church of England as laden with a worldly and immoral clergy who were too preoccupied with their financial needs or scandalous behavior to tend to the needs of colonists. This model greatly distorts the Anglican Church and clergy and ignores the deep piety of many Anglicans. Instead, Rhys Isaac argues that dissenting sects like the Baptists built their appeal as part of a countercultural movement that contributed to a larger redefinition of authority in the pre-Revolutionary era. As evangelicals joined other Virginians in challenging traditional structures of deference to social and political authorities, they undermined the gentry's values by redefining them as ungodly. In this way, Isaac argues, people on the economic and social margins carved out a place for themselves in both this world and the next.[4]

While this argument is both persuasive and influential, we need to look not only at the cultural appeal of these sects, but also at the seismic changes in religion during the mid-eighteenth century. The 1730s and '40s were a dynamic era of communal and individual religious enthusiasm that extended across geographic and denominational lines. A variety of different sects, including Presbyterians in Scotland and New Jersey, Anglicans in England and Pennsylvania, Congregationalists in Massachusetts and Connecticut, and the Dutch Reformed in New York and New Jersey, all experienced religious revivals marked by conversions, great fervor, and emotional, experiential forms of religious practice. These revivals, known collectively as the Great Awakening, were a transatlantic phenomenon built and connected by the movement of both people and ideas. In the 1740s, the Great Awakening reached Virginia, as the revivalist or New Side Presbyterians, followed a decade later by the Separate Baptists, brought an evangelical style of worship, a renewed emphasis on a new birth experience, and an ecclesiology that defined the church as a community of converted members rather than as a building or a geographic area.[5]

The revivalists' message and method suited the Virginia landscape and appealed to many residents. While the focus on a conversion experience and a convert's direct relationship to God can appear individualistic, these churches were deeply communal. Membership demanded accountability to all the members of the church, and members watched over each other's conduct in public and private matters. This watchfulness could be intrusive, but these churches intended it to be a loving vigilance that replicated a strict family structure, even calling members "brother" and "sister" to create the bonds and duties of spiritual kinship. In these actions, evangelical churches had much in common with the Society of Friends. Quakers too had high expectations of conduct and communal accountability, and they also utilized the language of family to demonstrate a bond deeper than that of neighbor and parish. These commonalities suggest that Virginians who joined dissenting churches valued close ties and a community, both of which could be hard to achieve within the social geography of rural Virginia, particularly its backcountry.

Moreover, these dissenting churches, like the Society of Friends, did not require great resources to establish new congregations. The evangelical focus on the preaching of the Word as the conduit of God's saving grace allowed many congregations to meet in homes or barns to read, pray, or hear lay preaching. Nascent Presbyterian churches were aided by northern presbyteries, which sent traveling ministers to preach among them for extended stays. But even in their absence, many evangelical Presbyterians worshiped, read, and prayed with lay leaders. Similarly, Baptists' emphasis on the spiritual power of the unfettered spoken Word meant that they valued lay preaching and allowed men without education to be ordained. The true measure of a preacher was not his worldly education or learned theology; it was instead demonstrated by his ability to make an audience hear—and more accurately, feel—the power of God flowing through a humble instrument. Free of requirements for buildings, education, or salary, Baptist churches could easily proliferate.

The growth of these sects is all the more remarkable because of the demands they made of their members. In creating a godly church, each sought to make membership the defining aspect of their congregants' behavior. Membership, though, was not conferred simply through attendance. These sects sought to erase the line between sacred and secular life. They thus disregarded the distinction between sacred and secular time and space by holding services on all days of the week and in a variety of places such as homes and barns. These choices were shocking to Anglicans because for them the demarcation between sacred and secular was what sacralized the time and place of their worship, removing it from the mundane. In addition, church expectations extended into members' social and domestic lives and at times into their economic and political lives as well. Members were encouraged to watch over each other and to report unrepented misdeeds. Baptists, for instance, expelled members for dancing, drinking to excess, marital discord, hard business practices, horse racing, and disorderly speech. The wide array of potential sins ensured that any active church was involved in a number of disciplinary proceedings at any given time.[6]

It is likely that the rigors of membership were part of these churches' appeal for some eighteenth-century Virginians because the seriousness of their enterprise reflected the significance of their mission. In their different ways, these sects believed they were part of an extraordinary moment in human history. One of the leaders of the evangelical Presbyterian meetings, Samuel Morris, recalled, "'Tis hard for the liveliest Imagination to form an Image of the Condition of the Assembly [congregation] on these glorious Days of the Son of Man."[7] Baptists too exalted in their ability to participate in what they saw as glorious times. Believing themselves to be heirs to the Primitive Christians, and thus uniquely able to spread God's kingdom, they were determined to strip away what they saw as centuries of invented rituals, unbiblical beliefs, adopted superstitions, and indulged laxity. They wanted to return to the purity of biblical precepts. When large numbers of conversions, many dramatic in nature, occurred against the backdrop of government persecution, it seemed to many that the age of the apostles was again at hand. This identity as the glorious remnant of true Christianity gave them a claim to religious surety, which was likely an enticing claim in a rapidly changing world. In much of this, Baptists resembled other dissenting sects. They each treasured their sense of chosenness, and they could look around at the growing numbers of believers and feel this was a unique time in human history. This fueled a sense of joy in their missions. In order to build God's kingdom, they happily and eagerly preached wherever they could—whether invited or not, to whomever would listen—and cheerfully dismissed such human inventions as an educated, elevated clergy, grand buildings for worship, and a passive laity.

Beyond the religious and social appeal of their beliefs, these dissenting sects were able to proliferate by means of practices and networks that allowed them to build churches more cheaply and easily than could the Anglicans. Anglican worship necessitated a number of significant expenses, including ordination abroad and a dignified (preferably grand) church structure complete with communion vessels and specific interior designs such as raised pulpits, tiers, and at least some specialized seating for gentry.[8] The Presbyterians were able to reduce many of these expenses by having clergy educated and ordained in nearby colonies, utilizing missionaries sent by other synods, and employing humbler buildings for their meetings. Baptists and Quakers went even further, explicitly rejecting these costly items altogether, insisting that these material elements did not mark a godly church. Freed from these material expenses, these sects could more easily negotiate the difficult social geography of the colony, while the Anglicans struggled to gather enough residents in their large parishes to cover expenses. By using traveling ministers and by meeting in homes, evangelical churches could proliferate, building on small memberships and developing unsalaried and often unordained spiritual leaders from within.

SEVENTEENTH-CENTURY FOUNDATIONS: QUAKERS AND THE ENGLISH TOLERATION ACT

Eighteenth-century dissenters found their world profoundly shaped by the legacy of dogged dissent of the Quakers in seventeenth-century Virginia and the passage of the English Toleration Act in 1689. In 1655, when George Fox, the founder of Quakerism, called his fellow believers to "let all nations hear the sound by word or writing[,] Spare no place," Virginia surely would not have been the easiest mission.[9] In addition to the hardships of the journey and the still-dangerous conditions for newcomers in the mid-seventeenth century, Virginia authorities were diligently seeking opportunities to shore up the Anglican establishment. Orthodoxy in Virginia, they discovered, had to be tenaciously built and conscientiously maintained; it was not inherited, nor could it be decreed. As warnings were dispatched from London about these accused heretics, early Quaker missionaries to Virginia were jailed and banished. But traveling by foot and boat, Quaker missionaries nonetheless made their way through Virginia settlements seeking to spread their message to the population. Believing that God speaks to all people in all times, Friends believed they, like the Primitive Christians of old, could hear and know God's will, aided by an "inner light." They did not disregard Scripture but believed that it was a divine guide rather than the totality of God's message to his people and that each person could interpret it for him- or herself without the aid of an ordained clergy. In invoking the Primitive Christians, they envisioned not just a code of beliefs but also a code of behavior. They intended—often in radical ways—to imitate the ways of Christ and his first followers, rejecting oaths, military service, and social conventions that honored rank. Whatever oratory skills they may have possessed, Quaker missionaries shared a remarkable surety and commitment to their faith. And some Virginians—whether out of curiosity or sympathy—were willing to listen to these individuals who risked everything to give their testimony.

Just as in other parts of the English Empire, small bands of Friends began to meet together for worship. Beginning in the 1650s, missionaries, including a number of women, traveled to and through Virginia to give testimony of their faith. These missionaries made converts who established spiritual communities that allowed them to sustain their faith for decades, primarily in the southeastern corner of the colony. They left few records, but if they followed the pattern of other devout Quakers in the mid-seventeenth-century English colonies, they would have made dissent from the Church of England visible (through their plain dress and simple ornamentation), verbal (through proselytizing and distinct language patterns), and provocative (through their abstinence from civil oaths and militia duty). However, beyond the traveling missionaries, there is no indication the Virginia Quakers were noisy or obtrusive, but they certainly were a thorn in the side of the parishes and Virginia authorities in their overt defiance of religious, civil, and social norms.

In the 1660s, the Virginia Assembly took steps to attack the Quaker menace, assailing Quakers on a variety of fronts. A number of acts in these years defined the sect as not just a religious abomination, but a civil threat as well, authorizing fines and other penalties. Quakers could be fined for missing Anglican services, for not having a child baptized, and for assembling in groups of five or more. At the same time, civil officials enacted penalties for those who facilitated the Friends' efforts, such as ship captains who brought Quakers into the colony, individuals who hosted Quaker preachers or distributed their literature, and even civil officials who did not prosecute them.[10] Under these directives, local authorities disrupted Quaker meetings; fined, imprisoned, whipped, and banished Quakers; and fined offending ship captains and Quaker supporters. One missionary who had been banished from the colony in 1660 returned approximately a year later to continue his work and was imprisoned in irons in a dark, airless room in which the windows had been blocked with brick and lime; he died as a result of wounds sustained from the irons.[11] Two women, traveling as missionaries, were whipped.[12] A member of the House of Burgesses was accused of being "loving to the Quakers" and subsequently expelled from that body.[13] Prosecution of Quaker and Quaker-leaning Virginians often exceeded directives from London. The Crown in 1662 instructed Governor William Berkeley to tolerate dissenting worship in order to encourage settlements in Virginia. But Virginians, particularly under Berkeley's leadership, continued their efforts to undermine and eliminate the Quaker heresy. While some Virginia Friends found the conditions in Maryland far more hospitable and migrated, others persisted in efforts to retain what they could of their goods and to gather freely together.[14]

As the remaining Friends pursued the right to preach and worship, Parliament laid the foundation for a new legal framework to govern dissenters' rights. Passed in 1689, the English Act of Toleration guaranteed the rights of Protestant dissenters to worship without harassment and exempted them from particular penalties. This act was never intended to be comprehensive or to guarantee religious liberty. It was instead an enumeration of the conditions under which particular dissenters could worship without financial penalties. It applied only to those dissenters who acknowledged the Trinity and the divine origin of the Bible and whose faith was consistent enough with the Church of England that they could give an oath supporting most of the thirty-nine

Articles of the Church (with a few specific articles excepted). To qualify, dissenters had to be willing to take an oath, or make a declaration if their faith forbade oaths, affirming their loyalty to the Crown and renouncing Catholicism. Furthermore, each minister had to be examined and licensed by civil authorities and assigned to a designated, licensed meeting house. If they fulfilled all of these conditions, dissenters would not be liable for penalties relating to nonattendance of Anglican services and participation in dissenting worship. This act did not, however, absolve them of their financial responsibilities to support the established church or of their civil duties. In Virginia, this meant that Quakers and other pacifists would still be fined for absence from militia duty. Significantly, this version of toleration was an indulgence offered by the government, rather than a right guaranteed by nature. As such, its interpretation and application were mediated through the judgment of civil officials. Moreover, the Toleration Act granted the right to worship, but not necessarily the right to practice one's faith in other contexts. This distinction was important to those whose religion demanded that there be little if any divide between their secular and sacred worlds. Those sectarians who refused to limit the manifestations of their faith to designated meetings of worship collided with the limits of this model.

In the half century following passage of the Toleration Act, Quakers reaped its benefits and learned its limits. They were willing to conform to the law insofar as they were able, for example by agreeing to register their meeting houses.[15] In return, they received a degree of toleration from courts and officials. Moreover, after a generation of living together, Quakers and their non-Quaker neighbors shared a quiet coexistence, where religious identity could be noted but not stigmatized. However, in fulfilling the demands of their faith beyond Sunday worship, they could not conform to Virginia law or authorities' expectations. For instance, as ardent pacifists, Friends would not allow their resources, financial or human, to be used for military purposes. When Virginia was threatened by the French in the early eighteenth century, this stand, which in times of peace seemed "only" a heresy, now seemed treasonous. The lieutenant governor declared his unwillingness to offer them the degree of toleration they had previously been granted, insisting that their doctrines were "so monstrous as their Brethren in Engl^d have never owned, nor indeed can be suffered in any government." He then declared his intention to force the Quakers, under threat of civil penalty, to assist as he saw fit.[16] Even in times of peace, Quakers were fined, and their property was seized for refusing to pay church tithes and for missing musters. Friends, for their part, persisted in petitioning for relief from these penalties, arguing that these practices were fundamental components of their faith and that the penalties were onerous.[17] In so doing, the Quakers sought to broaden the meaning of toleration by claiming rights beyond the right to worship communally, which was the only indulgence currently granted dissenters. They thus became the first of the major dissenting sects to demand religious rights that extended beyond the sphere of worship, a point to which the Baptists would return.[18]

PRESBYTERIANS AND THE LEGAL REGULATION OF WORSHIP

In the eighteenth century, dissenters continued to be subject to significant restrictions on their religious practice. Unlike the Quakers and, later, evangelical Baptists, the Presbyterians carefully sought to conform to Virginia's legal restrictions and to exhibit religious respectability. Their efforts produced two results: first, they carved a space for reputable dissenting worship in the colony, and second, they served notice that, far from deterring Southerners from joining, dissenters' peculiar place under Virginia law drew more popular attention to their work.

In the 1740s, the Presbyterians faced the brunt of Virginia authorities' renewed determination to enforce a limited interpretation of the Toleration Act. There had been a few Presbyterians in the colony at the turn of the eighteenth century willing to conform to legal regulation. As a result, they were allowed to worship, and a few ministers received licenses to preach beginning as early as the 1690s. Even as their numbers increased due to the migration of the Scotch-Irish from Pennsylvania into the western counties during the following decades, there seems to have been little alarm. For example, in 1738, the Synod of Philadelphia inquired about the feasibility of "a considerable number" of their sect migrating to the backcountry. The lieutenant governor of Virginia responded positively, declaring, "you may be assured, that no interruption shall be given to any minister of your profession" who conformed to the Toleration Act.[19] As settlers moved into the backcountry, Virginia authorities found that a more densely populated frontier would be more valuable than religious homogeneity.

However, two things changed in the 1740s that directed renewed attention toward the Presbyterians and brought them into conflict with reigning interpretations of the Toleration Act. First, revivalist New Side Presbyterians began to move through communities, seeking to aid struggling congregations and bring in new converts. This was quickly defined as a violation of Virginia law and seen as a dangerous road to demagoguery. That some of these evangelicals were unordained and uneducated men heightened these worries. Second, large crowds now gathered to hear these impassioned believers. Meetings were crowded, newcomers were swept up, and more people stopped attending their local Anglican services. In short, while Anglican authorities reluctantly allowed dissenters to practice so long as they were inconspicuous and numerically unobtrusive, in the 1740s, it became clear that the Presbyterians were neither.

The New Side Presbyterians built a solid base in the west when a small group of dissatisfied believers in Hanover County began to meet, read, and pray together. They soon attracted the attention of local and colonial authorities. Having no affiliation with an existing church, they were asked to identify their faith so they could be categorized within the existing religious order. They initially called themselves Lutherans because they had read and embraced commentaries by Martin Luther, claiming membership by affinity rather than through institutional ties, but upon closer examination of their beliefs, they quickly accepted the designation of Presbyterian.[20] They believed in a new birth experience and justification by Christ alone, and they practiced their faith by gathering to read and hear sermons on these topics, which often inspired emotional and physical responses by the audience. These nascent congregations received institutional support from the northern New Side synods, which sent temporary preachers to sustain and expand this small evangelical presence in the backcountry. These preachers also sought to bring the congregations into greater alignment with Presbyterian doctrine. They traveled through the area by the invitations of those who were interested in, or simply curious about, these meetings. Given what believers said about the assemblies, it is no wonder that settlers and authorities watched with interest (or alarm): "a whole House-full of People was quite over-come with the Power of the Word . . . they could hardly sit or stand, or keep their Passions under any proper Restraints."[21]

The Presbyterians' growth—and their implicit and explicit critiques of the Church of England—inspired hostility in many quarters, and Virginia authorities moved to enforce the restrictions on dissenting worship. Governor William Gooch sounded the alarm in 1745 when he denounced the Presbyterian ministers as "false teachers" and "seducers" and warned with a ringing rhetorical flourish that not stopping them would be "unjust to God, to our king, to our country, to ourselves, and to our posterity."[22] Anglican ministers, local sheriffs, and the courts took this warning seriously. In some cases, preachers and prominent laypeople were summoned to answer charges of violating the requirements for toleration. Some individuals were accused of blasphemy, and others were accused of slandering the doctrines or personnel of the Church of England. With this antievangelical campaign encouraging neighbors to turn on neighbors, many Presbyterians had cause to worry about additional fines, costly summonses to the Governor's Council, and even the possibility of banishment. Some ministers were threatened. James Waddell, for example, found himself denounced by a local Anglican minister as a "pick pocket, dark-lantern, moon-light preacher, and an enthusiast." Having denounced Waddell, the Anglican minister subsequently called upon his godly listeners to capture the preacher and drag him to the whipping post.[23] In 1747, the governor took stronger steps to limit Presbyterian practice and growth, issuing a proclamation requiring local magistrates to restrain all itinerant preaching. Since all of their ministers had been on loan from northern synods and had traveled to a number of scattered congregations, this was a direct blow to their ability to continue their meetings.[24]

The arrival of Samuel Davies in 1747 created a new Presbyterian strategy in the region. Born in 1723 in Delaware and ordained at age twenty-three, Davies was politically savvy and determined to assist the struggling congregations. In Virginia, he embarked on a campaign with two central and linked elements: first, to distinguish New Side Presbyterians from more "unruly" dissenters as well as from Quakers, and second, to demonstrate his sect's conformity to Virginia law in word and deed. This was a conservative strategy in many ways, particularly as it sought to extend the protections of the existing law to Presbyterians rather than to challenge the law or demand an interpretation that would protect other dissenting sects. While explaining his practices to Lieutenant Governor Robert Dinwiddie, Davies insisted he was not an itinerant preacher, declaring it a "character he abhor'd."[25] On another occasion, he affirmed very modest aims on behalf of his congregants: to "claim no liberties than those granted by the act of toleration and those only upon our compliance with all its requirements."[26] In a letter intended for publication, Davies vowed he had no intention of complaining about civil authorities, "especially when there is in Truth so little Occasion for it."[27] In this way, Davies and other Presbyterian ministers hoped to disarm many of their opponents' objections to the sect. Aware that Presbyterians had been accused of disparaging the Anglican ministry (an allegation frequently lodged against dissenters), Davies was careful to praise Anglican ministers as "gentlemen of learning, parts, and morality."[28] So too he praised the governor and the Governor's Council, insisting he had the "profoundest veneration" for the civil leadership.[29] Even when he criticized the established clergy, Davies insisted that he did so to honor God by showing the unaided work of the Presbyterians, rather than to "asperse another denomination."[30] This was a subtle distinction that may not have satisfied the Anglicans, but it was one the Baptists did not bother to make.

If Davies reiterated his loyalty to and respect for civil and religious authorities, he also displayed his willingness to submit to civil oversight, performing conformity in word and deed. Before he notified the Hanover congregations of his intention to minister to them, he presented himself to the General Court for examination and to give the required oaths. He also requested the first licenses for all of the meeting houses he intended to serve.[31] As opportunity and interest increased, other ministers also presented themselves for examination and licensing. In agreeing to have preachers examined by authorities, the Presbyterians signaled their full faith in the spiritual orderliness of their ministers. By complying with these requirements for toleration, they sought to persuade Virginia authorities to formally recognize the legal authority of the English Toleration Act, which some persisted in denying even as late as the 1750s. Appearing before the Governor's Council in 1755, Davies found that some members argued that the "Act of Toleration is not in Force in Virginia; & consequently that the Dissenters lie wholly at the Discretion of the Courts." In that spirit, the council even identified additional restrictions it wanted to see.[32] It was in this context that the Presbyterians appealed for the enforcement of the Toleration Act and accepted civil regulation of churches, rather than resisting government authority over religious worship and practice. Moreover, there is no indication that the Virginia Presbyterians rejected the *principle* of government oversight, only the *practice* of it in the colony. They consistently used the language of religious toleration rather than religious freedom, as when Davies explained that he sought a "Security & Enlargement of the Privileges," a far cry from what the Baptists would demand.[33] In short, Davies and the other Presbyterians did not challenge the government's right to regulate dissenters; they instead sought to demonstrate that their sect met those regulations. With all of these policies, Presbyterians declared in word and deed their religious respectability and demanded Virginia conform to English law. Cannily positioning themselves as a law-abiding and respectable sect, they could appeal to Virginia authorities for greater access to religious toleration.

To say that the Presbyterians performed civil subordination and conformed to the legal restrictions is not to suggest that the strategy was not in many ways radical or that it did not produce powerful results. In the pursuit of the free exercise of their faith, they diligently worked to force the colony to abide by the Toleration Act when it aided their efforts, and when it did not, they exploited loopholes, challenged contradictions, and pushed for a reevaluation of dissenters' so-called itinerancy. Morris and his fellow believers were careful to call the physical spaces they gathered in "reading houses" rather than "meetinghouses," which would have required a license and a licensed minister. Davies applied for, and was granted, licenses to preach at seven different meeting houses across five counties, an area of two hundred miles.[34] When opponents, including the commissary and the bishop of London, argued that this made him an itinerant and thus unprotected by the Toleration Act, Presbyterian supporters argued that such ministers were not itinerants but were designated ministers for multiple licensed meeting houses. In making this case, they accurately suggested that this situation resembled that of some Anglican clergy in Virginia who had equally large parishes and traveled to local chapels to serve outliers. Davies was (politely) relentless in making his arguments. At various times he met with the acting governor and the Governor's Council; argued his case with the attorney general; and wrote to the bishop of London and prominent supporters in London, New England, and New York, asking them to advocate for these issues. In 1753, he even traveled to England and Scotland to "seek a Redress" for the "intolerable Restraints" on Virginia Presbyterians, consulting with civil and religious leaders and circulating a petition among ministers of a number of denominations.[35]

By pushing against the boundaries of the Toleration Act, even as they expressed and generally performed compliance, Presbyterians successfully laid claim to dissenters' rights even as they broadened its application. This made it far more difficult for officials to ignore or deny legal toleration. These tactics worked, and Virginia authorities grudgingly ceased most of the harassment of the Presbyterians by 1760. In a tacit agreement between this sect and civil authorities, religious regulation would govern the establishment of new churches to ensure their orderliness, allowing Anglican authorities to keep a watchful eye on their activities. Preaching to existing dissenters would be tolerated; seeking to convert new individuals who rightfully belonged to the Anglican Church would not.

GENDER, BAPTISTS, AND THE RIGHT TO PRACTICE

In the 1750s, this tacit agreement faced new challenges when the Separate Baptists exposed its limits. There were some Baptists who were willing and able to conform to the regulations laid out by Virginia authorities. But a new evangelical strain of Baptists found that they could not conform because conformity to the religious regulations was inconsistent with their faith. For this group, the right to worship could not be equated with the right to practice, because as with the Quakers, the practice of their faith spilled out of their meeting houses and into the spaces of their communities. Their faith could not be rendered private by the walls of a church, and so they broke the unspoken agreement that sustained the rights of dissenters by insisting on a more fundamental right of unfettered religious expression. As Baptists began to pursue a new vision of the relationship between church and state, they broadened the narrative of religious liberty and thus reexposed the fragility of Virginia's structure of state-granted toleration of worship.

Following the Presbyterian challenges of the midcentury, the grudging acceptance of regulated dissenting churches extended to other sects, including the Particular Baptists. These Baptists had been recently reenergized and reorganized with assistance from Pennsylvania congregations, which brought increased orthodoxy along Calvinist lines. That this reorganization, occurring only ten years after Virginia's Presbyterians had experienced a similar revitalization, did not spark new civil restrictions suggests how effective the Presbyterian campaign had been.

By this time, a far more disorderly religious presence had begun to appear on the scene, one that made sects like the Presbyterians and Particular Baptists seem less threatening. Beginning as a small group of missionary families, the Separate Baptists arrived in northern Virginia in the 1750s. Having emerged out of the evangelical revivals in New England, these individuals were zealous believers, enthusiastic worshippers, and ardent missionaries. They had a number of unusual practices that made them odd, not just to Anglicans, but, at least initially, to other Baptists as well. First, they were willing to ignore social conventions in pursuit of their spiritual mission. They thus allowed women to exhort, give testimony, and pray publicly. They also preached to audiences that included slaves. These practices were deeply threatening to Anglicans, who often associated heresy with civil disorder. Second, their worship included enthusiastic elements, such as lay preaching, physical and verbal responses to preaching, and intense emotional experiences ranging from exuberant joy to desperate weeping. Third, they refused to have their worship regulated. These revivalists believed that a true minister was chosen by God and that the validity of a call could be determined only by a godly church made up of converted members and other similarly chosen ministers. Government officials, to their mind, had neither the ability nor the authority to judge the work of God. That they sought to do so was proof enough of a dangerous arrogance that threatened a true gospel church. Invoking the first-century Christians' resistance to the unrighteous authority of the Romans, Separate Baptists gloried in their steadfast opposition to civil regulation of religion. Willing to "render to Caesar the things that are Caesar's," they did not resist civil authority in other respects, but they insisted that they must give "to God the things that are God's." In that spirit, they refused to allow Virginia's civil and social restrictions to govern their mission. They did not register their meeting houses and refused to confine their meetings to designated buildings or even indoors. Ministers did not submit to examination by civil authorities; in fact, one Baptist association that included many Virginia ministers threatened to discipline any preacher who voluntarily submitted to an exam.[36] They also authorized unordained members, including women and slaves, to give testimony and exhort. Their final affront was not a violation of law but a violation of custom: they sought to evangelize any who would listen, without regard to their status (in the case of slaves) or religious affiliation (in the case of Anglicans).

This overt defiance of social and civil norms appalled Virginians and gave civil authorities the opportunity to move against this disruptive sect. In the 1760s and 1770s, Virginia officials, often at the instigation of Anglican ministers, targeted many Baptists preachers. In 1771, an Anglican minister, a local sheriff, and a group of other men dragged Baptist preacher John Waller from his pulpit, and he was whipped by the sheriff.[37] One minister was attacked by a magistrate carrying a warrant and a club. Others were arrested and jailed for preaching without a license and disturbing the peace. They were often offered the chance to go free if they would give a bond promising not to teach or preach for some period of time, usually a year; instead they chose jail. One minister, told that he "must give security not to teach, preach, or exhort, for twelve months and a day, or go to jail," stated simply, "I chose the latter alternative."[38] As with the Quakers and Presbyterians, some of the fiercest opposition came from the Baptists' own neighbors. A mob dragged two preachers to some nearby water, and, to ridicule the Baptist practice of full baptismal immersion, they forced the men's heads into the muddy water, demanding to know if they "believed."[39] In addition to attacking ministers, officials and mobs targeted congregations as they met for worship or baptisms, turning normally joyful gatherings into occasions fraught with drama and danger. One Stafford County church suffered repeatedly. At one time a gang of forty men barged into the meeting and began a bloody riot; on other occasions, opponents threw a live snake and a hornets' nest into the meeting and tried to disperse congregants by brandishing firearms.[40]

For Baptists, persecution proved to have a complicated meaning that shaped their identity and their own historical memory of the early movement. On the one hand, they fiercely opposed the legal harassment and restrictions and mobilized a public campaign to pressure the government. On the other hand, Baptists were energized by opposition and knew that it drew curious audiences who otherwise might not have heard their message. Moreover, the persecution became a defining component of their identity because they believed it was an honor to suffer for Christ, one they shared with the apostles and the first Christians.[41] This identity, and the inherent drama of the imprisonment of sincere believers, encouraged the emotionally charged atmosphere that brewed outside James Greenwood's jail: "as the sound of salvation was heard from the grated windows of his cell, the multitudes without, wept, and many believed unto eternal life."[42] Others, perhaps scornful of Baptists' unlawfulness, came simply to be amused and entertained or to express their outrage. The curious came too, hoping to see the spectacle: undaunted ministers preaching through the grates, converts in the throes of spiritual rapture, and opponents gathering for mischief and malice. Whatever the crowds' motives in coming, Baptists were galvanized by the suffering of their ministers and the swelling audiences. They could find no better proof of the righteousness of their cause than when the "wicked designs of [a jailed minister's] persecutors were utterly defeated: for the word of the Lord mightily prevailed. Many believed the gospel, and acknowledged the Lord Jesus."[43]

In response to these experiences, Baptist associations began to construct a political protest campaign that would eventually take them from advocating for dissenters' rights to insisting on the withdrawal of state authority over ministers, churches, and the religious choices of Virginians. In the years before the American Revolution, Baptists submitted a variety of petitions protesting the imprisonment of ministers, requesting rights granted to other dissenters, and asking for a broader interpretation of the Toleration Act. In so doing, they, like the Presbyterians, called upon the model of religious *toleration* rather than religious *liberty*.[44] For instance, in 1772, some Baptists in Amelia County complained that no local authorities would grant licenses for meeting houses, necessitating a costly journey to Williamsburg, and that only one meeting house was permitted per county. Another petition from Sussex County objected that "the Benefits of the Toleration Act [were] denied them" and asked that they "be treated with the same kind Indulgence in religious Matters as Quakers, Presbyterians, and other Protestant Dissenters enjoy."[45] After the start of the Revolution, Baptists shifted to an even more radical demand. In one petition circulated by Baptists, the petitioners objected to being forced to pay to support the established church and asked that "this, as well as every other yoke, may be broken, and that the oppressed may go free."[46] This demand marked a new phase in the reenvisioning of church-state relations, one that involved new players in the legislative assembly, substantial challenges for the Church of England, coalitions between groups of dissenters, and shifting alliances of significant individuals and sects.

While many historians have rightly focused on the Baptists' emerging political campaign for religious liberty, the Baptists did not recount those efforts in their own narratives of the era, choosing instead to include in their records of ministers' work a different kind of battle, this one fought by women.[47] These narratives were first and foremost the histories of ministers and their ministries, but they also documented the ways in which the struggle for religious liberty occurred in the domestic arena as well. The right and ability of domestic dependents to worship according to their own consciences was both a significant part of the struggle for liberty and a central means by which Baptists might spread their faith. In the histories they recorded and collected, the Baptists documented the persecution of female believers, usually at the hands of their husbands. According to ministers' narratives of the early evangelical movement, women often converted to the faith despite their husbands' fierce opposition. A woman named Mrs. Baily approached a traveling preacher and explained that she wanted to be baptized, "but her husband had told her, if she was ever baptized he would whip her within an inch of her life, and kill the man that should baptize her." Like the ministers who suffered for a righteous cause, she too invoked the holiness of suffering, stating, "if I am whipped, my Savior had long furrows ploughed upon his back." With that she bravely chose to be baptized, and her husband did in fact whip her.[48] Another woman was certain her husband would kill her for joining the Baptists. She chose to be baptized nonetheless but kept her baptism a secret, attending meetings for years sitting "in some by-corner covered with a large handkerchief."[49] In these narratives, a wife often became the first convert in a family, who then had to justify her new faith, her new church community, and her absence from the services of the Church of England. Many husbands clearly perceived this as a betrayal that was both intimate, because it struck at the heart of patriarchal authority and familial tranquility, and public, because their wives' absence from Anglican services and full-immersion baptism would be visible.[50]

In describing a virtuous wife's righteous resistance to the arbitrary authority of a husband, these stories recast the traditional story of religious oppression told in Virginia, which usually featured a preacher resisting civil authority. By describing these two models in tandem, wives joined preachers in becoming the heroic and godly sufferers for God's kingdom. (Interestingly, there are no comparable tropes about suffering laymen in these histories). While these disputes occurred in "private" familial settings, Baptists chose to make these stories public: women told them to ministers, ministers repeated them to individuals writing histories, and those writers chose to include and often to highlight them. In other words, women were not accidental heroes of the battle for religious liberty; many Baptists writers recognized women as the human impetus for family members' conversion and believed that they stood on the front line of the battle for domestic liberty of conscience. Thus, in the early histories, preachers and wives fought for liberty of conscience against Anglican ministers, civil authorities, violent mobs, and angry husbands.[51]

As these stories praised and memorialized the commitment of these women, the Baptists presented a vision of godly womanhood that was in stark contrast to eighteenth-century ideals of white womanhood, particularly women's roles as wives. In religious and popular texts of the era, women were defined as subordinate, a status given them by nature and God and thus immutable. Wives, in particular, were encouraged to demonstrate obedience and meekness. But in these Baptist narratives, women received the highest accolades for abandoning conventional gender roles and for behaving in ways that were far more independent, defiant, and strong—in short, adopting the characteristics typically assigned to men. At one Baptist meeting, it was a woman who stepped in to save an endangered preacher. When an armed man broke in on an assembly and drew a sword to attack the preacher, his wife, "like a female angel, sprang like the lightning of heaven, clasped her arms within his elbow, around his body, locked her hands together, and held him like a vice," until some men disarmed him. Whether challenging husbands or challenging opponents of evangelicalism, these women were portrayed as heroes of the efforts to build God's kingdom. In pursuit of their mission, Baptists were willing to embrace a distinctly evangelical vision of womanhood, one that was characterized by steadfastness and strength, rather than submission and meekness.[52]

As with the persecuted ministers, women's steadfastness in the face of persecution ultimately led to others' conversions. In many of the stories, wives' ardent faith, courage, and suffering inspired their husbands to agonize over their own spiritual well-being. After John Poindexter's wife converted, he expressed "surprise and rage" and forbade her baptism. She prayed, and soon her husband began to "feel his own guilt and ruin, and to sue for mercy."[53] When Mrs. Reese was baptized in her church, her husband "was thrown into monstrous temptation," and in a rage, he left her on a muddy and impassible road with her child, insisting he would never live with her again. Before he had gone half a mile, he repented of his actions and begged his wife to pray for him.[54] More generally, ministers' narratives lauded women for assisting the evangelical movement in a variety of ways. Writers frequently credited women with hosting meetings and giving powerful testimony, and wives of ministers were often recognized for their labors. For instance, at the time James Read was ordained, "he could neither read nor write. Under the tuition of his wife, he was soon able to peruse the pages of unerring truth" and became an effective itinerant.[55] John King's wife transformed his ministry when he "received much valuable information under her tuition. She appropriated much of her time in affording such assistance as he needed. A great improvement in his manner of preaching was perceptible."[56] Many of the recorded contributions of laywomen were undramatic, such as hosting meetings, assisting ministers, giving testimony, and praying. And yet by including these in their narratives, Baptists suggested that the pursuit of their holy mission in the face of persecution required men and women laboring together, albeit in their own ways.

WHILE THERE were some similarities in their tactics, particularly between the Baptists and the Quakers, each of the major dissenting sects fought on their own terms, developing different strategies in their campaign against destructive regulations. That each fought their own campaign with little connection to others' was, of course, a function of historical circumstance in many ways. Since each sect faced its greatest opposition in the first decades of rapid expansion, it is perhaps not surprising that these sects argued their own cases with little or no reference to other dissenters. Their individual strategies emerged, first and foremost, out of their religious missions and had to suit the needs of their respective faiths. While dissenters did not seek to build cross-sect alliances until after the start of the Revolution, there were always multiple groups of dissenters laboring under substantial restrictions whose struggles gradually destabilized the colonial arrangement of church and state. Like a military campaign testing for weak spots on the flanks before embarking on a frontal assault, dissenters functioned together—albeit unintentionally—to weaken the status quo by consistent pressure at a variety of stress points.

Liberty of conscience and the right to religious free exercise without restriction can appear to be predominately political and legal topics. But many colonial dissenters would not have defined the issues so narrowly. To be sure, they sought to have their rights enshrined in law, but for many of them this was a theological issue, designed to protect God's work. The practice of their faith ensured that their religion spilled into civic identities, family structures, gender norms, and even, at times, racial matters. Within the messiness of evangelical faiths, a religious tolerance based on dissenters' unobtrusiveness became increasingly problematic. For some sectarians, like the Baptists, tolerance was an unsustainable model, and they challenged it by spurning legal and social conventions, choices that ultimately contributed to their religious identity as a persecuted and holy remnant. Thus, if dissenters influenced the exercise of Virginia law, so too did Virginia shape the nature of dissenters' worship. This extended dialogue between dissenters and authorities formed the context for a new model of church-state relations.

NOTES

1. For work on the Society of Friends in seventeenth-century Virginia, see Kenneth L. Carroll, "Quakerism on the Eastern Shore of Virginia," *Virginia Magazine of History and Biography* 74 (1966): 170–89; Jay Worrall, *The Friendly Virginians: America's First Quakers* (Athens, GA: Iberian Publishing, 1994), chapters 1–8.

2. For recent work on the rise of the evangelical Baptists in colonial Virginia, see Monica Najar, *Evangelizing the South: A Social History of Church and State in Early America* (New York: Oxford University Press, 2008); Jewel L. Spangler, *Virginians Reborn: Anglican Monopoly, Evangelical Dissent, and the Rise of the Baptists in the Late Eighteenth Century* (Charlottesville: University of Virginia Press, 2008).

3. For recent work on early Virginia Methodism, see Cynthia Lynn Lyerly, *Methodism and the Southern Mind, 1770–1810* (New York: Oxford University Press, 1998). See also John Wigger, *Taking Heaven by Storm: Methodism and the Rise of Popular Christianity in America* (New York: Oxford University Press, 1998); Dee Andrews, *The Methodists and Revolutionary America, 1760–1800: The Shaping of an Evangelical Culture* (Princeton, NJ: Princeton University Press, 2000).

4. Rhys Isaac, *The Transformation of Virginia, 1740–1790* (Chapel Hill: University of North Carolina Press, 1982). Isaac focuses on Baptists, but his argument has implications for Presbyterians and Methodists as well.

5. For treatment of the transatlantic movement of ideas and people, see particularly Thomas Kidd, *The Great Awakening: The Roots of Evangelical Christianity in Colonial America* (New Haven, CT: Yale University Press, 2007). The classic work on the Great Awakening in Virginia is Wesley Gewehr, *The Great Awakening in Virginia, 1740–1790* (Durham, NC: Duke University Press, 1930).

6. For more on this topic, see Najar, *Evangelizing the South,* chapters 1 and 2.

7. Samuel Morris quoted in Samuel Davies, *The State of Religion among the Protestant Dissenters in Virginia; in a Letter to the Rev. Mr. Joseph Bellamy* (Boston, 1751), 13.

8. See Dell Upton, *Holy Things and Profane: Anglican Parish Churches in Colonial Virginia* (Cambridge: MIT Press, 1986).

9. George Fox, *A Journal or Historical Account of the Travels, Sufferings, Christian Experiences, and Labours of Love in the Work of the Ministry* (1694; repr. Philadelphia, 1839), 1:231.

10. For examples of these laws, see William Waller Hening, ed., *The Statutes at Large: Being a Collection of all the Laws of Virginia from the first session of the Legislature, in the Year 1619* (Richmond, 1809–23), 1:532–33, 2:48, 165–66, 180–83. Among the insidious components of the law was one that encouraged neighbors to report on neighbors by promising that the informer would receive half of the fines collected. Ibid., 2:48. See also William Henry Foote, *Sketches of Virginia: Historical and Biographical* (Philadelphia, 1850), 1:34–36.

11. Kenneth L. Carroll, "Quakerism on the Eastern Shore of Virginia," *Virginia Magazine of History and Biography* 74 (1966): 173.

12. One of the women became gravely ill and died shortly thereafter. Joseph Besse, *A Collection of the Sufferings of the People Called Quakers* (London, 1753), 2:234. See also Carroll, "Quakerism," 175.

13. Hening, *Statutes at Large,* 2:198. He was also expelled for refusing to give the required oaths, which the other burgesses likely demanded in their effort to prove he was himself a Quaker.

14. Henry R. McIlwaine, *The Struggle of Protestant Dissenters for Religious Toleration in Virginia* (Baltimore: Johns Hopkins University Press, 1894), 23.

15. Carroll, "Quakerism," 180.

16. Letter from Col. Spotswood, Oct. 15, 1711, in *Historical Collections Relating to the American Colonial Church,* ed. William Stevens Perry, D.D. (1870; repr. New York: AMS Press, 1969), 1:189.

17. See, e.g., *The Journal of the House of Burgesses* (Williamsburg, VA), Aug. 1736, 22, Nov. 1738, n.p., Apr. 1757, 30. While Quakers were sometimes granted exemptions (to give an affirmation rather than an oath or to send a substitute for their military duties), their petitions for relief from church tithes and militia fines were often rejected, in part or in whole. See ibid., Aug. 1736, 26, Apr. 1757, 34.

18. Many early scholars of dissenters in Virginia downplayed the work of Quakers. H. J. Eckenrode quickly dispensed with their political work, concluding that "the Quakers, after their first period, were not aggressive and they never threatened the supremacy of the establishment." H. J. Eckenrode, *Separation of*

Church and State in Virginia: A Study in the Development of the Revolution (Richmond, VA: D. Bottom, 1910), 31. While he was right that they did not, and could not, threaten the establishment, they nonetheless shaped the terrain of dissent, sustained a pattern of protest and dissent, and even laid the path (albeit unintentionally) for Presbyterians to successfully claim their "orderliness."

19. Minutes of the Pennsylvania Synod from A.D. 1717 to 1758, in *The Records of the Presbyterian Church in the United States of America* (Philadelphia, 1841), 140, 145.

20. Davies, *State of Religion,* 11.

21. Samuel Morris quoted in Davies, *State of Religion,* 14. For more on Morris and his evangelical community, see Rodger M. Payne, "New Light in Hanover County: Evangelical Dissent in Piedmont Virginia, 1740–1755," *Journal of Southern History* 61 (1995): 665–94.

22. William Gooch, in *Records of the Presbyterian Church,* 180–81.

23. *Virginia Gazette* (Rind), July 21, 1768, 2–3; see also Aug. 18, 1768, Nov. 15, 1768. For an exploration of Anglican concerns and efforts to contain enthusiasts, see Dan M. Hockman, "'Hellish and Malicious Incendiaries': Commissary William Dawson and Dissent in Colonial Virginia, 1743–1752," *Anglican and Episcopal History* 59 (1990): 150–80.

24. Davies, *State of Religion,* 18.

25. Mr. Dinwiddie to the Bishop of London, June 5, 1752, in Perry, *Historical Collections,* 1:396. For an excellent study of Davies and his work in Virginia, see George William Pilcher, *Samuel Davies: Apostle of Dissent in Colonial Virginia* (Knoxville: University of Tennessee Press, 1971).

26. Extract of a Letter from the Reverend Mr. Sam. Davies in Hanover County, Virginia, to Dr. Doddridge, Oct. 2, 1750, in Perry, *Historical Collections,* 1:371.

27. Davies, *State of Religion,* 41.

28. Davies to Bishop of London, in Foote, *Sketches of Virginia,* 1:202.

29. Davies, *State of Religion,* 41.

30. Extract from Davies to Doddridge, Oct. 2, 1750, 1:368.

31. Davies, *State of Religion,* 19; see also 42.

32. Samuel Davies to Dr. Stennett, Apr. 25, 1755, Hanover, VA, Samuel Davies Collection, box 1, folder 10, Department of Rare Books and Special Collections, Princeton University Library. Davies also debated the applicability of the Toleration Act to Virginia with the attorney general and discussed the matter with civil and religious authorities in London. See Diary of the Revd. Samuel Davies, From July 2 A.D. 1753 to April 28 [A.]D. 1754. Carefully Transcribed, Compared and Corrected by Philander Camp, 1845, Samuel Davies Collection, box 1, folder 13.

33. Davies, Diary, 7.

34. Dinwiddie to Bishop of London, June 5, 1752, 1:396.

35. See Davies, Diary, passim, quote on 6.

36. Many Particular Baptists complied with Virginia regulations and were granted the requested licenses. See David Benedict, *A General History of the Baptist Denomination in America, and Other Parts of the World* (Boston, 1813), 2:31.

37. John Williams, Journal, MS, May 10, [1771], Virginia Baptist Historical Society, University of Richmond.

38. James Barnett Taylor, *Lives of Virginia Baptist Ministers,* 2d ed., rev. and enlarged (Richmond, 1838), 120; for other examples, see ibid., 148, 149.

39. Ibid., 157.

40. Morgan Edwards, *Materials toward a History of the Baptists* (Danielsville, GA.: Heritage Papers, 1984), 2:38.

41. For an example of that explicit connection, see Taylor, *Lives,* 48–49, when he notes of one minister, "During his incarceration, he enjoyed much of the Divine presence. And, as it was with the Apostle, his trials only promoted the furtherance of the gospel." See also ibid., 121.

42. Ibid., 126.

43. Ibid., 148.

44. For an extended treatment of the important difference between these two ideas, see Daniel L. Dreisbach's discussion in chapter 6 of the present volume.

45. *Journals of the House of Burgesses,* Feb. 24, 1772, 35.

46. *Journal of the House of Delegates of Virginia* (Williamsburg, 1776), Oct. 16, 1776, 20.

47. In the ministers' personal narratives and the early histories that result, there is little mention of Baptists' efforts in petitions, newspaper debates, networking, and alliances. There are excellent studies of dissenters' involvement in political campaigns; see particularly Thomas E. Buckley, S.J., *Church and State in Revolutionary Virginia, 1776–1787* (Charlottesville: University Press of Virginia, 1977); Rhys Isaac, "'The Rage of Malice of the Old Serpent Devil': The Dissenters and the Making and Remaking of the Virginia Statute for Religious Freedom," in *The Virginia Statute for Religious Freedom: Its Evolution and Consequences in American History,* ed. Merrill D. Peterson and Robert C. Vaughan (New York: Cambridge University Press, 1988), 139–69; John A. Rogosta, "Virginia Dissenters' Struggle for Religious Liberty during the American Revolution," *Virginia Magazine of History and Biography* 116 (2008): 226–81. For more specific studies, see Paul Longmore, "'All Matters and Things Relating to Religion and Morality': The Virginia Burgesses' Committee for Religion, 1769–1775," *Journal of Church and State* 38 (1996): 775–95; Thomas E. Buckley, S.J. "Keeping the Faith: Virginia Baptists and Religious Liberty," *American Baptist Quarterly* 22 (2003): 421–33.

48. The minister, John Leland, moved on before harm came to him. John Leland, *The Writings of the Late Elder John Leland Including Some Events in his Life Written by Himself,* ed. L. F. Greene (New York, 1845), 20.

49. William Hickman, "A Short Account of my Life and Travels. For More than fifty years; A Professed Servant of Jesus Christ" (1828), Virginia Historical Society, Richmond, 15–17.

50. Besides wives' overt disobedience, these stories also had other dangerously threatening elements. These stories posit a triangle with the minister coming between a husband and wife, as the wife undergoes an emotional, even passionate, experience. The husbands often respond in the manner of a jealous lover, threaten-

ing the minister and wife with violence. Adult baptism itself was often seen as an immodest or sexual act. For more, see Najar, *Evangelizing the South*, chapter 2.

51. Examples of histories that juxtapose these stories include Leland, *Writings*; Taylor, *Lives*; John Taylor, *A History of Ten Baptist Churches*, 2d ed. (Bloomfield, 1827).

52. Leland, *Writings*, 27. See also Najar, *Evangelizing the South*, chapter 2. Baptists also constructed evangelical versions of manhood; see Janet Moore Lindman, "Acting the Manly Christian: White Evangelical Masculinity in Revolutionary Virginia," *William and Mary Quarterly*, 3d ser., 57 (2000): 393–416.

53. Taylor, *Lives*, 340. For other examples of wives' conversion inspiring their husbands, see Taylor, *Ten Baptist Churches*, 28, 47.

54. Taylor, *Lives*, 340; Taylor, *Ten Baptist Churches*, 74.

55. Taylor, *Lives*, 24.

56. Ibid., 227; see also ibid., 330; Taylor, *Ten Baptist Churches*, 47.

FIVE   Establishing New Bases for
         Religious Authority

THOMAS E. BUCKLEY, S.J.

FOR MANY IF NOT MOST VIRGINIANS ON THE EVE OF THE
Revolution against Great Britain, the idea of religious freedom as
their descendants would later envision it made no sense whatsoever. Religion was too important to let any Tom, Dick, or Harry
believe whatever nonsense came into his head, much less spread
it through the neighborhood. Instead, the value Virginians placed
on religion found expression in a formal religious establishment
that linked church and state together by law, custom, and practice. This arrangement was the locus of religious authority, and it
demanded religious conformity. As had their ancestors, eighteenth-
century colonists conceived of their society in organic terms. Just
as all the inhabitants belonged to a single political entity—the English colony of Virginia governed from Williamsburg—so all should
be members of the Church of England, sitting in their proper places
in their parish churches on Sunday, hearing the word of God, and
absorbing a decent sermon read by a properly ordained clergyman
or a duly appointed layman. Church polity and a common faith
knit them together as one people under one civil and religious government. Such a church-state relationship proved mutually beneficial. The church supported the state by its public worship and by its
teaching of the Christian gospel, the moral law, and the obligations
of good subjects of the Crown. The government supported the
church by favorable laws, public taxes, and benevolent oversight.
Church and state, clergy and laity, worked together in friendly
alliance for the well-being of the whole society.[1]

    At least that was the theory. For a church that claimed an episco-
pal polity (i.e., governed by bishops), however, the Church of En-

gland in Virginia was in an anomalous position. By the eighteenth century, the Bishop of London maintained a nominal oversight through a commissary or personal representative in Williamsburg, but no bishop was on hand to provide ordination and confirmation or to supervise the clergy. The clerical ranks were filled by ministers who came from Great Britain or Virginians who traveled to England to be ordained. The laity, particularly those sitting on parish vestries, essentially governed the colonial church. Their relationship with the clergy sometimes proved contentious, particularly when the latter challenged the gentry's dominance and attempted to assert their rights. The Parson's Cause, in which the ministers unsuccessfully challenged a General Assembly act that effectively reduced their salaries, is a well-known case in point.[2]

Moreover, colonial authorities recognized—grudgingly—the existence of religious "dissenters," principally Quakers, Presbyterians, and Baptists. Before the 1740s, however, they comprised only a tiny minority of the population, whose presence necessitated a bare toleration. The civil authorities allowed a restricted space for the relatively few nonconformist preachers in the colony, provided they registered with the government, swore the oaths required by the English Toleration Act of 1689, and preached within the confines of a licensed meeting house. Their numbers did not significantly increase until what historians later called the "Great Awakening" began to sweep through Virginia in the mid-eighteenth century. The revivals led by Anglican George Whitefield and Presbyterian Samuel Davies stirred parts of the Tidewater and the central Piedmont, and other evangelists of various persuasions and lesser abilities followed in their wake. By 1745, furious at their attacks on the doctrine and liturgy of the established church, the usually amiable Governor William Gooch in a charge to the grand jury of the General Court vigorously denounced "false teachers" who were leading "innocent and ignorant people into all kinds of delusion." The next year Gooch levied severe penalties against meetings of "Moravians, New Lights, and Methodists."[3]

The rising religious heterogeneity annoyed the governor, but only the arrival of the Separate Baptists in the decade and a half before the Revolution presented a major threat to the authority of the established church. Unlike other dissenters, they refused to cooperate with the procedures set forth by the Virginia authorities. They would not apply to magistrates for licenses or register their meeting houses. Instead, they preached wherever they chose and whenever the spirit moved them to whatever audience they could gather. They needed no human permission to preach the Gospel; their mandate came from God. They demanded complete religious freedom. And as they grew in numbers, they appeared to strengthen the resistance of other recalcitrant Virginians to the religious authority of the establishment.

The authorities struck back. People who refused to attend parish church services were presented before the county justices.[4] They were frequently joined in court by those who, "without having Episcopal Ordination or a license from the General Court," preached "contrary to the Act of Tolleration."[5] Yet throw these firebrands into jail, and they would preach through the bars. Sentences usually included a period of confinement plus a stiff fine, but persecution worked in their favor by winning converts and sympathizers.[6]

The application and extension to Virginia of the English Toleration Act of 1689 had been contested for many decades. In an effort to settle this issue and bring colonial law into conformity with English law, the Virginia Assembly debated a toleration act in 1772. Patrick Henry, already famous for his Stamp Act Resolves challenging British taxation of the colonies, proved the most notable courtroom defender of toleration in colonial Virginia. The Hanover lawyer had been a staunch advocate for exempting the pacifist Quakers from the militia laws even before he argued for the conscience rights of the Baptists.[7] Henry served on the drafting committee and spoke warmly in support of the toleration bill in the House of Burgesses. But even his oratorical skills proved insufficient to overcome the persistent conservatism of the laymen who controlled both the religious establishment and the colonial government.[8]

Yet all was not lost. Within Virginia's gentry class, a small element, educated in Enlightenment thought about the rights of conscience, had become sympathetic to the dissenters and hostile to the exclusive prerogatives of the established church. One of them, a young James Madison, wrote angrily to a friend in January 1774 of the persecution Baptist preachers were suffering from the Anglican clergy as a result of a "Hell conceived principle of persecution."[9] Like many among the college-educated segment of his generation, including his closest future collaborator, Thomas Jefferson, Madison was a nominal member of the established Anglican Church. He and his friends were not antireligious, but antiestablishment. Many of them, and particularly Jefferson, equated religion with morality; thus, religion depended upon reason and calculation rather than revelation. One's beliefs were a purely private matter beyond the purview of the state. Yet the majority in the colonial assembly rejected this perspective. In 1774 and again in 1775, the House of Burgesses received petitions from Baptists and other dissenting groups and ordered various bills to be drawn up, but nothing came of these efforts.[10] It would take a political revolution to effect a religious revolution.

CHURCH AND STATE DURING THE REVOLUTION

The political revolution began in earnest in May and June of 1776 when the Revolutionary Convention in Williamsburg took charge of Virginia's government. After resolving on independence from Great Britain, the convention drafted a republican form of government and a Declaration of Rights written by George Mason. In committee, Henry proposed that it include an article on religious toleration, and Mason's initial draft stated "that Religion, or the Duty which We owe to our Creator, and the Manner of discharging it, can be directed only by Reason & Conviction, not by Force or Violence, and therefore that all men shou'd enjoy the fullest Toleration in the Exercise of Religion." Madison was instrumental in having "fullest toleration" of religion replaced by "the free exercise of religion."[11] Some thought this was a matter of semantics, but Madison knew the difference between "toleration"—which the state could grant or withhold at its pleasure—and "free exercise of religion," which belonged to the category of natural rights that every human being enjoyed prior to any claim of the state. His intervention changed the language of the sixteenth article, but the convention rejected further efforts to disestablish the Church of England.

When Virginia's General Assembly met in the autumn of 1776, Jefferson was home from the Continental Congress in Philadelphia and happily back in the state legislature. Jefferson proposed an end to the church establishment and all laws tying church to state. Much later he remembered that the objections of his fellow legislators brought on "the severest contests" he ever faced.[12] Their proposal was very different from his. While the Assembly ended the taxation of dissenters to support the Church of England and suspended it for Anglicans, it left open the possibility of an assessment or tax on everyone for the general support of religion.

The argument that religion was essential for a republican political society carried the day. Henry was particularly vocal on this subject. Together with the article on religious toleration, he proposed what became the fifteenth article of the Declaration of Rights. Unlike the others, this article imposed obligations on Virginians by linking rights with responsibilities. Predicating the future success of the republican experiment on their behavior, it stated "that no free Government or the Blessing of liberty, can be preserved to any people but by a firm adherence to justice, moderation, temperance, frugality, and virtue, and by frequent recurrence to fundamental principles."[13] Similar themes appeared in Virginia's first constitution, in which the state was styled as the Commonwealth of Virginia. That is, the purpose of this new republic was to be the commonweal or common good of all the people it encompassed. Interestingly, Massachusetts and Pennsylvania would also use this term. For eighteenth-century republicans, virtue meant allowing the common good to set the standard for collective as well as individual behavior. In the final analysis, the success or failure of these societies would depend on the civic virtue of both the people and those they elected to govern them.[14] Because religion grounded both virtue and morality in public and private life, it was in the best interest of the state publicly to support religion. Most Americans in Virginia and elsewhere in the nascent republic accepted the logic of that position. Their differences revolved around the forms such public support might take.

During the Revolutionary years, Virginians developed four alternative perspectives on the proper relationship between church and state. First, traditionalists such as Robert Carter Nicholas, Archibald Cary, and Edmund Pendleton embraced the proestablishment position that the clergy also defended.[15] They belonged to the older generation of revolutionaries who were devoted to independence but also wanted to maintain the established church in its accustomed role as an essential component of their society. From their perspective, this system of religious authority had worked well enough for over a century. By the 1770s, with a hundred parishes served by more than a hundred clergymen, the colonial church appeared strong. This was a familiar world in which conservative churchmen were comfortable, not least of all because they controlled it.

Jefferson, Madison, and their allies represented a second position, directly counter to the conservatives. A generally younger group of politicians, they supported immediate disestablishment and complete religious equality. They would leave all religious groups to fend for themselves with voluntary support. The self was the basis for religious authority. This position found its fullest expression in Jefferson's proposed religious liberty statute.[16]

During the war years, Jefferson served on a small legislative committee charged with revising the entire code of colonial laws in accordance with Virginia's newly independent status. His statute "for establishing religious freedom" became Bill #82 of the revised code submitted to the General Assembly for its approval in 1779. The title was deliberate. Jefferson sought to replace an established church with an establishment of complete religious freedom, the most sweeping guarantee of conscience rights in America.

He began his composition by equating religion or belief with an opinion a person forms from evidence that the human mind recognizes as reasonable and true. Because "God hath created the mind free," religious belief cannot be coerced, but only persuaded by the evidence available to human reason. This process is not voluntary. As Jefferson understood it, belief was not an act of the will, something that one deliberately chose, but rather an acknowledgment of the truth of self-evident propositions, much like the opening lines he composed for the Declaration of Independence. Divine revelation had no place in this schema. Rather, God chose "to extend [religion] by its influence on reason alone." The Assembly would later erase much of this argument in support of the supremacy of reason but leave intact the phrase about the "mind free."

In terms of public life, Jefferson's bill argued that it mattered not a whit what religious opinions a person might hold. Civil government had no place in the realm of religious thought and its expression, either to coerce or to support, often a form of coercion. Instead, people should be left entirely free to believe and to practice whatever religion they found persuasive. Jefferson stated this as a matter of "natural rights" that were antecedent to the authority any government might possess. No state had any business intruding in matters of religious "opinion"; if it did so, it "destroys all religious liberty." Following this lengthy preamble, a brief clause guaranteed complete freedom of religious belief, speech, and practice. His final paragraph warned future assemblies that this statute expressed "the natural rights of mankind." While another assembly could revoke this law, if it did so, it would be violating "natural right."

A few years later, frustrated perhaps by the failure of the wartime Assembly to pass his statute, Jefferson distinguished in his *Notes on the State of Virginia* between activities appropriate to civil government and to the individual: "The legitimate powers of government extend to such acts only as are injurious to others. But it does me no injury for my neighbor to say there are twenty gods, or no god. It neither picks my pocket nor breaks my leg." Belief and conduct were unrelated, and religion utterly private. Replacing government as teacher and enforcer, Jefferson would set up truth, reason, and open discussion. Only "error needs the support of government," he wrote. "Truth can stand by itself." His statute echoed this viewpoint: "Truth is great and will prevail if left to herself." Jefferson thought that education could best achieve this purpose.[17]

Patrick Henry disagreed. Henry and those revolutionaries who agreed with him represented yet a third position. They struggled with the tension between two values: freedom of conscience and the public importance of religion. They favored religious equality and were not necessarily opposed to the disestablishment of the church, but they viewed the Christian religion as an essential support for republican government. In the words of Mason's sixteenth article in the Declaration of Rights, religion was the "duty which we owe to our Creator." The intellectual gap between Jefferson and Henry can be measured by the difference between those two words with which they defined religion. For Jefferson it was an "opinion"; for Henry it was a "duty." People who thought like Henry, while accepting religious freedom, wanted the government to support the Christian ministry as it had always done, but on a broader basis. They were chiefly concerned that the state foster the civil virtue needed for a republic.

The evangelicals, principally Presbyterians and Baptists, agreed on the importance of Christianity for the well-being of the republic, but they spelled out a fourth position on church-state relations. Praising the Declaration of Rights as Virginia's "Magna Charta," Hanover Presbytery called in 1776 for the complete equality of all denominations and an end to the state's support of the establishment. In their quest for religious freedom, these dissenters shared the objectives but not the rationale of Jefferson and his allies. They understood from Scripture that the success of Christianity did not depend upon "civil aid" because Christ had renounced "all dependence upon State Power."[18] They would develop that approach and add to it a particular interpretation of history during the postwar campaign against the assessment and in support of Jefferson's statute.

While these perspectives circulated among Virginians, delegates to the General Assembly introduced two measures in the fall of 1779. The first, a bill "concerning religion," was closely modeled after a statute enacted the previous year in South Carolina. It would establish the Protestant Christian religion with a general assessment or tax on everyone to support the church or clergyman of their choice. The second measure was Jefferson's statute "for establishing religious freedom." Both alternatives were tabled in 1779. In effect, the legislature postponed the church-state contest for the postwar world to settle.[19]

RECALIBRATING CHURCH AND STATE
AFTER THE REVOLUTION

By the time the Assembly convened in May 1784 at Richmond, the state's new capital, the legislators knew they faced multiple religious issues. The legislative petitions that session spelled them out. Urging the need for state support for religion in general, some voiced strong demands for a general assessment.[20] Baptists insisted on changes in the marriage and vestry laws that still privileged the Church of England, now called the Protestant Episcopal Church in Virginia. Hanover Presbytery included those issues in its larger complaint against the "superiority and distinction" that church still enjoyed as "the established church" and its retention of all the church property.[21]

Many if not most Episcopalians, on the other hand, realized that their church was in dire straits. At least half of its ministers had either died or resigned during the Revolution, and those who remained in active service now relied on purely voluntary support from their parishioners. England had sent no replacements for the thinning ministerial ranks in almost a decade, and the war and general neglect had caused enormous damage to church property. But the largest problem the clergy confronted involved religious authority. By severing the ties to the Church of England across the sea, the Revolution eliminated whatever episcopal oversight and support had previously existed.

Yet because of the church's established status in Virginia, a web of laws still bound it to the state. As the Assembly convened, a group of ministers under the energetic leadership of David Griffith, the rector of Christ Church in Alexandria, met in Richmond and petitioned for an act of incorporation that would enable them to manage their church's affairs. Neither clergy nor laity could envision taking any steps to organize the Virginia church without the government's approval. Indeed, a June petition to sell a glebe (the land and dwelling used to support a minister) in Halifax County reminded the legislators that control over church affairs continued to rest with them.[22]

When the Assembly reconvened in the fall session, sentiment was running strongly in favor of an assessment for religion. Even Hanover Presbytery was open to this, provided it was done "on the most liberal plan."[23] After his successful tenure as governor ended in 1779, Patrick Henry was back in the House of Delegates, and he introduced a bill establishing a provision for "teachers of the Christian religion." The preamble spelled out its justification: "a general diffusion of Christian knowledge hath a natural tendency to correct the morals of men, restrain their vices, and preserve the peace of society." The county sheriff would collect from property holders a percentage of their property tax, and each taxpayer could designate the church or minister that would receive the funds. After extensive discussions, this measure was postponed so that it could be printed and debated across the state. A shrewd James Madison had engineered this maneuver by encouraging the Assembly to return Henry to the governor's seat, a largely honorific position that erased his capacity for influencing legislation.

Madison also supported the bill for "incorporating the Protestant Episcopal Church" in Virginia. As he later reported to Jefferson, something was needed to regulate the church's property.[24] But the passage of that act roused the fury of the former dissenters. Evangelical Christians objected to the Incorporation Act for three reasons. First, its provisions spelled out the governing polity of the Episcopal Church in Virginia.[25] From an evangelical perspective, the state had no business intervening in the internal affairs of any religious group. The legislators, however, possessed a very different mindset. Mainly Episcopalians, these men and their ancestors had always controlled the temporal affairs of the church in the colonial assembly and in the vestries. The clergy worked for them. Now, without any interference from English bishops or the Crown, they saw themselves with complete authority to determine the parameters within which the Virginia church would operate.

Second, in confirmation of the 1776 statute exempting dissenters from church taxes, the act reaffirmed the Episcopal Church's title to all the buildings, farm lands, slaves, and other property that the colonial parishes had held. Finally, the evangelicals read into this law an obvious predilection by the legislators for the old hated church establishment. Incorporation reminded the Presbyterians, the Baptists, the newly organized Methodists, and other smaller religious groups that the Episcopal Church still retained its favored position. If they had ever had any doubts about the purposes of the assessment, they now understood the bill as a measure designed primarily for the revival of that church and its clergy.

While the erstwhile dissenters fumed, the Episcopalians held a convention in May 1785 to organize their church along lines specified by the Incorporation Act. The fate of what would become the Diocese of Virginia now rested in the hands of over one hundred delegates. Two-thirds were laymen, and they dominated the meeting with proposals for broad changes in doctrine and liturgy far beyond anything required by the necessary separation from the Church of England. These resolutions passed despite the objections of most of the clerical delegates, but with the support of the convention's presiding officer, the Reverend James Madison, president of the College of William and Mary and cousin to the other Madison. Known for his religious rationalism, he had backed Jefferson's efforts to eliminate the chair of theology at the college in 1780 on the grounds that the subject was inappropriate in a republican institution. With Madison as chair, the convention also adopted a series of canons that placed all religious authority in the hands of a unicameral body of clergy and laity to whom the bishop, when the Virginia diocese received one, was to be "amenable." Apart from being the full-time rector of a parish, the bishop's duties were limited to ordaining, confirming, and presiding at church functions. Any other episcopal role was purely advisory.[26] As George MacLaren Brydon pointed out, these canons "wrecked the Church in Virginia and brought it to destruction within twenty-five years."[27] They effectively emasculated the religious authority of an episcopal polity.

Meanwhile, during the spring and summer of 1785, a petition war unmatched in Virginia history raged across the Commonwealth over the assessment issue. With at least a dozen petitions favoring its passage, the printed bill drew what would ordinarily be regarded as strong support. But the opposition produced an avalanche. At the urging of some friends, Madison drafted his "Memorial and Remonstrance against Religious Assessments," a lengthy statement that reviewed in fifteen points all the political, philosophical, secular, and religious arguments he could muster against the assessment. Designed for broad appeal, Madison's composition was printed and copies circulated widely for signatures. Moreover, for every person who signed this memorial, ten more signed an explicitly religious petition sponsored mainly by Baptist or Presbyterian organizations and churches opposed to both assessment and incorporation.

The implications of these two measures outraged the evangelicals, and their petitions challenged the legislature's exercise of religious authority. A summer convention of Presbyterians attacked the presumption of "Civil Rulers" to assume "the exercise of Spiritual powers." The Incorporation Act "which authorizes and directs the Regulation of Spiritual concerns" violates "Divine Prerogative." The church possessed "sufficient authority" directly from God to govern itself, rather than rely upon "fallible men" and "the Sanction of Civil Law."[28] The Baptists agreed. A general association meeting in Orange County objected vigorously to any religious assessment as beyond the authority "of any Legislature on earth" and to incorporation as an equivalent to the "royal establishment." Another group of Baptist associations called implicitly for the separation of church and state. "The Church as a Spiritual body" could "govern itself," they insisted, and it should be "distinct from and independent of all Combinations of Men for Civil Purposes."[29] Several "formula" petitions based their arguments against the assessment mainly on religious grounds. Circulated and signed extensively at church meetings and on court days in numerous counties, they basically argued that any assessment for religion violated "the Spirit of the Gospel and the Bill of Rights."[30]

When the Assembly met in the fall of 1785, the demonstration of popular opposition was so overwhelming that the legislature never considered the assessment. The Presbyterian convention had explicitly requested the passage of the bill in the revised code for "establishing religious freedom."[31] Madison seized the moment to bring forward Jefferson's statute, which had been tabled in 1779; it passed easily through the Assembly after senate amendments trimmed back the more rationalistic elements of the preamble. A powerful alliance of evangelicals and rationalists had given Virginians the most sweeping guarantee of religious freedom in the new nation. The key element was the evangelical bloc that had been rapidly growing in numbers and influence since the outset of the Revolution a decade earlier. They all agreed with Madison and his allies on freedom of conscience as foundational to religious liberty, the voluntary nature of religion, and man's relationship to God as prior to the authority of the state. They also wanted the churches separated from civil government.

But each side also possessed a distinct perspective that its new-found ally tended to overlook. Rationalists emphasized natural rights, stressed the use of reason in pursuit of truth, and privatized religion. They were not particularly concerned about the well-being of the churches and preferred to manage the state, and by implication society at large, outside the churches' influence. The Baptists, Presbyterians, and other evangelicals focused on the scriptural commands and teachings of Christ, the need for believers to respond to God's grace without the constraints imposed by the old religious establishment, and the historical opportunity that political independence offered to recapture the situation of the New Testament churches. They were vitally interested in Christianity's future in America. Church-state separation promised the opportunity to transform their society and the whole nation by the Gospel message. Jefferson's legislation ended the threat of a revived establishment in the guise of the Episcopal Church.

The very next year, the evangelicals joined their forces for the successful repeal of the Incorporation Act. This repeal declared that all religious bodies were free to manage their own affairs, thus ending Virginia's religious establishment. But some evangelicals, led by the Baptists, now insisted that the government should go further and seize all the buildings and land that had belonged to the established church in the colonial era. This proved to be a much more arduous task because of the assault it represented on the rights of private property and the repeated guarantees the government had made to the Episcopal Church.[32]

Ultimately, a two-step process evolved. In 1799 the Assembly repealed every law that pertained to religion, except the statute "for establishing religious freedom," and it declared that Jefferson's work was to be regarded as the "true exposition of the principles of the Bill of Rights and Constitution." Three years later a new law permitted the Episcopalians to keep their churches and churchyards but provided for the eventual seizure and sale of the glebe lands and other property unless it had come to the church by private donation. Its purpose was stated in its title: "to reconcile all the good people of this commonwealth."[33] This confiscation of property that Assemblies in 1776, 1784, and 1786 had guaranteed to the Episcopal Church marked a major socioeconomic revolution. This happened in part because the Episcopal Church leadership was seriously distracted by its own internal argument over religious authority and who should wield it.

THE EPISCOPALIAN CONFLICT OVER
RELIGIOUS AUTHORITY

Two clergymen, James Madison from Williamsburg and David Griffith, a transplanted New Yorker, represented the opposing forces in the Episcopal convention of 1785 that had passed the canons for the church's government. At that meeting, the delegates had also elected a standing committee composed of two laymen and two ministers, plus Madison as chair, to oversee the church's regular operation and to examine possibilities for obtaining a bishop for a Virginia diocese. The choice of Madison is understandable, as many of the delegates had attended William and Mary and knew its president personally, but it proved a fateful one. Together with John Page, a liberal layman and close friend of Jefferson, Griffith was elected to attend a General Convention in Philadelphia that would organize a national Episcopal church, but Madison in Williamsburg controlled the Virginia church. Their disagreement over liturgy, theology, and polity sharpened when the Virginia convention met in May 1786 to complete the work of restructuring the church and to respond to the conservative proposals of the General Convention in Philadelphia. Participants there had rejected many of the Virginia church's suggestions. Indeed, one New Jersey minister privately called the 1785 convention's work a "motley mixture of Episcopacy, Presbytery and Ecclesiastical Republicanism."[34]

Attendance at the 1786 Virginia convention was off from the previous year, with sixty-three delegates, of whom only seventeen were clergymen. Elected again to preside, Madison preached on the second day. Griffith and most of the clergy present must have writhed in their seats when he urged the convention to eliminate "every system, as the fallible production of human contrivance, which shall dictate articles of faith, and adopt the gospel alone." Arguing in Jeffersonian tones that Episcopalians should endorse "free inquiry" as their norm, he supported the abandonment of all doctrinal systems and creedal statements. For a church accustomed to the rituals of the Book of Common Prayer, the formulations of ancient creeds, and the theological verities expressed in the Thirty-

Nine Articles, this was heady advice. But orthodoxy for Madison meant simply an opinion that agreed with the scriptures. Even Page, who had previously urged significant alterations to the traditional creeds, found that position too simplistic.[35] The convention spent most of its time discussing the Philadelphia convention's actions, and by a roll-call vote of thirty-two to twenty, it accepted the proposed changes to the Book of Common Prayer, while asking for revisions of certain articles of religion. Griffith and Page supported the measure, while Madison opposed it, probably because of his vocal opposition to any articles of faith. Only three other clerical delegates supported his position. Then, after these fateful decisions, the convention, on its sixth and final day, finally elected a bishop. On the first ballot, the delegates gave Griffith thirty-two votes, John Bracken ten, and Samuel Sheild seven.[36]

Madison was not in the running, and Griffith had no real competition for the position.[37] Though born in New York, he had accepted a Virginia parish in 1771, preached before Virginia's General Convention in 1775, and served as chaplain and surgeon in the Third Virginia Regiment during the Revolution. The state's most illustrious citizen, George Washington, was his good friend and parishioner. Ever since the Revolution ended, Griffith had labored incessantly to revive the state's "Mother Church" and adjust its worship and polity to the radically new social, political, and economic realities. He had proven that he could work collaboratively with both ministers and laity. They had insisted that nothing be done without legislative approval, so he had proposed the Incorporation Act to the Assembly. At the 1785 state Episcopal convention, some delegates had pushed for liturgical and doctrinal alterations that he personally found objectionable. Yet after that meeting approved the changes, he had followed its instructions at the General Convention and had not attempted to undermine Page's liberal efforts. Despite their differing views on liturgy and theology, the two men had cooperated in Philadelphia for the good of Episcopalian unity. Page later acknowledged Griffith's "indefataguble efforts" in the church's service, not only in Virginia but nationally. Griffith's contacts with other church leaders, especially in New York and Pennsylvania, proved crucial in the church's reorganization. Samuel Sheild, a conservative leader among the Virginia clergy and

Griffith's good friend, praised his "unremitting zeal for the Prosperity of our Church."

Even though Griffith appeared to be the convention's leader as
it ended, Madison outmaneuvered the transplanted New Yorker
and seized control of the church's future. The meeting had already
appointed a new standing committee, all from the Williamsburg
area, to be chaired by Madison. With newly expanded authority
to govern the Virginia church, they, rather than any bishop, were
responsible to provide its leadership, supervision, and discipline.
The standing committee was a new entity in Episcopalian polity;
nothing like it existed in the Church of England. Repudiating both
hierarchical and representative structures, Virginia Episcopalians
chose oligarchy—a government by committee with Madison in
charge.[38] Their most pressing order of business from the convention was to assist Griffith in obtaining consecration as a bishop.
That required a voyage to England and the willingness of the bishops there to consecrate him. Immediately after the meeting ended,
John Buchanan, a clergyman and treasurer for the church, sent a
printed letter to all the vestries, informing them of the convention's work and asking them to take up a collection for Griffith's trip
to England, to which some parishes responded quickly.[39] Before
the convention adjourned, it chose Griffith and Cyrus Griffin, a layman who had supported Madison's views, to attend the national
General Convention in Philadelphia.[40]

That June, with Griffith presiding, the General Convention's
principal business was obtaining the consent of the English bishops to consecrate three Americans in order to secure apostolic
succession for their new branch of the church. The bishops were
balking, mainly out of concern that American Episcopalians would
not be faithful to the church's liturgy and doctrine. So the June
meeting drafted a letter to the English hierarchy, assuring them of
their intention to maintain the worship, doctrines, and discipline
of the Church of England, "as far as was consistent with our civil
Constitutions." After a second letter arrived from London, however, the Americans realized that they would have to reverse some
of the decisions taken at their 1785 national meeting.[41] They moved
quickly to reconvene in Wilmington, Delaware, in October and
restore to the Book of Common Prayer a number of items dropped

the previous year at the instigation of Page. This meeting also fulfilled another condition of the English bishops by signing testimonials for the consecration of Griffith and the bishops-elect of Pennsylvania and New York.

OPPOSITION TO A BISHOP

Griffith had absented himself from this assemblage because he and Cyrus Griffin, Virginia's lay delegate, believed that to attend they needed either reappointment or another election. Madison had told him, however, that there was insufficient time to call a Virginia convention and also that the standing committee had decided there was "no cause" to hold one until Parliament had passed the enabling act for the consecration.[42] By this time, Griffith knew that Madison and at least some of the standing committee were deliberately stalling his efforts to obtain consecration. The English bishops had also requested testimonials from state conventions. Madison had assured him that as soon as the committee received word that Parliament had passed the enabling act, it would call a convention to provide this document. Once Parliament acted, Griffith sent Madison a copy of that act, the press published it, a month passed, and nothing happened. Stung by this deliberate obstruction by people who should be fostering the development of the church, Griffith poured out his frustrations to William White, the bishop-elect of Pennsylvania and a close friend. He now expected only "delays and difficulties" from the current members of the standing committee. Some, he thought, were "unfriendly to Episcopacy," while others only wanted a "pliant" bishop from the Williamsburg area who would let them run the church as they saw fit. A few days later, Madison informed Griffith that the committee had decided not to call a convention because, despite the enabling act, the English bishops might yet refuse to consecrate the Americans. Madison and his cabal would not provide Griffith with testimonials. As White and Joseph Provoost of New York prepared to sail for England, Virginia's bishop-elect cooled his heels in Alexandria. Madison also reported that funds were insufficient for the trip, but as Griffith pointed out, a convention would be just the thing to raise the money.[43]

Opposition to a bishop certainly existed among Virginia Episcopalians, as the 1785 canons demonstrated. On the back of one of

Buchanan's printed solicitations for funding Griffith's consecration, one respondent scratched a series of "Quaries." Attacking the
convention delegates as "a set of Ninnihammers" who were mix-
ing "oil with cold water" in trying to adapt the Church of England
to a republic, he wondered whether anyone would ever contribute
to Griffith's attempt to become "Bishop of Virginia." The press
produced further diatribes against the introduction of episcopacy
into Virginia. For example, two articles in the *Virginia Gazette* (Petersburg) argued that bishops were simply incompatible with republican government. Operating under the presupposition that
"Bishops are the creatures of Kings," the writer invented an ecclesiastical domino theory that began with the Incorporation Act and
ended in religious "oppression" under an episcopal yoke. In their
efforts to inaugurate a bishop with purely spiritual authority within
a particular church, and chosen by the vote of clergy and laity of
that church, the Episcopalians were proposing what Frederick
Mills aptly styled an "ecclesiastical revolution."[44]

The May 1787 Virginia convention, while it elected Griffith its
presiding officer, kept the reins of influence and decision in the
hands of the Williamsburg junto that formed the standing committee. Not wanting Griffith as their bishop, they endorsed a new
delaying tactic. The manipulated convention asked the newly consecrated bishops White and Provoost to consecrate Griffith either
together or separately. This violated Episcopal tradition, which
called for three consecrating bishops, as well as the agreement between the General Convention and the English bishops, as Griffith
explained to the delegates. But even the letters he produced from
White did not sway the Virginians. Madison and most of the standing committee opposed Griffith. Virginia's bishop-elect thought
they used "great art" and "popular arguments" to persuade even
"well disposed persons" to their point of view. The name of the
game was delay.[45]

Griffith also explained to White that his opponents alleged financial reasons as an obstacle to his consecration in England, but
they also wanted to change the canons to keep the bishop from
having a voice in approving men for ordination, and, asserting the
equality of bishops and presbyters in the early church, they tried
to eliminate the bishop's precedence in church functions. "What

more," Griffith asked White, "could the most zealous Presbyterian have proposed to abolish all distinctions in the Orders of the Ministry, and overturn the Episcopal church?" Other foes tried to prevent Griffith's testimonial from being signed, but their intentions became so obvious that on the last day almost all the delegates affixed their signatures. The convention had been a great ordeal for the bishop-elect, but he refused to yield to discouragement or quit. The delegates had chosen him to preside and elected him over Madison to serve as a delegate to the next General Convention. As the meeting ended, they urged the parishes to contribute to his voyage, and, he told White, as soon as the funds arrived, he would sail for England.[46]

He never made the trip. Although some parishes launched subscription drives, the amount collected was insufficient, and prospects worsened as Virginia suffered an acute shortage of specie. In accepting the episcopal office in 1786, Griffith had reasonably expected that the diocese and his parish in Alexandria would support him financially. But yearly parish contributions averaged only about fifty pounds in the postwar era, and his only other income derived from a mediocre glebe. Hard-pressed to support a wife and nine children, Griffith resolved to relinquish the episcopal nomination at the 1788 convention, but a quorum failed to appear, and his resignation letter was returned unopened. Over the next months, he and White considered other ways to pay for his consecration in England, including appeals to the Society for the Propagation of the Gospel or even to the English bishops themselves.[47] Ultimately, these proved infeasible, and Griffith drafted a fresh letter of resignation that the 1789 convention accepted. But the delegates did not elect another bishop at that meeting. Perhaps they hoped he would change his mind, and moreover, they kept Griffith as their representative to the coming General Convention. He accepted that task, he explained to White, to show his goodwill and continued interest in "the cause of the Church," as well as to prevent "certain troublesome innovators" from disturbing the meeting. Then, shortly after the convention opened in Philadelphia that August, Griffith died suddenly at Bishop White's home.[48]

THE "FEEBLE EXERTIONS" OF BISHOP MADISON

The 1789 Virginia convention had directed the standing committee to draft a new appeal for funding a bishop's consecration in England. "It is time to awake," their address announced, lest "inattention . . . prove fatal to the Protestant Episcopal church." But the committee's delaying tactics had achieved its purposes. Perhaps Griffith had been too orthodox in his advocacy of normative church polity and doctrine. Despite almost twenty years of service in Virginia, he remained an outsider and might have appeared much too zealous in his efforts to remodel the church. For those of the old school persuasion, legislative control of ecclesiastical matters had suited Virginia's Episcopalians well enough. Those who regarded a bishop as at best a necessary evil to be carefully controlled could now select a candidate after their own hearts. In 1790 a convention of twenty-seven ministers and thirty-four laymen elected James Madison. The perennial head of the standing committee received forty-six votes to Sheild's nine. Madison was also reappointed to chair that committee, the locus of real power in the Virginia church.[49] He now held all the reins. It remained to be seen how he would direct the carriage.

Suddenly, funding a bishop's consecration ceased to be a problem. Urged on by his standing committee, Madison sailed for England within two months of his election. Requesting the necessary testimonials from Bishop White, he wrote with a newfound awareness of the church's crisis that in Virginia "not a Moment is to be lost. The Situation of the Church is truly lamentable. We want Discipline, Zeal, Talents." But they had lost five years. Griffith had possessed all those abilities, but Madison and his collaborators had preferred their own weak oligarchic rule. By Christmas 1790, the new bishop had returned to Williamsburg. A creature of the canons that severely limited the scope of normal episcopal authority, Madison would prove incapable of providing the energetic, creative leadership the church needed. Reporting to White on the warm reception the English bishops had proffered, Madison pledged his cooperation "for the general welfare of our Church" and pointed out the task: "Much indeed is necessary to be done in this State. I will not be deficient on my Part, as far as my feeble

Exertions may extend." The bishop accurately appraised his challenge: "Ignorance and Enthusiasm are Hydras which require a powerful arm to oppose them."[50]

To move his church from a de facto congregational system to an episcopal polity, Madison would have to overcome a mountain of ignorance, prejudice, and suspicion. John Tyler, the future governor and father of the future president, served as a lay deputy from Westover parish in the convention of 1785. Five years after Madison returned from England as bishop, Tyler expressed his private reservations: "I feel the highest veneration for his character as a Man, but I like him not the better for his canonicals." The Virginia mind associated episcopacy with monarchy and papacy, a toxic triumvirate, as a Richmond newspaper expressed in verse: "Lo! A Bishop without a King! / Poor lifeless, senseless, Popish thing."[51] No wonder that in a newspaper testimonial to the good character of a recently hired clergyman, the bishop simply signed himself as "James Madison, William and Mary College," or that from time to time he contemplated retiring to a farm.[52] The governing structure Virginians understood was the parish, not the diocese, and the size of the state made the task even more daunting. A clergy so dispersed across the countryside was not accustomed to consultation and collaboration, or to the supervision that was ordinarily part of a bishop's mandate.

Meanwhile, the forces of "enthusiasm" wanted the church's property, and the evangelical revivals in the late 1780s shifted the balance of denominational power. An amazed Isaac Backus, writing to a New England Baptist friend in 1789, thought the religious transformation of Virginia "unparalleled in any history I ever read." Stripped of its position as "the ruling sect," the defunct establishment had been "reduced to a small, feeble party."[53] Madison could become enthusiastic when he engaged in Republican politics, but outside of the church convention setting, he seemed incapable of lobbying for his church's interests despite his extensive political contacts. Instead he consulted lawyers and relied on the courts. His confidence there was misplaced. Real energy remained in individual parishes throughout these years, but it was not tapped.[54]

The struggles over church property, and especially the struggles within the Episcopalian Church, demonstrate that the consequences of religious disestablishment were as much ecclesiastical as they were legal and social. The Revolution removed the authority the Church had long enjoyed from the English Crown; Jefferson's statute now withdrew the authority it had derived from the state. The church in Virginia was left to fend for itself. Yet in the wake of disestablishment, it was unprepared to exercise its new freedom. In the next century, a new generation would have to start practically from scratch, and it would take another transplanted New Yorker, Bishop Richard Channing Moore, to establish religious authority in Virginia's "Mother Church."[55]

JEFFERSON'S STATUTE IN VIRGINIA

The glebe struggle ensured that the act "for establishing religious freedom" would not simply be one law among many. It received paramount status when the Assembly in 1799 repealed all other laws dealing with religion except Jefferson's statute and declared it authoritative in understanding Virginia's church-state relationship. But what did the statute mean? Certainly it made the self the chief religious authority in all matters of conscience. But beyond that, both Bishop Madison and St. George Tucker, Virginia's most distinguished jurist, evidently thought it permitted religious assessments. The bishop proffered such an idea at the Episcopal convention in 1799. Then in his 1803 edition of *Blackstone's Commentaries*, Tucker urged public taxes to build and support "places of worship, and public schools" and to employ "teachers of religion and morality."[56] Nothing came of such proposals, but the correct interpretation of Jefferson's statute remained a matter of public debate in Virginia for over a century.[57]

Meanwhile, another religious authority was developing in the Old Dominion. The eighteenth-century fight over the statute had revealed the political leverage of a potent evangelical bloc. This group of churches and conservative religionists would now use their considerable political clout to ensure that Virginia acknowledged its identity as a Christian state. Jefferson's statute certainly guaranteed the freedom to believe without hindrance from the government or from an established church. But these evangelicals viewed freedom of belief as but one dimension of the statute "for establishing religious freedom." Freedom for organized religion represented another. From their perspective, Jefferson's text did not require the state to maintain religious neutrality, much less separate religion or religiously based moral or ethical values from society or political life. This religious authority would mandate for Virginia the social establishment of evangelical Christianity through the nineteenth century and well into the twentieth.

NOTES

1. Two excellent recent studies of the colonial church are Edward L. Bond, *Damned Souls in a Tobacco Colony: Religion in Seventeenth-Century Virginia* (Macon, GA: Mercer University Press, 2000); and John K. Nelson, *A Blessed Company: Parishes, Parsons, and Parishioners in Anglican Virginia, 1690–1776* (Chapel Hill: University of North Carolina Press, 2001).

2. See Rhys Isaac, "Religion and Authority: Problems of the Anglican Establishment in Virginia in the Era of the Great Awakening and the Parsons' Cause," *William and Mary Quarterly*, 3d ser., 30 (1973): 3–36 (hereafter *WMQ*). For a wonderful example of the prickly relationship that could develop between clergy and laity, see Peter Henriques, "Major Lawrence Washington Versus the Reverend Charles Green: A Case Study of the Squire and the Parson," *Virginia Magazine of History and Biography* 100 (1992): 233–64 (hereafter *VMHB*).

3. John Burk, *The History of Virginia, from its First Settlement to the Present Day* (Petersburg, VA, 1805), 3:119–20, 125. For the colonial revivals and dissent in Virginia, see Wesley Marsh Gewehr, *The Great Awakening in Virginia, 1740–1790* (Durham, NC: Duke University Press, 1930); George William Pilcher, *Samuel Davies: Apostle of Dissent in Colonial Virginia* (Knoxville: University of Tennessee Press, 1971); and especially Rhys Isaac, *The Transformation of Virginia, 1740–1790* (Chapel Hill: University of North Carolina Press, 1982). For further treatment of the dissenting churches' struggles with the established authorities, see chapter 4 of the present volume.

4. See, e.g., Grand Jury Presentments, "For not frequenting their parish church," May 12, Nov. 10, 1768, May 12, Nov. 9, Dec. 15, 1769, Caroline County Court Order Book, 1767–70, 142, 272–73, 348, 86, microfilm, Library of Virginia, Richmond (hereafter LVA); Grand Jury Presentments, June 23, 1763, 143; Fauquier County Minute Book, 1763–64, microfilm, LVA; William Fristoe, *A Concise History of the Ketocton Baptist Association* (Staunton, VA: William Gilman Lyford, 1808), 69–71.

5. Caroline County Court Order Book 1770–72, June 13, July 11, Aug. 11, 1771, 211, 241–42, 255, microfilm, LVA.

6. For Baptist hagiography, see Lewis Peyton Little, *Imprisoned Preachers and Religious Liberty in Virginia* (Lynchburg, VA: J. P. Bell, 1938). For further treatment of Baptist dissenters, see chapter 4 of the present volume.

7. Robert B. Semple, *A History of the Rise and Progress of the Baptists in Virginia* (Richmond, 1810), 23–24; Edmund Randolph, *History of Virginia*, ed. Arthur H. Shaffer (Charlottesville: University of Virginia Press, 1970), 179; Robert Douthat

Meade, *Patrick Henry: Patriot in the Making* (Philadelphia: J. P. Lippincott, 1957), 244–50.

8. William Wirt Henry, *Patrick Henry: Life, Correspondence, and Speeches* (New York: Charles Scribner's Sons, 1891), 1:112–16. For the text of this proposal, see Act of Toleration Engrossed by the Virginia House of Burgesses, Mar. 1772, Colonial Papers, box 149, LVA; for the petitions supporting it and subsequent legislative action, see *Journal of the House of Delegates of Virginia*, Feb. 27, 12, 24, Mar. 17, 1772, 160–61, 185–86, 194, 197, 249 (hereafter *JHDV*).

9. William T. Hutchinson and William M. E. Rachel, eds., *The Papers of James Madison* (Chicago: University of Chicago Press, 1962–), 1:106. For a helpful introduction to this mentality, see Henry F. May, *The Enlightenment in America* (New York: Oxford University Press, 1976).

10. *JHDV*, May 12, 16, 1774, 5, June 13, 1775, 92, 102, 189, 225. See Monica Najar's discussion of the Baptist petitions in chapter 4 of the present volume.

11. Robert A. Rutland, ed., *The Papers of George Mason, 1725–1792* (Chapel Hill: University of North Carolina Press, 1970), 1:274–92; Hutchinson, *Papers of Madison*, 1:174. Henry's role is explained by Randolph, *History of Virginia*, 254. See also Daniel L. Dreisbach, "George Mason's Pursuit of Religion Liberty in Revolutionary Virginia," *VMHB* 108 (2000): 5–44. For the text as passed, see William Waller Hening, ed., *The Statutes at Large: Being a Collection of all the Laws of Virginia, from the First Session of the Legislature, in the Year 1619* (Richmond, 1809–28), 9:111–12.

12. Thomas Jefferson, *Autobiography*, in *The Life and Selected Writings of Thomas Jefferson*, ed. Adrienne Koch and William Peden (New York: Modern Library, 1944), 41. For the work of the Assembly in effecting the religious revolution, see Thomas E. Buckley, S.J., *Church and State in Revolutionary Virginia, 1776–1787* (Charlottesville: University of Virginia Press, 1977).

13. Rutland, *Papers of Mason*, 1:289; Randolph, *History of Virginia*, 254.

14. H. Jefferson Powell, *The Moral Tradition of American Constitutionalism: A Theological Interpretation* (Durham: Duke University Press, 1993), 67–72.

15. For the clergy's defense of the establishment, see Miscellaneous Petition, Nov. 8, 1776, Legislative Petitions, RG 78, LVA (hereafter LP).

16. For the text of this act as it evolved during the legislative process, see Julian P. Boyd, ed., *The Papers of Thomas Jefferson* (Princeton, NJ: Princeton University Press, 1950–), 2:545–53.

17. Thomas Jefferson, *Notes on the State of Virginia*, ed. William Peden (New York, 1982), 159, 160; Boyd, *Papers of Jefferson*, 2:547. Jefferson's proposal for an educational system in Virginia was Bill no. 79, "for the More General Diffusion of Knowledge." It was never enacted. See Boyd, *Papers of Jefferson*, 2:526–35.

18. Miscellaneous Petition (Hanover Presbytery), Oct. 24, 1776, LP.

19. James Lowell Underwood, *Church and State, Morality and Free Expression*, vol. 3 of *The Constitution of South Carolina* (Columbia: University of South Carolina Press, 1992), 42–43, 63–72. For the legislative battles that year, see Buckley, *Church and State*, 46–62.

20. Warwick County, May 15, 1784, LP; Powhatan County, June 4, 1784, LP.

21. King and Queen County (Baptist petition), May 26, 1784, LP; Miscellaneous Petition (Hanover Presbytery), May 26, 1784, LP. The property had been guaranteed to the established church in 1776 by the same law that ended taxes for its support by the dissenters.

22. Miscellaneous Petition (Episcopal Clergy), June 4, 1784, LP. For this mentality, see the correspondence between Griffith and John Buchanan in William Meade, *Old Churches, Ministers, and Families of Virginia* (Philadelphia: J. P. Lippincott, 1906), 1:264–67; *Virginia Gazette and Weekly Advertiser* (Richmond), Nov. 6, 1784; Halifax County, June 12, 1784, LP.

23. Miscellaneous Petition (Hanover Presbytery), Nov. 12, 1784, LP.

24. James Madison to Thomas Jefferson, Jan. 9, 1785, in Boyd, *Papers of Jefferson*, 7:594.

25. For the text of this act, see Hening, *Statutes at Large*, 11:532–37. It made no difference that the Assembly offered to incorporate any other church that applied.

26. *Journal of a Convention, 1785*, 3–11, in Francis L. Hawks, ed., *A Narrative of Events Connected with the Rise and Progress of the Protestant Episcopal Church in Virginia*, vol. 1 of *Contributions to an Ecclesiastical History of the United States*, Appendix: *Journals of the Conventions of the Protestant Episcopal Church in Virginia from 1785 to 1835* (New York, 1836–39). For a firsthand account of the convention, see Notebook of John Page, typescript, Earl Gregg Swem Library, College of William and Mary, Williamsburg, VA. For Madison, see Charles Crowe, "Bishop James Madison and the Republic of Virtue," *Journal of Southern History* 30 (1964): 58–70 (hereafter *JSH*); and [Rev.] James Madison to Ezra Stiles, Aug. 27, 1780, in *The Literary Diary of Ezra Stiles*, ed. Franklin Bowditch Dexter (New York: Charles Scribner's Sons, 1901) 2:446.

27. George MacLaren Brydon, *Virginia's Mother Church and the Political Conditions under Which It Grew* (Richmond: Virginia Historical Society, 1948; Philadelphia: Church Historical Society, 1952), 2:460.

28. Miscellaneous Petition (Presbyterian Convention), Nov. 2, 1785, LP. For the campaign against the assessment, see Buckley, *Church and State*, 130–55.

29. Orange County (General Association of Baptists), Nov. 17, 1785, LP; Powhatan County (Baptist Associations), Nov. 3, 1785, LP.

30. This was the most common formula in dozens of petitions that in other respects varied their arguments against the assessment. See, e.g., Cumberland Co., Oct. 26, 1785, LP; Hanover Co., Nov. 17, 1785, LP; Northumberland Co., Nov. 28, 1785, LP.

31. Miscellaneous Petition (Presbyterian Convention), Nov. 2, 1785, LP.

32. Hening, *Statutes at Large*, 12:266–67. For the politics of the church property issue, see Thomas E. Buckley, S.J., "Evangelicals Triumphant: The Baptists' Assault on the Virginia Glebes, 1786–1801," *WMQ*, 3d ser., 45 (1988): 33–69.

33. Samuel Shepherd, ed., *The Statutes at Large of Virginia, 1792–1806: Being a Continuation of Hening* (Richmond, 1835–36), 2:149, 314–16.

34. Thomas B. Chandler to William Samuel Johnson, Dec. 28, 1785, in *Life and Correspondence of Samuel Johnson, D.D.: Missionary of the Church of England in Connecticut, and First President of Kings' College, New York*, ed. E. Edwards Beardsley (New York, 1874), 370. For the General Convention, see Clara O. Loveland, *The Critical Years: The Reconstitution of the Anglican Church in the United States of America, 1780–1789* (Greenwich, CT: Seabury Press, 1956), 152–58.

35. James Madison, *A Sermon Preached before the Convention of the Protestant Episcopal Church in the State of Virginia, on the Twenty Sixth of May, 1786* (Richmond, 1786), 8, 10; Notebook of John Page.

36. *Journal of a Convention, 1786*, 12, 16–17.

37. For Griffith, see a series of articles by William Sydnor: "David Griffith—Chaplain, Surgeon, Patriot," *Historical Magazine of the Protestant Episcopal Church* 44 (1975): 247–56 (hereafter *HMPEC*); "Doctor Griffith of Virginia: Emergence of a Church Leader, March 1779–June 3, 1786," ibid., 45 (1976): 5–24; "Doctor Griffith of Virginia: The Breaking of a Church Leader, September 1786–August 3, 1789," ibid., 45 (1976): 113–32.

38. *Journal of a Convention, 1786*, 14, 15; Loveland, *Critical Years*, 252–53.

39. John Buchanan to Lee Massey, June 6, 1786, Papers of the Protestant Episcopal Church in the United States of America, Virginia Diocese, Virginia Historical Society, Richmond (hereafter ViHi). Also, Quaries to the Gentle Reader, ViHi. For parish subscription efforts, see St. John's Vestry Book, Henrico County, June 28, 1786, 11, ViHi; Wicomico Parish Vestry Book, Northumberland County, Aug. 11, 1786, LVA; Fredericksville Parish Vestry Book, Albemarle County, Sept. 14, 1786, 125, LVA.

40. *Journal of a Convention, 1786*, 17; Meade, *Old Churches*, 1:333; Notebook of John Page; Samuel Sheild to David Griffith, Dec. 20, 1784, David Griffith Papers, ViHi.

41. William Stevens Perry, ed., *Journals of General Conventions of the Protestant Episcopal Church in the United States, 1785–1835* (Claremont, NH, 1874), 1:44. The English bishops' letters are in ibid., 1:36, 51–55. New England already had a bishop in Samuel Seabury, consecrated by the nonjuring bishops of Scotland. Seabury and his clergy also had problems with the work of the 1786 meeting, as did some other Episcopalians in the mid-Atlantic and South. For these developments, see Loveland, *Critical Years*, 167 et seq.

42. Perry, *Journals of General Conventions*, 1:58–62; David Griffith to William White, Sept. 16, 26, Oct. 6, 1786, William White Papers, Church Historical Society, Austin, TX.

43. David Griffith to William White, Oct. 20, 26, 1786, ibid.

44. Quaries to the Gentle Reader; *Virginia Gazette* (Petersburg), Dec. 14, 28, 1786; Frederick V. Mills Sr., *Bishops by Ballot: An Eighteenth-Century Ecclesiastical Revolution* (New York: Oxford University Press, 1978), 243. Mills finds opposition to episcopacy within the convention that elected Griffith. He argues that Griffith received only a bare majority of votes because sixty-three delegates are listed in the *Journal*, but only forty-nine voted. Hence he surmises that fourteen of the

delegates, or about one-fourth, abstained. However, the record does not mention abstentionism, and the vote for bishop took place on the last day of the convention. According to the *Journal*, John Bracken, who had served as secretary, had already left the meeting. Undoubtedly, others had gone as well. The day before, only fifty-two members had voted on the roll-call vote. After Griffith's election, only forty-four voted for the two delegates to the next General Convention. *Journal of a Convention, 1786*, 16–17.

45. *Journal of a Convention, 1787,* 18–25; David Griffith to William White, Apr. 28, 1787, White Papers. For the letter of the standing committee, see James Madison to William White, June 4, 1787, White Papers. It was signed by all the members of the committee except Samuel Sheild, a conservative clergyman and friend of Griffith.

46. *Journal of a Convention, 1787,* 19–22; David Griffith to William White, May 28, 1787, White Papers; William White, *Memoirs of the Protestant Episcopal Church in the United States of America* (New York, 1880), 27–28, 162. For White's refusal, see "Copy of a Letter to the Standing Committee of the Church in Virginia: dated June 1787," Fullam Papers, XVII, 174, Lambeth Palace Papers, London. William Sydnor speculates that the standing committee opposed Griffith because he would be too independent of their control. William Sydnor, "Doctor Griffith of Virginia: The Breaking of a Church Leader, March, 1779–June 3, 1786," *Historical Magazine of the Protestant Episcopal Church* 45 (1976): 113–32, 117.

47. David Griffith to William White, July 4, 1787, June 12, July 9, Nov. 27, 1788, Feb. 10, Apr. 30, 1789, White Papers; *Journal of a Convention, 1789,* 26; Perry, *Journals of General Conventions,* 73. White explained to the Archbishop of Canterbury that Griffith had resigned either because of "a Neglect manifested by the Church in Virginia, or to some other Causes of which I am not competent to Judge." William White to Archbishop of Canterbury, Aug. 11, 1789, Fullam Papers, XVII, 173.

48. David Griffith to William White, June 18, 1789, White Papers. The convention *Journal* for 1789 does not list either Griffith or Madison in attendance. John Bracken was elected to preside, and Robert Andrews was chosen as secretary. Nor does the *Journal* record the appointment of delegates to the General Convention, only that those delegates were to notify the gathering that Griffith had resigned as bishop-elect. *Journal of a Convention, 1789,* 27–28. Robert Andrews was the lay delegate from Virginia at the General Convention. See William Smith, *Sermon Delivered in Christ-Church, Philadelphia, on Tuesday, August 4, 1789, at the Funeral of the Rev. David Griffith, D.C., Bishop-Elect of the Protestant Episcopal Church of Virginia,* in *The Works of William Smith D.D., Late Provost of the Academy and College of Philadelphia* (Philadelphia, 1803), 1:[38].

49. *Journal of a Convention, 1789 and 1790,* 28, 30, 31.

50. Standing Committee in Virginia to James Madison, July 13, 1790, Fullam Papers, XVII, 199; James Madison to William White, July 12, Dec. 19, 1789, White Papers.

51. *Journal of a Convention, 1785,* 3; John Tyler to St. George Tucker, July 10, 1795, John Tyler Papers, microfilm, Library of Congress; *Richmond and Manchester Advertiser,* Aug. 20, 1795.

52. *Virginia Gazette, and General Advertiser* (Richmond), Dec. 16, 1795; James Madison to James Madison, Nov. 12, 1794, in Hutchinson, *Papers of Madison*, 15:374; David Meade to Judge [Joseph] Prentis, Apr. 30, 1798, Webb-Prentis Papers, Accession #4136, Alderman Library, University of Virginia.

53. Isaac Backus to William Rogers, Oct. 21, 1789, Isaac Backus Papers, Franklin Trask Library, Andover Newton Theological School, Newton Centre, MA. For the shift toward the evangelicals in one county, see Catherine Greer Obrion, "A Mighty Fortress Is Our God: Building a Community of Faith in the Virginia Tidewater, 1772–1845" (Ph.D. diss., University of Virginia, 1997).

54. Twenty-eight parishes in twenty-one counties and Williamsburg submitted petitions in 1786 defending the Incorporation Act. For an example of a vigorous parish with an active vestry even when lacking a clergyman, see St. Paul's Vestry Book, Hanover County, VA, 1787–1802, Brock Collection, box 12, Henry E. Huntington Library, San Marino, CA.

55. Lawrence L. Brown, "Richard Channing Moore and the Revival of the Southern Church," *HMPEC* 35 (1966): 3–63; Susan H. Godson, "Bishop Richard Channing Moore and the Renewal of the Antebellum Episcopal Church of Virginia," *Virginia Cavalcade* 32 (1983): 184–91.

56. *Journal of a Convention, 1799*, 83; St. George Tucker, *Blackstone's Commentaries* (Philadelphia, 1803), 2:117–18. For a subsequent discussion of this proposal, see the *Enquirer* (Richmond), June 6, 9, 1804.

57. For these developments, see Thomas E. Buckley, S.J., "After Disestablishment: Thomas Jefferson's Wall of Separation in Antebellum Virginia," *JSH* 61 (1995): 445–80; "The Use and Abuse of Jefferson's Statute: Separating Church and State in Nineteenth Century Virginia," in James H. Hutson, *Religion and the Founding of the American Republic* (Washington, DC: Library of Congress, 1998), 41–64; " 'A Great Religious Octopus': Church and State at Virginia's Constitutional Convention, 1901–1902," *Church History* 72 (2003): 333–60. Jefferson's statute was incorporated into the state constitution in 1830.

six   Virginia's Contributions to the
       Enduring Themes of Religious Liberty
       in America

DANIEL L. DREISBACH

IN THE BICENTENNIAL YEAR OF THE U.S. CONSTITUTION, A
wordsmith for the Virginia Commission on the Bicentennial of the
United States Constitution coined a clever slogan that was displayed
prominently on commission literature and state promotional materials.[1] It read: "The Constitution: It has Virginia written all over
it." The tagline packs a lot of truth. The same could be said of religious liberty in the American experience: "It has Virginia written
all over it." The last third of the eighteenth century, especially, was
a time of great innovation in Western thinking about religious
liberty and church-state relationships, and Virginia played a crucial
role in shaping and promoting creative approaches to a persistent
and vexing controversy. The pursuit of religious liberty in Virginia
in the tumultuous decade between 1776 and 1787 is one of the great
stories in human history, and the lessons learned from the struggle to recognize religious liberty in Virginia's laws and public policies merit scrutiny.

In 1776 and the decade that followed, Virginia was the epicen-
ter of the former British colonies that would become the United
States of America. It was the largest, most populous, prosperous,
and influential of the former colonies. And, as the most central
geographically, it had the potential to unify or divide the southern
and northern extremities of the fledgling American confedera-
tion. Virginia also produced great leaders, respected throughout
the former colonies, who played decisive roles in the independence
movement. Events in the Commonwealth inevitably impacted
other states; thus, they were carefully scrutinized. As John Adams

of Massachusetts wrote to Patrick Henry of Virginia in the anxious days of June 1776, "we all look up to Virginia for examples."[2]

In the decades that followed independence, virtually every state scrambled to redefine the church-state arrangements they inherited from colonial times. In none was this process more dramatic and, in the end, momentous than in Virginia. From the first shots of the War for American Independence to the ratification of the national constitution, as Thomas J. Curry observes, "no state surpassed Virginia in speed and extent of alterations in Church-State relations."[3] By 1786, Virginia had replaced a policy of *toleration* with the principle of religious *liberty*, eliminated state restrictions on religious exercise, terminated direct tax support for the established church, and placed churches on a purely voluntary footing. Although none moved with the speed and decisiveness of Virginia, other states wrestled with the same issues, and some adopted similar policies. In many respects, "Virginia was a microcosm of the ferment taking place throughout the new nation."[4]

The struggle to redefine the Commonwealth's church-state arrangements was important to the entire nation. As Thomas E. Buckley observes:

> [The Old Dominion] provided the most critical experiment of the Revolutionary era, for Virginia served as a politicoreligious microcosm in which the whole nation could study the alternatives for a church-state relationship and then choose from among them. . . . From Chesapeake Bay across the mountains to the Shenandoah Valley there existed both a church established by law and a religiously diverse society. In this largest and most populous of the new states with a leadership noted for its intellectual and political talent, all sides of the church-state controversy were ably represented: the traditional religionists who clung to the establishment ideal and insisted upon civil support for religion; the rationalists who believed religion to be an entirely personal affair and fought for an absolute separation of church and state; and dissenters of every stripe who, despite their own differences in polity and theory, wanted equal religious rights and a church freed from state control. For over a decade these Virginians developed the full range of

arguments over the various alternatives presented for consideration: the retention of a single establishment, its replacement by a multiple system with state aid for all churches, the removal of religion from any relationship with civil authority, and the equality of religious groups without government assistance but free to influence society's morals and values.[5]

The dramatic story of religious liberty's emergence in Virginia has been recounted numerous times in the last two centuries, perhaps no more passionately than by the principal actors in this epic contest. Historians, not surprisingly, have been drawn to the saga of church and state in revolutionary Virginia because, as Leonard W. Levy observes, "the sources are uniquely ample, the struggle was important and dramatic, and the opinions of [James] Madison . . . and of [Thomas] Jefferson were fully elicited."[6] Also, as Buckley notes, Virginians confronted the full range of options regarding church-state relations available to the newly independent Americans. The struggle in Virginia reverberated far beyond the Commonwealth's borders, and indeed, the solutions worked out in the Old Dominion had a profound impact over the next two centuries on national and state church-state policies.

This dramatic and important story will not be recounted in this chapter. Rather, selected themes pertaining to religion in the American experience will be identified and considered, giving special (but not exclusive) attention to the part played by Virginia and Virginians. These themes are broad, important, and enduring. This chapter, in short, is concerned with broad themes, not minute details, relevant to the rise of religious liberty in Virginia and the new nation.

RELIGION'S PLACE IN THE NATIONAL NARRATIVE

Religion is woven into the fabric of the American experiment. In the traditional telling of the story, early colonists crossed the Atlantic Ocean to escape religious persecution in the Old World and to search for religious liberty in the New World. (Less noble motivations that drew immigrants to these shores—ambition, avarice, adventure—are typically omitted in more heroic versions of the story.) The Pilgrims, followed by the Puritans, were called by God, in the words of Matthew 5:14, to build a "city set upon a Hill," to create a new Zion in New England's wilderness. Even before they stepped ashore, as revealed in the Mayflower Compact (1620) and in John Winthrop's "Modell of Christian Charittee" (1630), these pious English settlers committed themselves to establish biblical commonwealths and remake the world in conformity with God's laws, as they understood them. They believed their political communities would become models for future commonwealths.

An invocation of divine blessing and acknowledgment of a sacred mission to spread the Gospel are recurring themes in colonial charters and other expressions of the colonists' political enterprises. The signatories to the Mayflower Compact affirmed that they had embarked on their voyage "for the Glory of God, and Advancement of the Christian Faith." "The Honour of our King and Country" ranked third among their expressed motivations.[7] The Pilgrims' English cousins to the south in Virginia, according to conventional wisdom, were motivated by gold and not God; yet their founding charters indicate that they similarly believed their venture was for the advancement of the faith. The First Charter of Virginia in 1606 commended the colonists' "humble and well intended desires" to further, "by the providence of Almighty God," a noble work "in propagating [the] Christian religion to such people, as yet live in darkness and miserable ignorance of the true knowledge and worship of God."[8] The Second Charter of Virginia in 1609, like the first, proclaimed that "the principal effect, which we can desire or expect of this action, is the conversion and reduction of the people in those parts unto the true worship of God and Christian Religion."[9] Virginia's "Articles, Lawes, and Orders," a legal code written in 1610 and enlarged in 1611, professed that the colonists owed their "highest and supreme duty" and all "allegeance to him, from whom all power and authoritie is derived, and flowes as from the first, and onely fountaine, and being especiall souldiers emprest in this sacred cause, we must alone expect our successe from him, who is only the blesser of all good attempts, the King of kings, the commaunder of commaunders, and Lord of Hostes."[10] Like legal codes subsequently framed in the Puritan commonwealths to the north, this code, the first written in British North America, bore the unmistakable imprint of the Ten Commandments.[11]

From the Pilgrim Fathers to the Founding Fathers, and even to the present day, Americans have seen themselves as a chosen people—God's new Israel. Early colonists thought they were re-living the Exodus story. The precise contours of the analogy differed depending on who made it and when, but they were often elaborate—sometimes tortured—comparisons. The politi-cal repression and religious persecution they had endured in En-gland and from which they fled was their Egyptian bondage. The Stuart monarchs (and, later in the revolutionary era, George III) were their intransigent Pharaoh; the treacherous waters of the At-lantic Ocean, which they traversed in search of the promised land, was their Red Sea. In the new Canaan, like the ancient Israelites, they had to contend with a forbidding terrain and hostile inhabit-ants. The native Americans they encountered were their Moabites and Philistines. Americans even observed that the population of the United States at the time of independence—three million people— was approximately the same as the number of Israelites with Moses in the wilderness.[12] (Many Americans of the founding era came to regard George Washington as their Moses who led them out of Egyptian bondage and to a "Promised Land.")[13] Accordingly, the providential history of the Hebrew commonwealth and Moses's in-structions for creating the legal and political institutions to govern that commonwealth recorded in the Old Testament had special meaning for these colonists and directed their ambitious errand into a new promised land.

These are among the defining themes of the American story that were perpetuated by the first English settlers and persist to this day. The notion that God directed the founding of America and continues to intervene in national affairs is a recurring fea-ture of American identity and mythology.

RELIGIOUS DIVERSITY IN THE AMERICAN EXPERIENCE

American culture has been characterized by an extraordinary diversity of religious sects, which has shaped church-state rela-tionships and fueled the drive for religious liberty. Many Europe-ans saw the New World as a refuge from religious oppression. The opportunity to worship God as one chooses, without fear of restraint or persecution, drew many early settlers to America's shores and continues to attract immigrants in the twenty-first century. This theme is ubiquitous in colonial rhetoric and literature.

As European settlements grew in number and size up and down the Atlantic seaboard, there was a corresponding increase in the religious diversity in colonial America. Why was there so much diversity? Religious pluralism was initially fueled by the migration of diverse sects to America. A splintering of familiar Christian denominations, triggered by rearticulations of doctrine and practice, and at times prompted by religious revivals, further increased sectarian diversity. The Great Awakening of the 1740s and 1750s convinced many Americans that meaningful, genuine religious experience could take place outside the walls and beyond the administration of an established church and crushed the notion that an established church was the only place for the elect. And indeed, many Americans began to migrate away from the established church into nonconforming, dissenting religious communities.

The sects that settled in British North America early in the colonial period were, for the most part, variant forms of Protestantism. The first New England settlers, the Pilgrims and the Puritans, for example, were offshoots of the Church of England. The Church of England, or Anglicanism, became firmly entrenched in Virginia and colonies to the south. The Reformed Church in America was established by Dutch and French settlers in New Netherland (later New York) before the Massachusetts Bay colony was founded. Around midcentury, French Huguenots (Protestants) began immigrating to North America in large numbers. In the 1630s, Swedish Lutherans settled territory along the Delaware River, and the first Baptists began arriving in North America.

Religious diversity in seventeenth-century America extended beyond Protestantism. The first Europeans in the New World encountered native people with various religious beliefs and practices. French and Spanish Catholics, arriving long before the English colonists, established North American settlements and missions to the north (Canada), south (Florida), and west (Mexico and California) of the territories that would later become the English colonies. African religions were introduced into the colonies by indentured servants and slaves, who began arriving in Virginia even before the Pilgrims set foot on New England's rocky coasts.

Maryland was established in the 1630s by the Roman Catholic Calvert family, in part as a haven for their coreligionists. In 1654, Sephardic Jews, fleeing Portuguese persecution in Brazil, landed in New Amsterdam (later New York City). The first Quakers arrived in Boston in the mid-1650s, where they met with severe persecution, including public executions. They thrived in the face of opposition, growing in numbers and influence throughout the colonies.

Meanwhile, diverse Protestant groups continued to arrive. Presbyterianism gained in strength from Connecticut to the Carolinas, accompanying a stream of Scotch-Irish immigration, starting in the late seventeenth century and continuing into subsequent centuries. Before the end of the seventeenth century, German Mennonites (Anabaptists) began to settle in Pennsylvania. Early in the next century, more Mennonites, Dunkers, Amish, Moravians, Brethren, Schwenkfelders, Lutherans, and the German Reformed arrived in the great German migration. A German Sabbatarian (Seventh-Day Baptists) community was founded in Ephrata, Pennsylvania, in 1732. Methodist societies began to spring up throughout the colonies by the 1760s. The Methodist Episcopal Church in America was formally organized in 1784. Mother Ann Lee, founder of the Shaker movement in America, arrived from England in 1774 with a small band of followers. A Universalist congregation was formed in Massachusetts in 1779, and the first organized convention of Universalists appeared in 1790 in Philadelphia, where a Unitarian congregation was also formed in 1796. This is only a sampling of the religious diversity in the colonies and the early republic. The nineteenth century witnessed an even greater proliferation of religious sects.[14]

What were the practical consequences of the extraordinary religious diversity in the New World? First, it was a source of rivalry and conflict among the sects competing for adherents and public recognition (and sometimes the legal and financial favor of the civil state). There are ample illustrations of such tension turning hostile and even bloody. Many sects suffered persecution and even death in their new homeland. Quakers, for example, were executed by public hanging on Boston Commons in the late 1650s and early 1660s. More than a century later, Baptist ministers were imprisoned in central Virginia for preaching without a license and, authorities alleged, disturbing the peace.[15]

This diversity was also an opportunity for accommodation and cooperation among the numerous sects. Although memory is more frequently drawn to dramatic sectarian clashes, the story of religions in America is, indeed, most remarkable for the amity and general respect among the diverse sects that were planted and flourished side by side in the American soil. Thomas Jefferson recounted an example of sectarian cooperation in his own richly diverse community of Charlottesville, Virginia: "In our village of Charlottesville," he reported, "there is a good degree of religion, with a small spice only of fanaticism. We have four sects, but without either church or meeting-house. The court-house is the common temple, one Sunday in the month to each. Here, Episcopalian and Presbyterian, Methodist and Baptist, meet together, join in hymning their Maker, listen with attention and devotion to each others' preachers, and all mix in society with perfect harmony."[16]

Second, this extraordinary religious diversity necessitated working out the terms of, initially, religious toleration and, eventually, religious liberty. In polities where citizens and rulers are all of one faith, there is little demand for a policy of religious liberty. But where citizens and those who wield state power come from many denominations, and where multiple sects compete for followers and public favor, peaceful coexistence requires a workable policy of toleration. Europeans learned this in the wake of the Protestant Reformation, which produced fractures in Christendom, and in the bloody wars of religion that followed. Very early in the colonial experience, American colonists began to grapple with these vexing issues, culminating in the bold policies of religious liberty enshrined in Article 16 of the Virginia Declaration of Rights (1776), the Virginia Statute for Religious Freedom (1786), and the First Amendment to the U.S. Constitution (1791).

This flourishing of religious toleration in the New World became an enticement for further immigration and resulted in even more sectarian diversity, especially on the frontiers. For example, in 1753, as an officer of the Ohio Company of Virginia, George Mason, along with his partners, prepared an advertisement that included religious liberty among the inducements to attract "foreign

Protestants" to the company's vast Western holdings.[17] In his "Memorial and Remonstrance against Religious Assessments" (1785), James Madison worried that a failure to respect religious liberty "will have a like tendency to banish our Citizens. . . . To superadd a fresh motive to emigration by revoking the liberty which they now enjoy, would be the same species of folly which has dishonoured and depopulated flourishing kingdoms."[18]

Third, America's extraordinary religious diversity, once manifested, made it difficult to establish and sustain a formal ecclesiastical establishment, such as had existed in Europe. Most of the original colonies had some form of religious establishment, but as sectarian diversity increased and the colonies transitioned from British colonies to independent republics, their ecclesiastical establishments became less and less viable. By the time the national constitution was crafted in the late 1780s, many influential citizens, despite some Enlightenment influences, continued to believe religion's place (and role) in the polity must be prominent and public. Some Americans continued to support the established church in their respective states, but very few advocated a national ecclesiastical establishment. The religious diversity in the new constitutional republic meant that the establishment of a national church was practically untenable. No denomination was sufficiently dominant to claim the legal favor of the national regime, and there was little likelihood that a political consensus would emerge as to which sect or combination of sects should constitute a "Church of the United States."

James Madison, an ardent foe of ecclesiastical establishments, thought religious pluralism contributed greatly to religious liberty in America. Drawing on Voltaire's famous aphorism,[19] Madison argued:

> Happily for the states, they enjoy the utmost freedom of religion. This freedom arises from that multiplicity of sects, which pervades America, and which is the best and only security for religious liberty in any society. For where there is such a variety of sects, there cannot be a majority of any one sect to oppress and persecute the rest. . . . The United States abound in such a variety of sects, that it is a strong security against religious persecution, and

is sufficient to authorise a conclusion, that no one sect will ever be able to out-number or depress the rest.[20]

Religious pluralism, in short, compelled a rethinking of the prudential and constitutional place of and role for religion, faith-based perspectives, and pious citizens in a society without a formal religious establishment.

Few Americans of the seventeenth and eighteenth centuries doubted the value and utility of a vibrant religious, specifically Christian, culture. The issue disputed in the eighteenth century was the most effective way to nurture popular religion and extend its influence in society. By the mid-eighteenth century, two distinct, conflicting schools of thought had emerged regarding how best to promote a vibrant religious culture in American civil society. The venerable Dr. Benjamin Rush described the stark choice: "There are but two ways of preserving visible religion in any country," he wrote. "The first is by establishments. The second is by the competition of different religious societies."[21] Nowhere was this choice of paths more vigorously debated and politically contested than in Virginia, especially during the bitter legislative battles over a general assessment for the support of Christian teachers in the late-1770s and, again, in the mid-1780s.[22]

The first way to encourage religion was to maintain a legally established church. This had been the practice in the Old World and in most of the colonies. The prevailing view of the early colonial period had been that insofar as religion was indispensable to social order and stability, it was the duty of all citizens to support religion through the auspices of the civil state, which officially and legally endorsed a particular sect or denomination. Establishmentarians feared that the failure to establish a church and to provide it with the civil state's sustaining aid would impair religion's vitality and influence in society.

By the second half of the eighteenth century, an unlikely coalition of religious dissenters, nonconformists, and moderate Enlightenment rationalists began to agitate for the second way to nurture a vibrant religious culture. In Virginia, this coalition was composed of rationalists like Thomas Jefferson, Anglican latitudinarians like George Mason, and evangelical dissenters like the Baptist parson

John Leland. Proponents of this approach advocated dismantling the old arrangement of one state, one church—that is, terminating legal privileges for one particular sect or combination of sects over all others—and replacing it with a disestablished regime in which all sects could compete for adherents and their support in an open marketplace of ideas. This approach ultimately prevailed in Virginia and throughout the former colonies. As jurisdictions abandoned ecclesiastical establishments toward the end of the eighteenth century and in the early nineteenth century, matters of one's belief or disbelief and association with and support of a particular minister or religious society were left to the voluntary choice of citizens; increasingly, the civil rights and prerogatives of citizens were no longer conditioned on their religious beliefs. Each religious belief system was free to compete in the open marketplace of ideas, where, as Jefferson confidently predicted, "truth is great and will prevail if left to herself."[23]

These opponents of state churches often argued that disestablishment and competition among religious sects in the marketplace of ideas, in the words of Madison, resulted "in the greater purity & industry of the pastors & in the greater devotion of their flocks."[24] Disestablishment required sects to compete to survive. Churches and their clergy had to be exemplary and industrious, demonstrating to the world the purity and efficacy of their faith. Churches were forced to rely on the voluntary support of adherents, rather than the benevolence of the civil state. Conversely, there was a growing belief in the founding era that religious establishments led to complacency, corruption, and intolerance, whereas the combination of competition among sects, religious liberty, and disestablishment created an environment in which religions could flourish and beneficently inform public culture.[25] Disestablishmentarians argued with growing confidence that the termination of state aid for one particular church facilitated a vibrant religious culture in which the best and purest religion would dominate. This, they said, was good for the church, good for society, and good for the civil state.

In the colonial and early national experience, it should be noted, the terms "disestablishment" and "nonestablishment" were not synonymous with the phrase "separation of church and state."

Philip Hamburger points out that the rhetoric, and attendant political and legal doctrines, of separation of church and state arrived much later in American political and legal thought than previously supposed.[26] In the second half of the eighteenth century, the precise meaning of "establishment" was increasingly debated. What institutions and practices constituted an "establishment of religion"? The definition of "establishment" varied from region to region and from denomination to denomination.[27] Advocates of a narrow institutional policy of disestablishment or nonestablishment did not necessarily embrace various conceptions of "separation of church and state." Furthermore, familiar concepts and terms, such as nonestablishment and free exercise of religion, did not necessarily mean the same thing in the founding era as they do today. For example, it was not uncommon for religious test oaths for public officials, along with other provisions supporting religion, to coexist in early state constitutions with nonestablishment and liberty-of-conscience provisions. Either such constitutions were contradictory, or these concepts did not mean the same thing then as they do today.

THE INDISPENSABLE SUPPORT OF RELIGION AND MORALITY

The religious beliefs of the Founding Fathers, as revealed in the record and their personal testimonies, ranged from orthodox Christianity to skepticism about Christian claims and doctrine. Despite these differences, there was broad agreement that religion and morality (informed by religious values) were "indispensable supports" for social order and political prosperity. Indeed, this was a virtually unchallenged assumption of the age.

The challenge confronted by the founders of the American constitutional regime was how to nurture personal responsibility and social order in a system of self-government. Tyrants and authoritarian rulers used the whip and rod to force people to behave as they desired, but clearly this was unacceptable for a self-governing people. The founders preferred that a pervasive civic virtue incline citizens to be self-controlled and self-regulating.[28] They concluded that religion—for either genuinely spiritual or merely utilitarian reasons—was indispensable to this project. "To promote true religion is the best and most effectual way of making a virtuous and regular people," the Presbyterian divine John Witherspoon opined.[29] Indeed, religion, and the virtue it fostered, was perhaps more important for a free, self-governing people than for any other society. Accordingly, the founders looked to religion to develop the internal moral compass that would prompt citizens to behave in a controlled, disciplined manner and thereby promote social discipline and a civil polity in which all citizens could enjoy life, liberty, and the pursuit of happiness.

James H. Hutson has called this "the founding generation's syllogism": "virtue and morality are necessary for free, republican government; religion is necessary for virtue and morality; religion is, therefore, necessary for republican government."[30] Furthermore, many founders believed that *religious liberty* was a desirable precondition for an effective republican government because it unleashed religion and religious expression in society. They knew from history that religion could survive in the face of state persecution;[31] however, they also believed that freedom—freedom of religious worship and expression—could facilitate a vibrant religious culture that, in turn, fostered virtue and political prosperity.

The literature of the founding era is replete with expressions of this vision for the role of religion in a republican system of government. No one made the argument more famously or succinctly than George Washington in his Farewell Address in September 1796:

> Of all the dispositions and habits which lead to political prosperity, Religion and morality are indispensable supports. In vain would that man claim the tribute of Patriotism, who should labour to subvert these great Pillars of human happiness, these firmest props of the duties of Men and citizens. The mere Politician, equally with the pious man, ought to respect and to cherish them. A volume could not trace all their connections with private and public felicity. Let it simply be asked where is the security for property, for reputation, for life, if the sense of religious obligation desert the oaths, which are the instruments of investigation in Courts of Justice? And let us with caution indulge the supposition, that morality can be maintained without religion. Whatever may be conceded to the influence of refined education on minds of peculiar

structure, reason and experience both forbid us to expect that National morality can prevail in exclusion of religious principle.

'Tis substantially true, that virtue or morality is a necessary spring of popular government. The rule indeed extends with more or less force to every species of free Government. Who that is a sincere friend to it, can look with indifference upon attempts to shake the foundation of the fabric.[32]

The theme that religion and morality are indispensable to civic virtue and social order is ubiquitous in the political literature of the era, espoused by Americans from diverse religious and intellectual traditions, walks of life, and regions of the country. John Adams, for example, wrote in 1776, "Statesmen, my dear Sir, may plan and speculate for liberty, but it is religion and morality alone, which can establish the principles upon which freedom can securely stand. The only foundation of a free constitution is pure virtue."[33] Again, in an 1811 letter to Dr. Benjamin Rush, Adams wrote, "Religion and virtue are the only foundations, not only of republicanism and of all free government, but of social felicity under all governments and in all the combinations of human society."[34] The Reverend Doctor Samuel Cooper, pastor of Boston's Brattle Street Church, similarly remarked in a sermon preached before Massachusetts' elected officials in October 1780:

> Our civil rulers will remember, that as piety and virtue support the honour and happiness of every community, they are peculiarly requisite in a free government. Virtue is the spirit of a Republic; for where all power is derived from the people, all depends on their good disposition. If they are impious, factious and selfish; if they are abandoned to idleness, dissipation, luxury, and extravagance; if they are lost to the fear of God, and the love of their country, all is lost. Having got beyond the restraints of a divine authority, they will not brook the control of laws enacted by rulers of their own creating.[35]

On October 11, 1782, the Continental Congress issued a Thanksgiving Day Proclamation, authored by the Presbyterian clergyman and signer of the Declaration of Independence John Witherspoon, declaring that "the practice of true and undefiled religion . . . is the great foundation of public prosperity and national happiness."[36] Benjamin Rush, another signer of the Declaration of Independence, opined in 1786, "The only foundation for a useful education in a republic is to be laid in RELIGION. Without this [religion], there can be no virtue, and without virtue there can be no liberty, and liberty is the object and life of all republican governments."[37] David Ramsay, physician, delegate to the Continental Congress, and the first major historian of the American Revolution, wrote in 1789, "Remember that there can be no political happiness without liberty; that there can be no liberty without morality; and that there can be no morality without religion."[38] Charles Carroll of Maryland, a Roman Catholic and signer of the Declaration of Independence, similarly remarked, "Without morals a republic cannot subsist any length of time; they therefore who are decrying the Christian religion, whose morality is so sublime & pure . . . are undermining the solid foundation of morals, the best security for the duration of free governments."[39] Writing in 1799, with the anti-Christian impulses of the French Revolution in mind, and employing imagery reminiscent of Washington's Farewell Address, Patrick Henry of Virginia stated, "The great pillars of all government and of social life . . . [are] virtue, morality, and religion. This is the armor, my friend, and this alone, that renders us invincible. These are the tactics we should study. If we lose these, we are conquered, fallen indeed."[40] The interdependence of religion, religious liberty, and political prosperity was acknowledged in the Northwest Ordinance (1787), one of the organic laws of the United States of America, which declared that, "Religion, Morality and knowledge being necessary to good government and the happiness of mankind," "no person" in the territories "demeaning himself in a peaceable and orderly manner shall ever be molested on account of his mode of worship or religious sentiments."[41]

Once conceded that religion is indispensable to civic virtue, social order, and political prosperity, it then follows that the enemy of true religion (or one who would undermine the public role of religion) is a danger to civil society and political prosperity. John Witherspoon said, in perhaps his most famous address, "that he is the best friend to American liberty, who is most sincere and active in promoting true and undefiled religion, and who sets himself with the greatest firmness to bear down profanity and immorality of every kind. Whoever is an avowed enemy to God, I scruple not to call him an enemy to his country."[42] George Washington came to a similar conclusion in his Farewell Address. In the sentence following his famous pronouncement that "religion and morality are indispensable supports" to "political prosperity," he warned, "In vain would that man claim the tribute of Patriotism, who should labor to subvert these great Pillars of human happiness, these firmest props of the duties of Men and citizens." Washington unabashedly challenged the patriotism of one who undermined or subverted a public role for religion and morality in political society. (Wags up and down the Atlantic seaboard wondered aloud whether the phrase "that man" was a generic reference or whether Washington had someone specific in mind. Among those concluding it was the latter, a consensus was soon reached that "that man" was a veiled reference to Jefferson.[43] This conclusion is lent credence by the fact that the line was suggested to Washington by Alexander Hamilton, Jefferson's political foe.) Reverend Doctor Isaac Lewis opined similarly in a 1797 election sermon before the governor and legislators of Connecticut:

> Public virtue, and political prosperity are intimately connected. Righteousness will exalt, and vice bring ruin on a people [Proverbs 14:34]. If then we are true patriots, if it is our glory *really to be*, as well as to be *esteemed* the friends of our country, we shall devote ourselves to the sincere practice of true godliness; and in our several stations faithfully endeavour its universal promotion. Enmity to religion is inconsistent with true patriotism. They who are either publicly or privately undermining the foundation of piety toward God, are weakening the force of moral obligation, and aiming a fatal blow against the dearest privileges resulting from the social compact.[44]

These are strong words, indeed, which remind us of religion's vital place and role in the founders' design for the American constitutional republic.

In summary, a vibrant religious culture, facilitated by religious liberty, was thought necessary to nurture civic virtue, preserve social order, and promote political prosperity. The free exercise of religion guarantee was written into the First Amendment in order to foster a society in which religion could flourish, free from the restraints or interference of the national government, and to create an environment in which moral leaders could speak boldly, without inhibition or fear of retribution, against immorality and corruption in the public arena. The extolling of morality was not only beneficial to the citizenry at large but also essential in preserving the "republican virtues" of the American system of self-government.

For this reason, public acknowledgments, exercises, and expressions of religion were not merely tolerated by the civil state as an act of benevolence or as a matter of human rights; rather, the expansive influence of religion (and religious values) in the polity and a vibrant religious culture were deemed essential to the very survival of the civil state. The civil state's respect for religion and religious liberty, in other words, was an act of self-preservation. The civil state's survival, the founders believed, was dependent on religious values and morality permeating the community, informing public values, softening the people's prejudices, guiding the consciences of political leaders, and shaping law and public policy.

This was not an argument in favor of an established church or compelled allegiance to a particular creed or bishop. Indeed, even critics of establishment often made this argument. Rather, the contention was that the political order must acknowledge and nurture basic religious values in order to prosper. Religious liberty created an environment in which religion and religious values could flourish and thereby foster the values that give citizens a capacity for self-government.

RELIGIOUS LIBERTY TRIUMPHS OVER RELIGIOUS TOLERATION

The triumph of religious liberty over mere toleration of religion is arguably America's greatest contribution to, and innovation of, political society. This principle was expressed in Article 16 of the Virginia Declaration of Rights, adopted by the Virginia Convention on June 12, 1776. George Mason, the declaration's architect and chief draftsman, initially framed Article 16 in the language of religious toleration, but in the course of legislative deliberations, toleration was abandoned in favor of liberty.

The convention, which convened in Williamsburg on May 6, 1776, was arguably the most noteworthy political body ever assembled in the Commonwealth's history. Composed largely of veterans of the old House of Burgesses, the convention on May 15 passed a resolution instructing the Commonwealth's delegates at the Continental Congress to press for a declaration of independence from England.[45] This bold initiative raised vexing questions about the nature of civil authority extant in the Commonwealth. Believing, perhaps, that they had reverted to a state of nature, the delegates thought it necessary to frame a new social compact, beginning with a declaration of man's natural rights, followed by a new plan of civil government. The assembly appointed a committee to prepare a state declaration of rights and constitution. Among those appointed to the committee were Mason and the young, untested delegate from Orange County, James Madison.

Although Madison was certainly interested in all portions of the declaration, only the final article, "providing for religious toleration, stirred him to action." In "his first important public act" in a long and distinguished public career, Madison objected to Mason's use of the word "toleration" because it dangerously implied that religious exercise was a mere privilege that could be granted or revoked at the pleasure of the civil state and was not assumed to be a natural, indefeasible right.[46] Mason's proposal reflected the most enlightened, liberal policies of the age and went further than any previous declaration in force in Virginia, but it did not go far enough to satisfy Madison. He wanted to replace "toleration" with the concept of absolute equality in religious belief and exercise.

As early as 1774, Madison had come to think of religious toleration, the ultimate objective of most reformers of his day, as an inadequate goal because, as Thomas Paine declaimed in 1791, "toleration is not the *opposite* of Intolerance, but is the *counterfeit* of it. Both are despotisms. The one assumes to itself the right of withholding Liberty of Conscience, and the other of granting it. The one is the Pope armed with fire and faggot, and the other is the Pope selling or granting indulgences."[47] Historically speaking, religious *toleration* is different from religious *liberty*. The former often assumes an established church and is always a revocable grant of the civil state rather than a natural, unalienable right. In Madison's mind, the right of religious exercise was too important to be cast in the form of a mere privilege allowed by civil authorities and enjoyed as a grant of governmental benevolence. Instead, he viewed religious liberty as a fundamental and irrevocable right, possessed equally by all citizens, that is located beyond the reach of civil magistrates and subject only to the dictates of a free conscience. He concluded, in short, that religious toleration, whether granted by the civil state or by a religious establishment, was inconsistent with freedom of conscience.

Madison proposed revisions to Mason's draft that punctuated his aversion to the concept of toleration. He proposed replacing Mason's statement, "all Men shou'd enjoy the fullest Toleration in the Exercise of Religion, according to the Dictates of Conscience," with the phrase, "all men are equally entitled to the full and free exercise of [religion] accord[in]g to the dictates of Conscience." He recognized that religious duties are prior to civil obligations. The logic of Mason's phrasing was that because religion "can be governed only by Reason and Conviction, not by Force or Violence," for practical reasons "all Men shou'd enjoy the fullest Toleration."[48] By contrast, the practical difficulty of governing religious opinion, whether by coercion or persuasion, concerned Madison less; rather, he sought to remove religion—and matters of conscience—from the cognizance of the civil state. Key to Madison's restatement was the word "equally," which the Virginia Convention retained in subsequent drafts. This language meant that the unlearned Separate Baptists of the central Piedmont had religious rights equal to those of the well-heeled Anglican aristocrats of the Tidewater. All citizens enjoyed absolute equality in religious belief.[49]

This great achievement of the American experiment was later enshrined in the Virginia Statute for Religious Freedom and the First Amendment to the U.S. Constitution. George Washington also recognized it in an eloquent 1790 address to a Hebrew congregation in Newport, Rhode Island:

> The Citizens of the United States of America have a right to applaud themselves for having given to mankind examples of an enlarged

and liberal policy: a policy worthy of imitation. All possess alike liberty of conscience and immunities of citizenship. It is now no more that toleration is spoken of, as if it was by the indulgence of one class of people, that another enjoyed the exercise of their inherent natural rights. For happily the Government of the United States, which gives to bigotry no sanction, to persecution no assistance requires only that they who live under its protection should demean themselves as good citizens, in giving it on all occasions their effectual support.[50]

There were differences of opinion in the founding era regarding the precise meaning of religious liberty in the American context. Among the issues debated were the extent to which the civil state, consistent with the principles of religious liberty, could identify with religion or cooperate with and aid religious institutions. Some Americans maintained that religious liberty did not preclude official recognition and even promotion of religion in general, while others argued that religious liberty necessitated a separation between the institutions of the church and the civil state.[51] The content, scope, and application of religious liberty were debated in the early republic, and they continue to agitate the public mind today.

FROM STATE CHURCH TO RELIGIOUS LIBERTY

The pursuit of religious liberty is appropriately woven into the narrative of the Virginian and American experience. Many of the early colonists were drawn to American shores by the promise of liberty in religious faith and practice. That promise, unfortunately, was not always honored. Most of the colonies established churches, following models they had known in Europe. Despite these religious establishments, an extraordinary diversity of religious sects, fueled by immigration and new expressions of doctrine and practice, blossomed in the New World. This placed increasing pressure on old models of exclusive ecclesiastical establishments and created an imperative for a practical regime of religious freedom. By the time the U.S. Constitution was crafted in Philadelphia in 1787, the prospect of a national ecclesiastical establishment was politically untenable, and existing religious establishments in the states were on the decline. The last state establishment was formally terminated in Massachusetts in 1833.

The decline in ecclesiastical establishments, however, did not diminish a public role for religion. Indeed, as Americans embarked on a bold experiment in self-government, religion assumed an increasingly vital role, replacing the authoritarian ruler's whip as an instrument for social control and discipline. The founders looked to religion to promote civic virtue and social order. Religion, in the words of George Washington, was an "indispensable support" for political prosperity in a regime of republican self-government. The essential role for religion, however, was not necessarily expressed in the form of a legally established church. An unlikely coalition of pious evangelical dissenters and Enlightenment rationalists in communities like central Virginia embraced disestablishment, believing an end to the ecclesiastical monopoly enjoyed by the established church and competition in an open marketplace of ideas would promote a vibrant religious culture that would beneficently influence social order and political prosperity. This vision, which eventually prevailed in the new nation, was debated and adopted in Virginia in the tumultuous decade between 1776 and 1786 and captured in seminal public expressions of religious liberty, such as Article 16 of the Virginia Declaration of Rights and the Virginia Statute for Religious Freedom.

No state in the fledgling union would forge a more bold and innovative path in this transition from state church to religious liberty than Virginia. Virginia was not the first American jurisdiction to disestablish, to separate church from state, or to champion liberty of conscience. The Old Dominion, however, crafted the model that mattered; she set the example other states followed. When it comes to religious liberty, all Americans can join John Adams in saying, "We all look up to Virginia for examples."

NOTES

1. Portions of this chapter are adapted from "Introduction: The Pursuit of Religious Liberty in America," in *The Sacred Rights of Conscience: Selected Readings on Religious Liberty and Church-State Relations in the American Founding*, ed. Daniel L. Dreisbach and Mark David Hall (Indianapolis: Liberty Fund, 2009), xxi–xxix.

2. John Adams to Patrick Henry, June 3, 1776, in *The Works of John Adams, Second President of the United States*, ed. Charles Francis Adams (Boston: Little, Brown and Company, 1850–56), 9:387.

3. Thomas J. Curry, *The First Freedoms: Church and State in America to the Passage of the First Amendment* (New York: Oxford University Press, 1986), 134.

4. Curry, *First Freedoms*, 134.

5. Thomas E. Buckley, S.J., *Church and State in Revolutionary Virginia, 1776–1787* (Charlottesville: University of Virginia Press, 1977), 6.

6. Leonard W. Levy, *The Establishment Clause: Religion and the First Amendment*, 2d ed. (Chapel Hill: University of North Carolina Press, 1994), 75.

7. "The Mayflower Compact" (1620), in Dreisbach and Hall, *Sacred Rights of Conscience*, 86.

8. "The First Charter of Virginia" (1606), in *The Statutes at Large; Being a Collection of all the Laws of Virginia, From the First Session of the Legislature, in the Year 1619*, ed. William Waller Hening (Richmond, 1809–23), 1: 58.

9. "The Second Charter of Virginia" (1609), in Hening, *Statutes at Large*, 1:97.

10. "Articles, Lawes, and Orders, Divine, Politique, and Martiall for the Colony in Virginea" (1610–1611), in *Colonial Origins of the American Constitution: A Documentary History*, ed. Donald S. Lutz (Indianapolis: Liberty Fund, 1998), 315–26.

11. Cf., e.g., "Articles, Lawes, and Orders, Divine, Politique, and Martiall for the Colony in Virginea" (1610–1611), with the "Massachusetts Body of Liberties" (1641), both in ibid., 315–26, 71–87.

12. See Ezra Stiles, *The United States Elevated to Glory and Honor. A Sermon, Preached before His Excellency Jonathan Trumbull, Esq L.L.D, Governor and Commander in Chief, and the Honorable the General Assembly of the State of Connecticut, Convened at Hartford, at the Anniversary Election, May 8th, 1783* (New Haven, CT: Thomas and Samuel Green, 1783), 6.

13. For discussions of Washington as an American Moses, see Robert P. Hay, "George Washington: American Moses," *American Quarterly* 21 (1969): 780–91; Garry Wills, *Cincinnatus: George Washington and the Enlightenment* (Garden City, NY: Doubleday, 1984), 27–37.

14. For a general introduction to the history of these groups, see Mark A. Noll, *A History of Christianity in the United States and Canada* (Grand Rapids, MI: W. B. Eerdmans, 1992), 9–113; Sidney E. Ahlstrom, *A Religious History of the American People* (New Haven, CT: Yale University Press, 1972), 124–384.

15. See Monica Najar's discussion of the persecution of Quakers and Baptists in Virginia in chapter 4 of the present volume.

16. Thomas Jefferson to Dr. Thomas Cooper, Nov. 2, 1822, in *Thomas Jefferson: Writings*, ed. Merrill D. Peterson (New York: Library of America, 1984), 1464.

17. "Proposal to Settle Foreign Protestants on Ohio Company Lands," Feb. 6, 1753, in *The Papers of George Mason, 1725–1792*, ed. Robert A. Rutland (Chapel Hill: University of North Carolina Press, 1970), 1:28.

18. James Madison, "Memorial and Remonstrance against Religious Assessments" [1785], in *The Papers of James Madison*, ed. William T. Hutchinson and William M. E. Rachal (Chicago: University of Chicago Press, 1962–), 8:302.

19. See Gaillard Hunt, "James Madison and Religious Liberty," in *Annual Report of the American Historical Association for the Year 1901* (Washington, DC, 1902), 1:170 (Madison was fond of quoting Voltaire's aphorism). See also Voltaire, *Letters Concerning the English Nation* (c. 1733), Letter VI: "On the Presbyterians," in *The Portable Enlightenment Reader*, ed. Isaac Kramnick (New York: Penguin Books, 1995), 133 ("If one religion only were allowed in England, the Government would very possibly become arbitrary; if there were but two, the people would cut one another's throats; but as there are such a multitude, they all live happy and in peace"); Voltaire, *Philosophical Dictionary*, "Tolerance," in *The Portable Enlightenment Reader*, 129–30 ("It has been said before, and it must be said again: if you have two religions in your land, the two will cut each other's throats; but if you have thirty religions, they will dwell in peace").

20. James Madison, Speech in the Virginia Convention, June 12, 1788, in Hutchinson, *Papers of James Madison*, 11:130–31. See also Publius (James Madison), "The Federalist Number 51," in ibid., 10:478–79 ("In a free government, the security for civil rights must be the same as that for religious rights. It consists in the one case in the multiplicity of interests, and in the other, in the multiplicity of sects").

21. Benjamin Rush to Granville Sharp, Apr. 27, 1784, in *Letters of Benjamin Rush*, ed. L. H. Butterfield (Princeton, NJ: Princeton University Press, 1951), 1:330–31.

22. See generally Daniel L. Dreisbach, "George Mason's Pursuit of Religious Liberty in Revolutionary Virginia," *Virginia Magazine of History and Biography* 108 (2000): 5–44. See Thomas E. Buckley's discussion of these legislative battles in chapter 5 of the present volume.

23. "A Bill for Establishing Religious Freedom," in *Thomas Jefferson: Writings*, 347. See also Jefferson, *Notes on the State of Virginia*, Query XVII, in ibid., 286 ("It is error alone which needs the support of government. Truth can stand by itself"); John Locke, "A Letter Concerning Toleration," in *The Second Treatise of Government (An Essay Concerning the True Original, Extent and End of Civil Government) and A Letter Concerning Toleration*, ed. J. W. Gough (New York: Macmillan, 1956), 153 ("For the truth certainly would do well enough if she were once left to shift for herself"); Benjamin Franklin to Richard Price, Oct. 9, 1780, in *The Papers of Benjamin Franklin*, ed. Barbara B. Oberg, et al. (New Haven, CT: Yale University Press, 1959–), 33:390 ("When a Religion is good, I conceive that it will support itself; and when it cannot support itself, and God does not take care to support [it], so that its Professors are oblig'd to call for the help of the Civil Power, 'tis a Sign, I apprehend, of its being a bad one").

24. James Madison to Jasper Adams, Sept. 1833, in *Religion and Politics in the Early Republic: Jasper Adams and the Church-State Debate*, ed. Daniel L. Dreisbach (Lexington: University Press of Kentucky, 1996), 118–20. See also Adam Smith, "The Wealth of Nations" (1776), in Dreisbach and Hall, *Sacred Rights of Conscience*,

76 (the exertion, zeal, and industry of religious teachers who rely "upon the voluntary contributions of their hearers" are "likely to be much greater" than for religious teachers who derive funds from legal establishments).

25. See James Madison, "Memorial and Remonstrance against Religious Assessments," in Hutchinson, *Papers of James Madison*, 8:301 ("What have been its fruits [fruits of ecclesiastical establishments]? More or less in all places, pride and indolence in the Clergy, ignorance and servility in the laity, in both, superstition, bigotry and persecution").

26. See Philip Hamburger, *Separation of Church and State* (Cambridge: Harvard University Press, 2002).

27. For useful analyses of the meaning of "an establishment of religion" in the late colonial and early national periods, see Thomas J. Curry, *The First Freedoms: Church and State in America to the Passage of the First Amendment* (New York: Oxford University Press, 1986); Donald L. Drakeman, *Church, State, and Original Intent* (New York: Cambridge University Press, 2010); Leonard W. Levy, *The Establishment Clause: Religion and the First Amendment*, 2d ed. (Chapel Hill: University of North Carolina Press, 1994).

28. See, e.g., Benjamin Franklin to Abbes Chalet and Arnaud, Apr. 17, 1787, in *The Works of Benjamin Franklin*, ed. John Bigelow, Federal Edition (New York: G. P. Putnam's Sons, 1904), 11:318 ("Only a virtuous people are capable of freedom. As nations become corrupt and vicious, they have more need of masters").

29. John Witherspoon, *Lectures on Moral Philosophy*, ed. Varnum Lansing Collins (Princeton, NJ: Princeton University Press, 1912), 110.

30. James H. Hutson, *Religion and the Founding of the American Republic* (Washington, DC: Library of Congress, 1998), 81.

31. See James Madison, "Memorial and Remonstrance against Religious Assessments," in Hutchinson, *Papers of James Madison*, 8:301 ("It is known that this Religion both existed and flourished, not only without the support of human laws, but in spite of every opposition from them").

32. George Washington, Farewell Address, Sept. 19, 1796, in *The Writings of George Washington*, ed. John C. Fitzpatrick (Washington, DC: Government Printing Office, 1931–40), 35:229–30. In a 1797 missive to the clergy of Philadelphia, Washington affirmed his belief "that *Religion* and *Morality* are the essential pillars of Civil society." Washington to the Clergy of Different Denominations Residing in and near the City of Philadelphia, [Mar. 3, 1797], in ibid., 35:416.

33. John Adams to Zabdiel Adams, June 21, 1776, in Adams, *Works*, 9:401.

34. John Adams to Benjamin Rush, Aug. 28, 1811, in ibid., 9:636.

35. Samuel Cooper, *A Sermon Preached before His Excellency John Hancock, Esq; Governour, the Honourable the Senate, and House of Representatives of the Commonwealth of Massachusetts, October 25, 1780. Being the Day of the Commencement of the Constitution, and Inauguration of the New Government* (Boston: Commonwealth of Massachusetts, 1780), 37.

36. Thanksgiving Proclamation of October 11, 1782, in *Journals of the Continental Congress, 1774–1789*, ed. Worthington Chauncey Ford (Washington, DC:

Government Printing Office, 1858–1941), 23:647. See also Jeffry H. Morrison, *John Witherspoon and the Founding of the American Republic* (Notre Dame, IN: University of Notre Dame Press, 2005), 21.

37. Benjamin Rush, *Thoughts upon the Mode of Education Proper in a Republic* (1786), in *American Political Writing during the Founding Era: 1760–1805*, ed. Charles S. Hyneman and Donald S. Lutz (Indianapolis: Liberty Press, 1983), 1:681.

38. David Ramsay, *The History of the American Revolution* (London, 1790), 2:356.

39. Charles Carroll of Carrollton to James McHenry, Nov. 4, 1800, in Bernard C. Steiner, *The Life and Correspondence of James McHenry* (Cleveland: Burrows Bros., 1907), 475.

40. Patrick Henry to Archibald Blair, Jan. 8, 1799, in *Patrick Henry: Life, Correspondence and Speeches*, ed. William Wirt Henry (New York: Charles Scribner's Sons, 1891), 2:592.

41. "Northwest Ordinance" (1787), articles 3 and 1, in Dreisbach and Hall, *Sacred Rights of Conscience*, 236, 238.

42. John Witherspoon, *The Dominion of Providence over the Passions of Men: A Sermon preached at Princeton, on the 17th of May, 1776, Being the General Fast appointed by the Congress through the United Colonies* (Philadelphia: R. Aitken, 1776), 51.

43. See Anonymous [William Loughton Smith], *The Pretensions of Thomas Jefferson to the Presidency Examined; and the Charges Against John Adams Refuted*, Part I (Philadelphia: n.p., Oct. 1796), 37–38 (Smith implied that Washington accused Jefferson of being "that man" who tried to subvert the great pillar of religion).

44. Isaac Lewis, *The Political Advantages of Godliness: A Sermon, Preached Before His Excellency the Governor, and the Honorable Legislature of the State of Connecticut, Convened at Hartford on the Anniversary Election. May 11, 1797* (Hartford, 1797), 31.

45. "Resolutions of the Virginia Convention Calling for Independence," in *The Papers of Thomas Jefferson*, ed. Julian P. Boyd, et al. (Princeton, NJ: Princeton University Press, 1950–), 1:290–91.

46. "Editorial Note," in Hutchinson, *Papers of James Madison*, 1:171.

47. Thomas Paine, *Rights of Man* (1791), in *The Writings of Thomas Paine*, ed. Moncure Daniel Conway (New York: G. P. Putnam's Sons, 1894), 2:325.

48. "Declaration of Rights and Form of Government in Virginia," [1776], in Hutchinson, *Papers of James Madison*, 1:172–75.

49. For Madison's account of this episode, see Douglass Adair, ed., "James Madison's Autobiography," *William and Mary Quarterly*, 3d ser., 2 (1945): 199.

50. George Washington to the Hebrew Congregation in Newport, Rhode Island, [1790], in *The Papers of George Washington*, Presidential Series, ed. Dorothy Twohig, et al. (Charlottesville: University Press of Virginia, 1987–), 6:285.

51. For further discussion of the historical origins and purposes of the free-exercise-of-religion guarantee, see Philip A. Hamburger, "A Constitutional Right of Religious Exemption: An Historical Perspective," *George Washington Law Review*

60 (1992): 915–48; Michael W. McConnell, "The Origins and Historical Under-standing of Free Exercise of Religion," *Harvard Law Review* 103 (1990): 1409–1517; Ellis M. West, "The Right to Religion-Based Exemptions in Early America: The Case of Conscientious Objectors to Conscription," *Journal of Law and Religion* 10 (1993–94): 367–401. Interestingly, guarantees of religious liberty coexisted with various manifestations of religious establishment in many late eighteenth- and early nineteenth-century state constitutions. See John Witte Jr., *Religion and the American Constitutional Experiment,* 2d ed. (Boulder, CO: Westview Press, 2005), 107–24.

CONTRIBUTORS

EDWARD L. BOND, Ph.D., is Professor of History at Alabama A&M University and editor-in-chief of *Anglican and Episcopal History*. He is editor of *Spreading the Gospel in Colonial Virginia: Preaching, Religion, and Community* (2005) and author of *Damned Souls in a Tobacco Colony: Religion in Seventeenth-Century Virginia* (2000), as well as many scholarly articles on the history of the church in Virginia.

RICHARD E. BOND, Ph.D., is Assistant Professor of History at Virginia Wesleyan College. He has coedited *Perspectives on Life after the History Ph.D.* (2006) and authored "Shaping a Conspiracy: Black Testimony in the 1741 New York Plot," in *Early American Studies* (2007).

THOMAS E. BUCKLEY, S.J., Ph.D., is Professor of Modern Christian History at the Jesuit School of Theology of Santa Clara University/ Graduate Theological Union. He is the author of *Church and State in Revolutionary Virginia, 1776–1787* (1977), *The Great Catastrophe of My Life: Divorce in the Old Dominion* (2002), and more than a dozen scholarly articles and book chapters on Thomas Jefferson and church-state issues in America. He is currently completing a study of the history of religious freedom and the implementation of Jefferson's Statute in Virginia before 1940.

DANIEL L. DREISBACH, J.D., D.Phil., is Professor in the Department of Justice, Law and Society at American University, School of Public Affairs. He is author of *Thomas Jefferson and the Wall of Separation between Church and State* (2002) and has edited or co-edited several volumes, including *The Sacred Rights of Conscience:*

Selected Readings on Religious Liberty and Church-State Relations in the American Founding (2009), *The Forgotten Founders on Religion and Public Life* (2009), and *The Founders on God and Government* (2004).

PHILIP D. MORGAN, Ph.D., is Harry C. Black Professor of History at Johns Hopkins University. He is author of *Slave Counterpoint: Black Culture in the Eighteenth-Century Chesapeake and Lowcountry* (1998) and coeditor of the volumes *Arming Slaves: From Classical Times to the Modern Age* (2006), *Atlantic Diasporas: Jews, Conversos, and Crypto-Jews in the Age of Mercantilism, 1500–1800* (2009), and *Atlantic History: A Critical Appraisal* (2009).

MONICA NAJAR, Ph.D., is Associate Professor of History at Lehigh University. She is author of *Evangelizing the South: A Social History of Church and State in Early America* (2008). Her article "'Meddling with Emancipation': Baptists, Authority, and the Rift over Slavery in the Upper South" was reprinted in *The Best American History Essays 2007.*

PAUL RASOR, J.D., Ph.D., is Director of the Center for the Study of Religious Freedom and Professor of Interdisciplinary Studies at Virginia Wesleyan College. He has published widely in both law and theology; his recent publications include *Faith without Certainty: Liberal Theology in the Twenty-first Century* (2005) and "Theological and Political Liberalisms," in the *Journal of Law and Religion* (2009).

BRENT TARTER is a founding editor of the Library of Virginia's *Dictionary of Virginia Biography* and an editor of the seven-volume *Revolutionary Virginia, the Road to Independence: A Documentary Record* (1973–83). He has published several articles on Virginia history in a variety of scholarly journals and is a cofounder of the annual Virginia Forum.